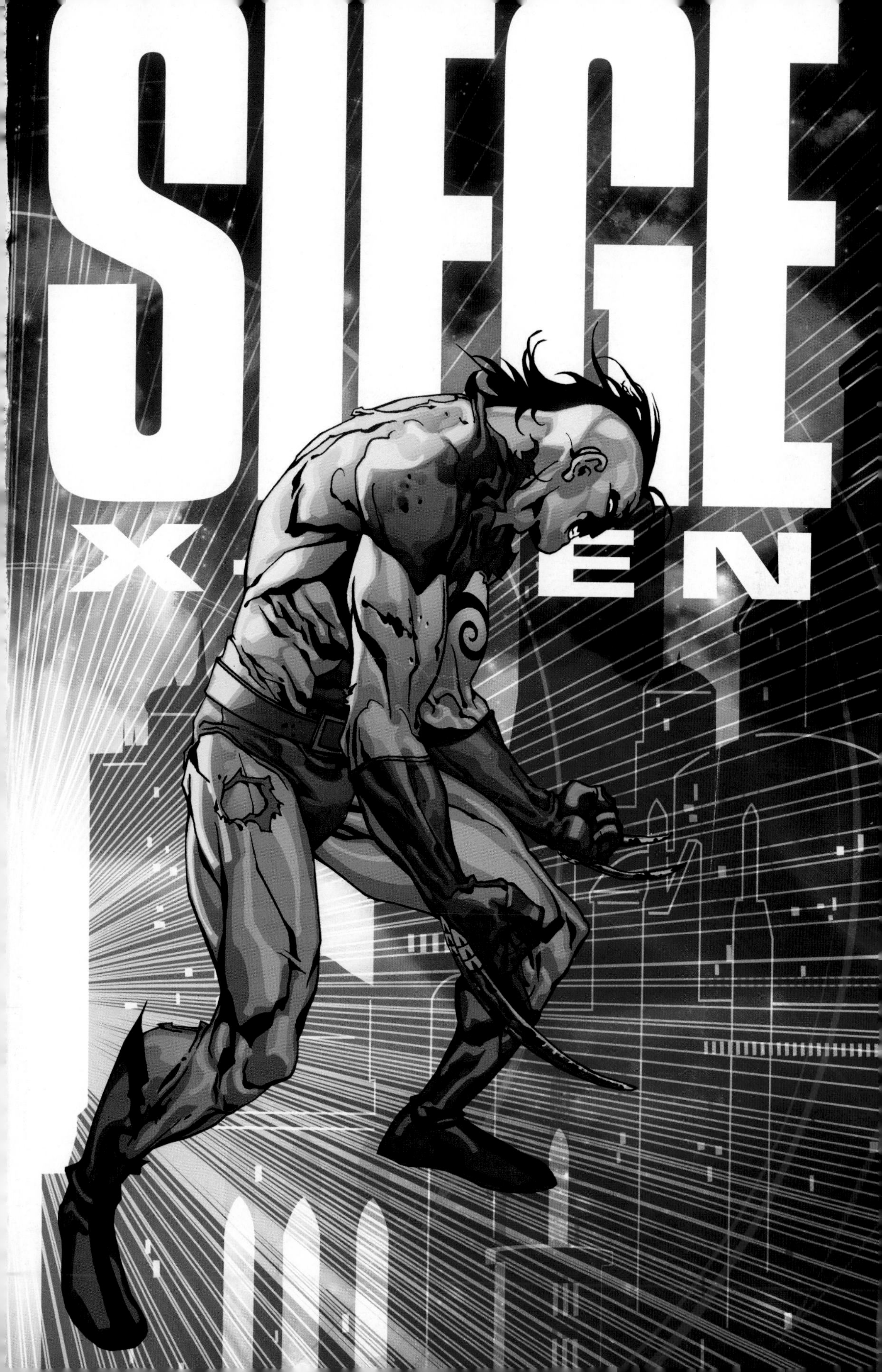
SIEGE
X-
EN

SIEGE
X-MEN

DARK WOLVERINE #82-84

WRITERS: **DANIEL WAY** & **MARJORIE LIU**
PENCILER: **GIUSEPPE CAMUNCOLI**
INKER: **ONOFRIO CATACCHIO**
COLORISTS: **MARTE GRACIA** WITH **ANTONIO FABELA**
LETTERER: **VC'S CORY PETIT**
COVER ART: **SALVADOR LARROCA** WITH **FRANK D'ARMATA**
LETTERER: **VC'S CORY PETIT**
ASSISTANT EDITOR: **JODY LEHEUP**
EDITOR: **JEANINE SCHAEFER**
EXECUTIVE EDITOR: **AXEL ALONSO**

NEW MUTANTS #11

WRITER: **KIERON GILLEN**
ART: **NIKO HENRICHON**
LETTERER: **VC'S JOE CARAMAGNA**
COVER ART: **TERRY DODSON** & **RACHEL DODSON**
ASSOCIATE EDITOR: **DANIEL KETCHUM**
EDITOR: **NICK LOWE**

SIEGE: STORMING ASGARD — HEROES & VILLAINS

HEAD WRITER/EDITOR: **JOHN RHETT THOMAS**
SPOTLIGHT BULLPEN WRITERS: **JESS HARROLD** & **DUGEN TRODGLEN**
COVER ART: **GREG LAND** & **JUSTIN PONSOR**
DESIGN: **BLAMMO! CONTENT & DESIGN, ROMMEL ALAMA** & **MIKE KRONENBERG**

COLLECTION EDITOR: **JENNIFER GRÜNWALD** • ASSISTANT EDITOR: **ALEX STARBUCK**
ASSOCIATE EDITOR: **JOHN DENNING** • EDITOR, SPECIAL PROJECTS: **MARK D. BEAZLEY**
SENIOR EDITOR, SPECIAL PROJECTS: **JEFF YOUNGQUIST**
SENIOR VICE PRESIDENT OF SALES: **DAVID GABRIEL** • BOOK DESIGNER: **RODOLFO MURAGUCHI**

EDITOR IN CHIEF: **JOE QUESADA** • PUBLISHER: **DAN BUCKLEY** • EXECUTIVE PRODUCER: **ALAN FINE**

SIEGE: X-MEN. Contains material originally published in magazine form as DARK WOLVERINE #82-84, NEW MUTANTS #11 and SIEGE: STORMING ASGARD - HEROES & VILLAINS. First printing 2010. ISBN# 978-0-7851-4815-9. Published by MARVEL WORLDWIDE, INC., a subsidiary of MARVEL ENTERTAINMENT, LLC. OFFICE OF PUBLICATION: 417 5th Avenue, New York, NY 10016. Copyright © 2010 Marvel Characters, Inc. All rights reserved. $19.99 per copy in the U.S. and $22.50 in Canada (GST #R127032852); Canadian Agreement #40668537. All characters featured in this issue and the distinctive names and likenesses thereof, and all related indicia are trademarks of Marvel Characters, Inc. No similarity between any of the names, characters, persons, and/or institutions in this magazine with those of any living or dead person or institution is intended, and any such similarity which may exist is purely coincidental. **Printed in the U.S.A.** ALAN FINE, EVP - Office of the President, Marvel Worldwide, Inc. and EVP & CMO Marvel Characters B.V.; DAN BUCKLEY, Chief Executive Officer and Publisher - Print, Animation & Digital Media; JIM SOKOLOWSKI, Chief Operating Officer; DAVID GABRIEL, SVP of Publishing Sales & Circulation; DAVID BOGART, SVP of Business Affairs & Talent Management; MICHAEL PASCIULLO, VP Merchandising & Communications; JIM O'KEEFE, VP of Operations & Logistics; DAN CARR, Executive Director of Publishing Technology; JUSTIN F. GABRIE, Director of Publishing & Editorial Operations; SUSAN CRESPI, Editorial Operations Manager; ALEX MORALES, Publishing Operations Manager; STAN LEE, Chairman Emeritus. For information regarding advertising in Marvel Comics or on Marvel.com, please contact Ron Stern, VP of Business Development, at rstern@marvel.com. For Marvel subscription inquiries, please call 800-217-9158. Manufactured between 6/7/10 and 7/7/10 by R.R. DONNELLEY INC., SALEM, VA, USA.

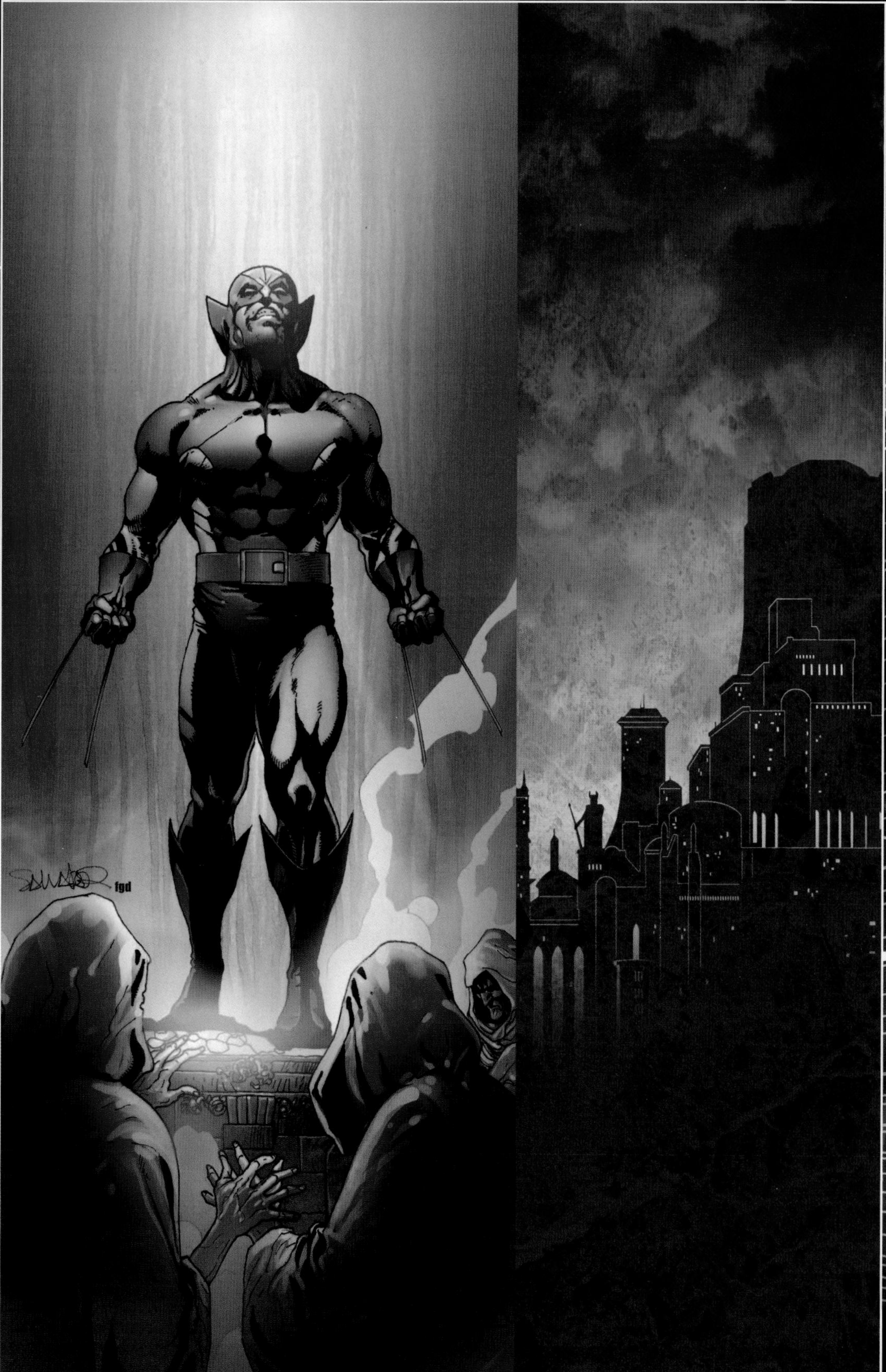

DARK WOLVERINE #82

Decades ago, the mutant known as Wolverine found peace in Japan and had a son with his wife, Itsu Akihiro. The peace was short-lived—Itsu was murdered and Wolverine believed his son died with her...but the boy lived. Like his father, the son possessed enhanced senses, a powerful healing factor, and razor-sharp claws on each hand. He became known by the name he was taunted with as a child: the Japanese term for "mongrel", Daken. As he grew, he blamed his father for his mother's death, and this resentment consumed him. Recently, Norman Osborn, the former costumed villain known as the Green Goblin, took the moniker Iron Patriot and became the Director of the U.S. government's espionage strike-team, H.A.M.M.E.R., as well as leader of its super hero team, the Avengers. Osborn then populated the Avengers with powered beings he felt he could trust along with a host of super villains and Daken as a...

DARK
WOLVERINE

Norman has been using Daken and his team of Dark Avengers to remake the country's status quo into his image of justice and fairness. An image that does not include mutant, monster or vigilante. And Osborn's more than willing to bend, break, or disregard basic human rights in order to achieve his dream.

Thor, the mighty god of thunder, has recently returned to Earth and brought the golden city of Asgard— and all the gods who call it home— with him. But Norman has secretly partnered with Thor's evil half-brother Loki in a plan to overthrow the golden city, covering his tracks by rallying the troops to defend American soil from the threat of Asgard. Now Osborn, H.A.M.M.E.R. and the Dark Avengers have laid siege to Asgard...and Daken...as always...has everyone right where he wants them...

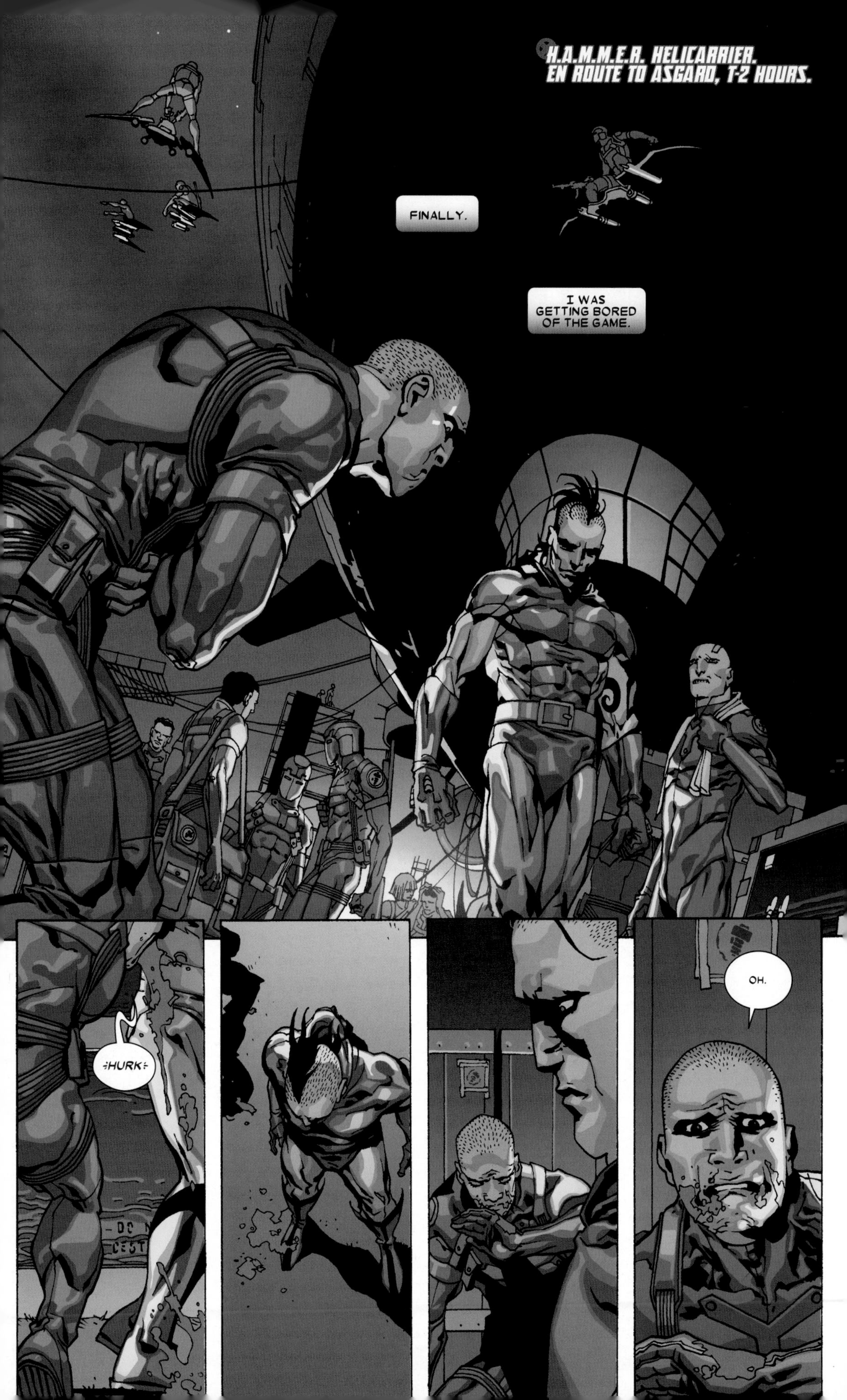
H.A.M.M.E.R. HELICARRIER.
EN ROUTE TO ASGARD, T-2 HOURS.
FINALLY.
I WAS GETTING BORED OF THE GAME.
=HURK=
OH.

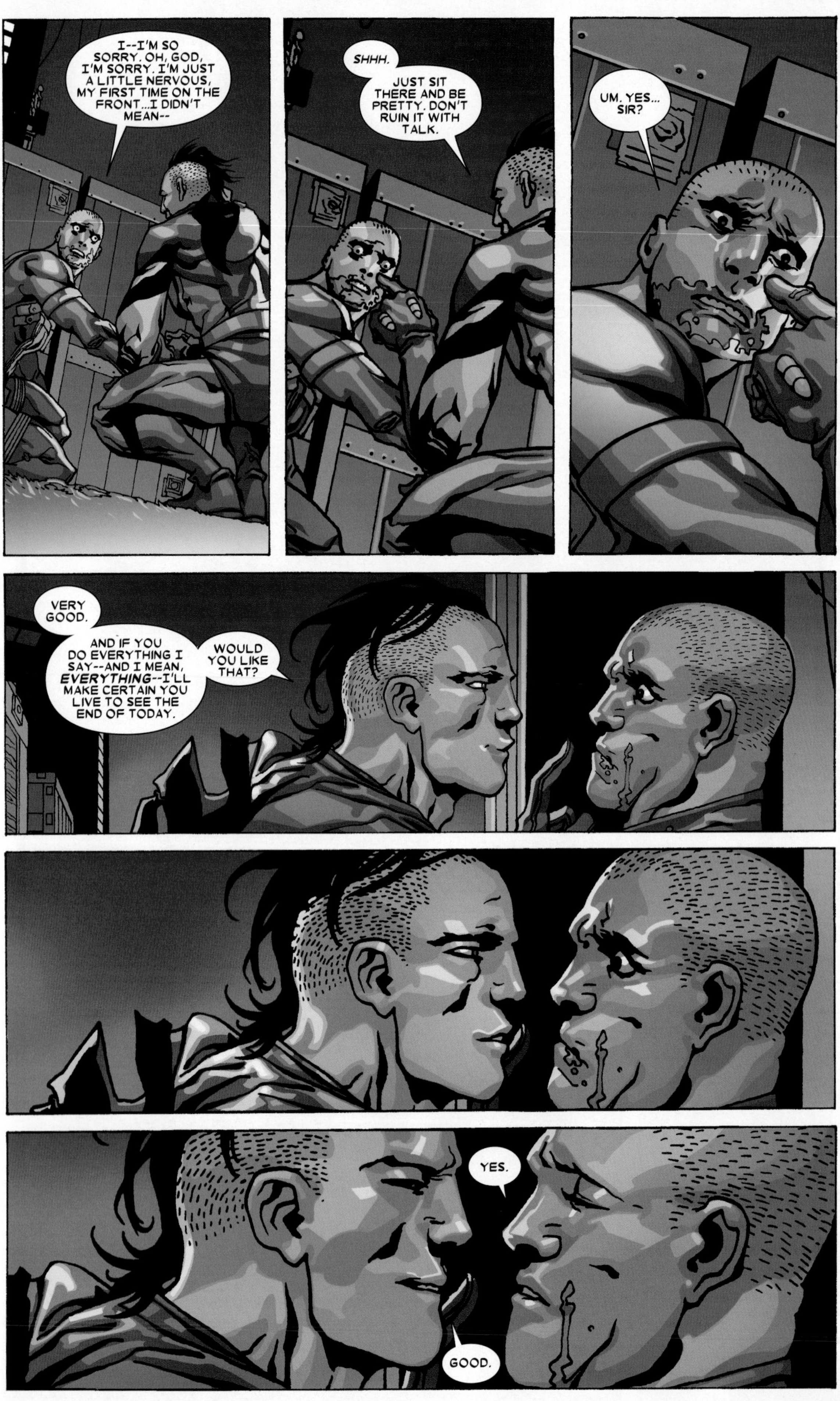
I--I'M SO SORRY. OH, GOD, I'M SORRY. I'M JUST A LITTLE NERVOUS, MY FIRST TIME ON THE FRONT...I DIDN'T MEAN--
SHHH.
JUST SIT THERE AND BE PRETTY. DON'T RUIN IT WITH TALK.
UM. YES... SIR?
VERY GOOD.
AND IF YOU DO EVERYTHING I SAY--AND I MEAN, EVERYTHING--I'LL MAKE CERTAIN YOU LIVE TO SEE THE END OF TODAY.
WOULD YOU LIKE THAT?
YES.
GOOD.

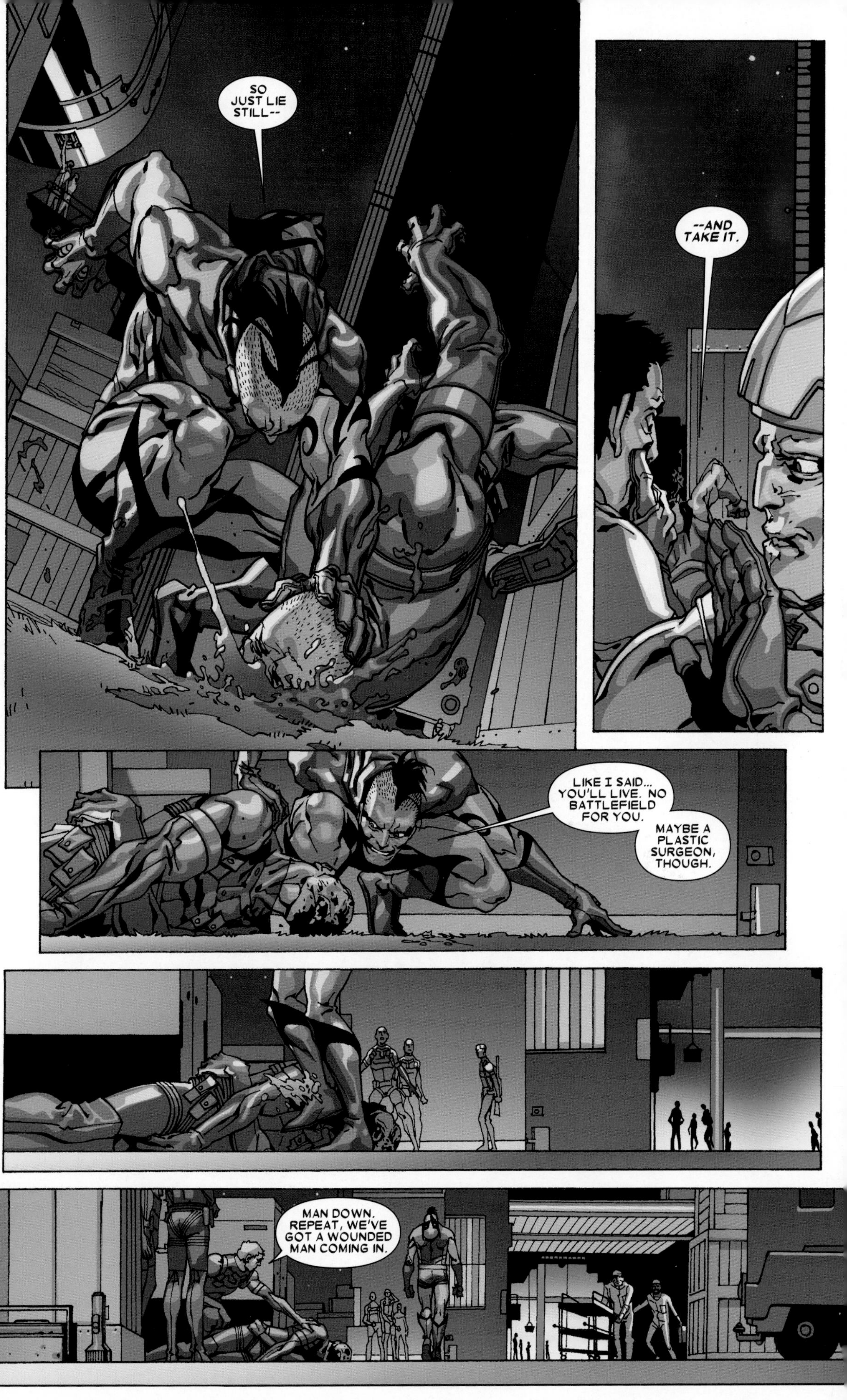
SO JUST LIE STILL--
--AND TAKE IT.
LIKE I SAID... YOU'LL LIVE. NO BATTLEFIELD FOR YOU.
MAYBE A PLASTIC SURGEON, THOUGH.
MAN DOWN. REPEAT, WE'VE GOT A WOUNDED MAN COMING IN.

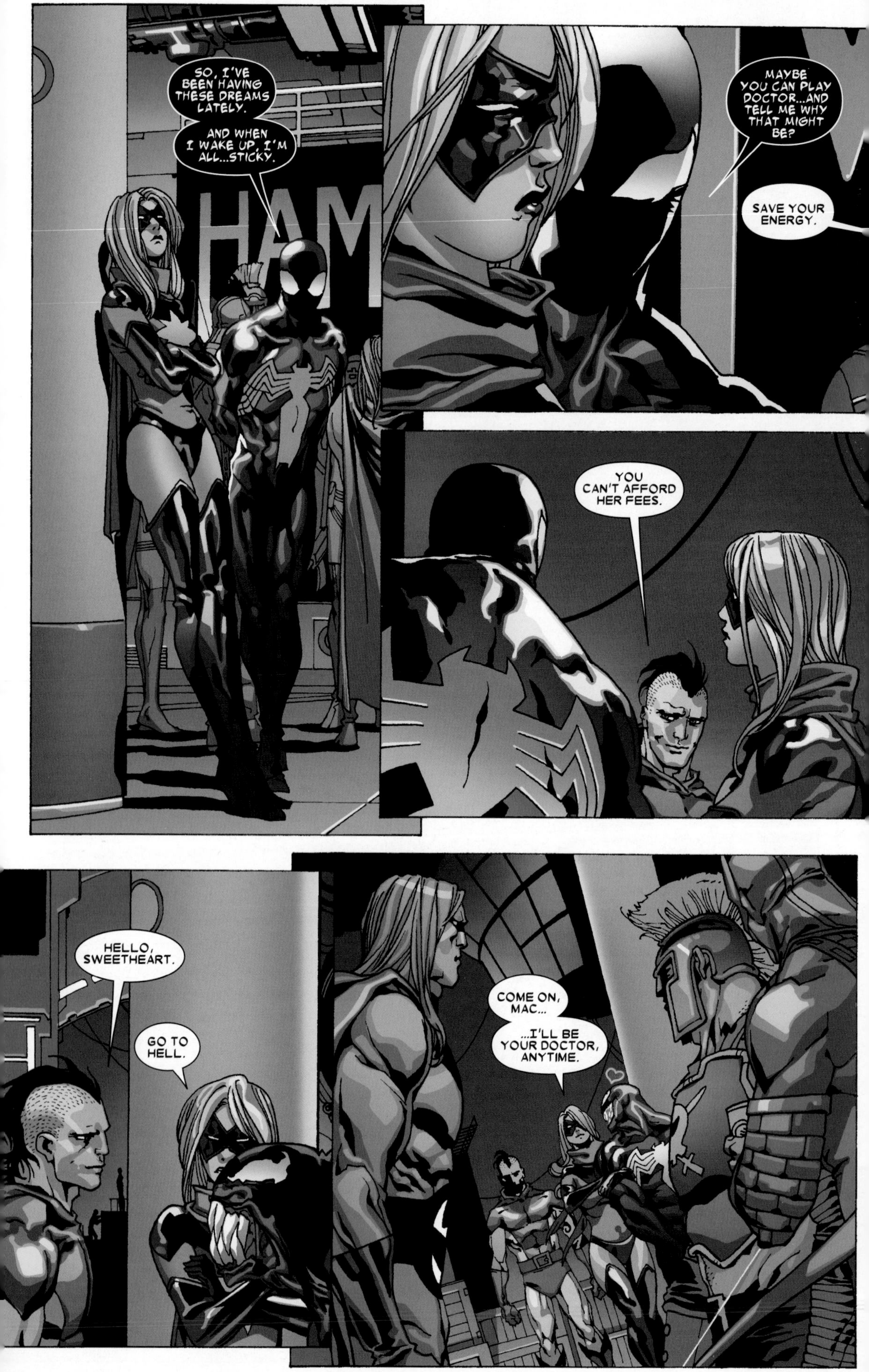
SO, I'VE BEEN HAVING THESE DREAMS LATELY.
AND WHEN I WAKE UP, I'M ALL...STICKY.
MAYBE YOU CAN PLAY DOCTOR...AND TELL ME WHY THAT MIGHT BE?
SAVE YOUR ENERGY.
YOU CAN'T AFFORD HER FEES.
HELLO, SWEETHEART.
GO TO HELL.
COME ON, MAC...
...I'LL BE YOUR DOCTOR, ANYTIME.

NO PLACE TO GO, KARLA. TRY IF YOU LIKE, BUT YOU CAN'T RUN. NONE OF YOU *HEROES* CAN.

AND YOU ALL KNOW IT.

OR ELSE YOU'RE TOO DUMB TO CARE.

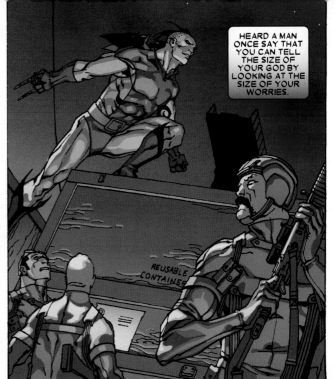

HEARD A MAN ONCE SAY THAT YOU CAN TELL THE SIZE OF YOUR GOD BY LOOKING AT THE SIZE OF YOUR WORRIES.

REUSABLE CONTAINER

LARGER YOUR WORRIES, THE SMALLER YOUR GOD.

AND HERE *WE* ARE, ABOUT TO DO BATTLE WITH HEAVEN.

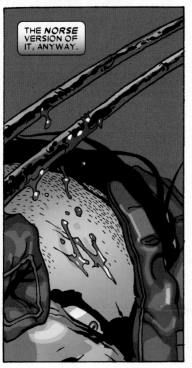

THE *NORSE* VERSION OF IT, ANYWAY.

I'M GUESSING THIS GUY DOESN'T SEE THE IRONY. I'D LAUGH IF I WEREN'T SO DISGUSTED.

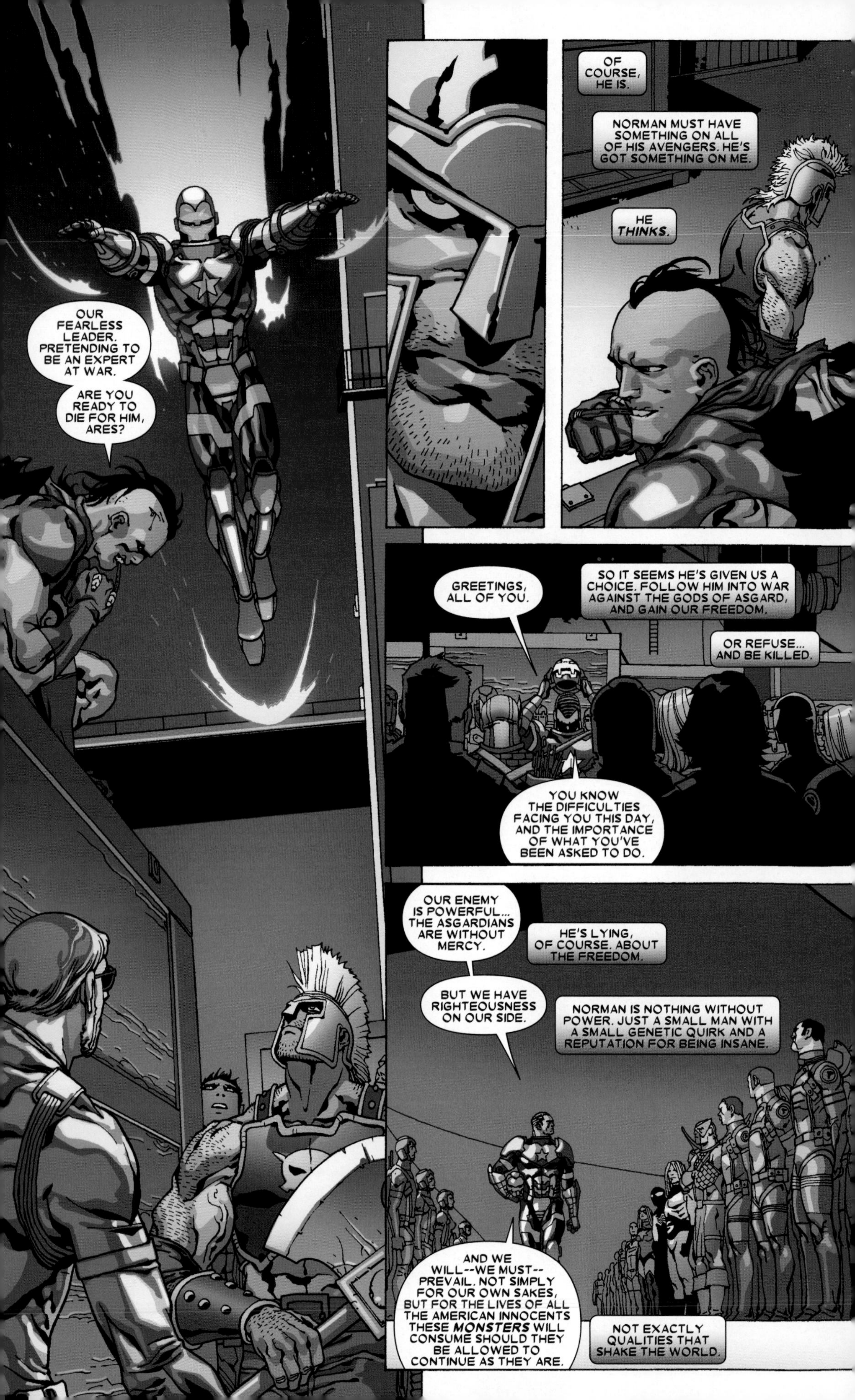
OUR FEARLESS LEADER. PRETENDING TO BE AN EXPERT AT WAR.
ARE YOU READY TO DIE FOR HIM, ARES?
OF COURSE, HE IS.
NORMAN MUST HAVE SOMETHING ON ALL OF HIS AVENGERS. HE'S GOT SOMETHING ON ME.
HE THINKS.
GREETINGS, ALL OF YOU.
SO IT SEEMS HE'S GIVEN US A CHOICE. FOLLOW HIM INTO WAR AGAINST THE GODS OF ASGARD, AND GAIN OUR FREEDOM.
OR REFUSE... AND BE KILLED.
YOU KNOW THE DIFFICULTIES FACING YOU THIS DAY, AND THE IMPORTANCE OF WHAT YOU'VE BEEN ASKED TO DO.
OUR ENEMY IS POWERFUL... THE ASGARDIANS ARE WITHOUT MERCY.
HE'S LYING, OF COURSE. ABOUT THE FREEDOM.
BUT WE HAVE RIGHTEOUSNESS ON OUR SIDE.
NORMAN IS NOTHING WITHOUT POWER. JUST A SMALL MAN WITH A SMALL GENETIC QUIRK AND A REPUTATION FOR BEING INSANE.
AND WE WILL--WE MUST--PREVAIL. NOT SIMPLY FOR OUR OWN SAKES, BUT FOR THE LIVES OF ALL THE AMERICAN INNOCENTS THESE MONSTERS WILL CONSUME SHOULD THEY BE ALLOWED TO CONTINUE AS THEY ARE.
NOT EXACTLY QUALITIES THAT SHAKE THE WORLD.

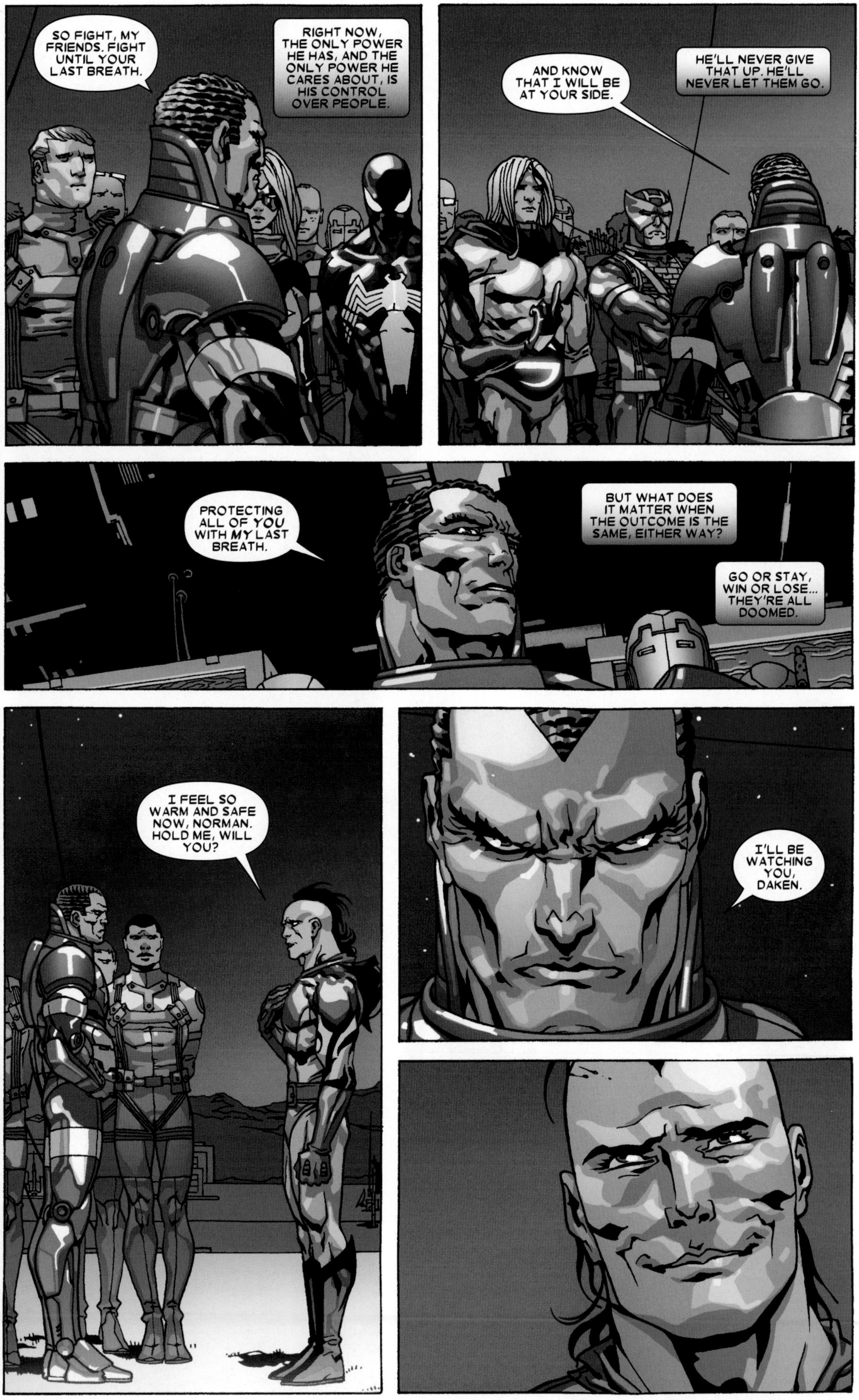
SO FIGHT, MY FRIENDS. FIGHT UNTIL YOUR LAST BREATH.
RIGHT NOW, THE ONLY POWER HE HAS, AND THE ONLY POWER HE CARES ABOUT, IS HIS CONTROL OVER PEOPLE.
AND KNOW THAT I WILL BE AT YOUR SIDE.
HE'LL NEVER GIVE THAT UP. HE'LL NEVER LET THEM GO.
PROTECTING ALL OF YOU WITH MY LAST BREATH.
BUT WHAT DOES IT MATTER WHEN THE OUTCOME IS THE SAME, EITHER WAY?
GO OR STAY, WIN OR LOSE... THEY'RE ALL DOOMED.
I FEEL SO WARM AND SAFE NOW, NORMAN. HOLD ME, WILL YOU?
I'LL BE WATCHING YOU, DAKEN.

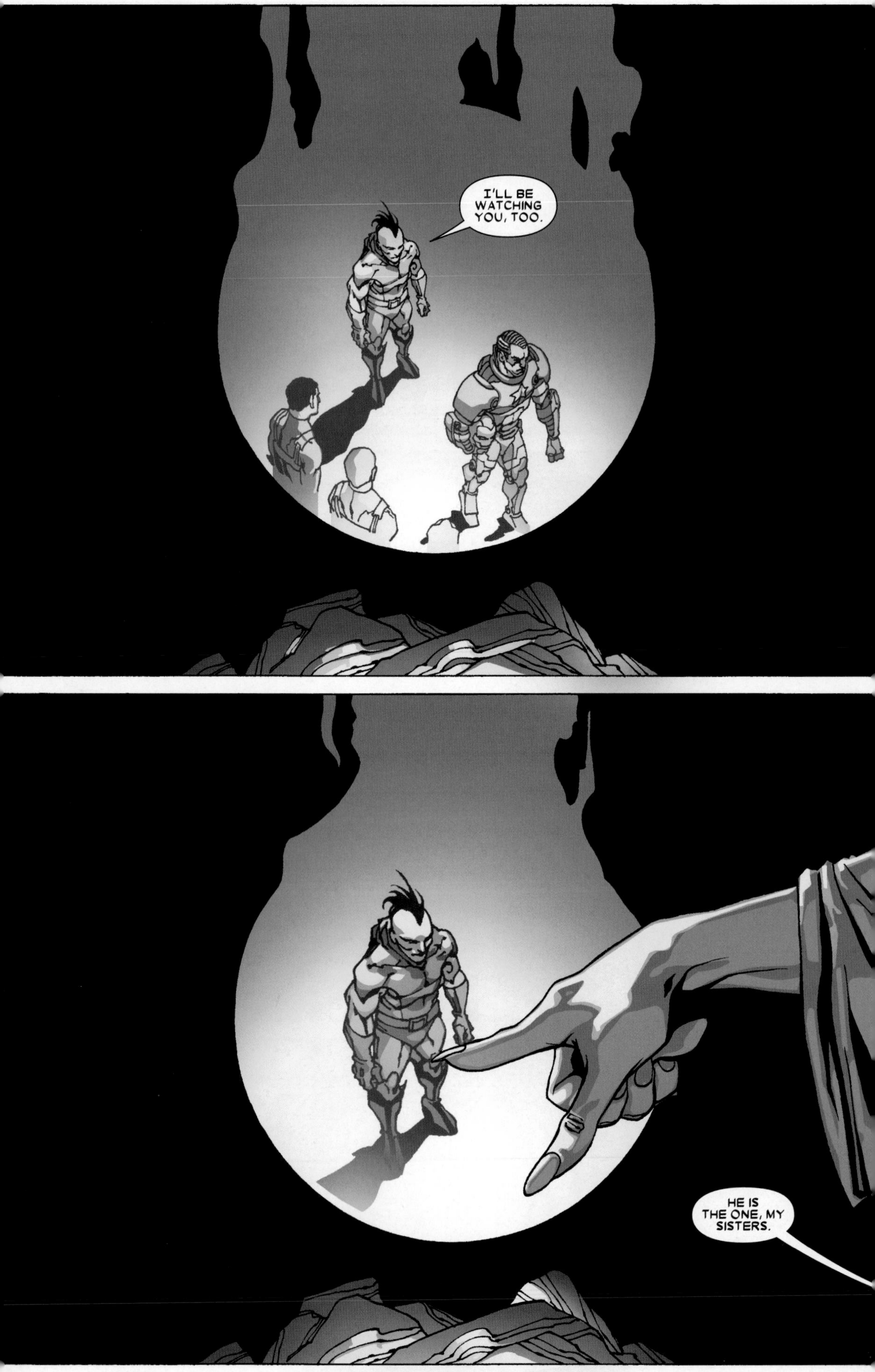
I'LL BE WATCHING YOU, TOO.
HE IS THE ONE, MY SISTERS.

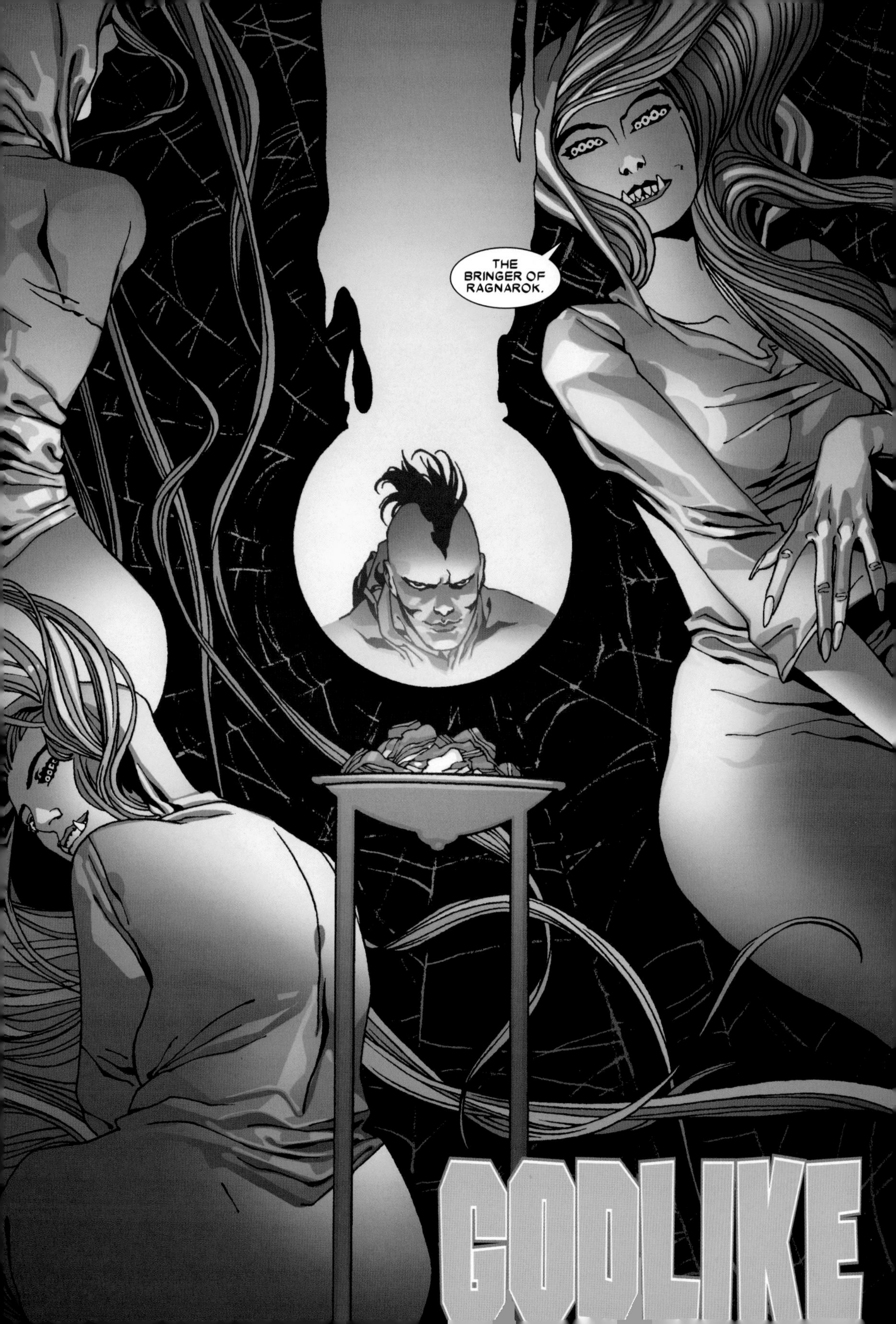
THE BRINGER OF RAGNAROK.
GODLIKE

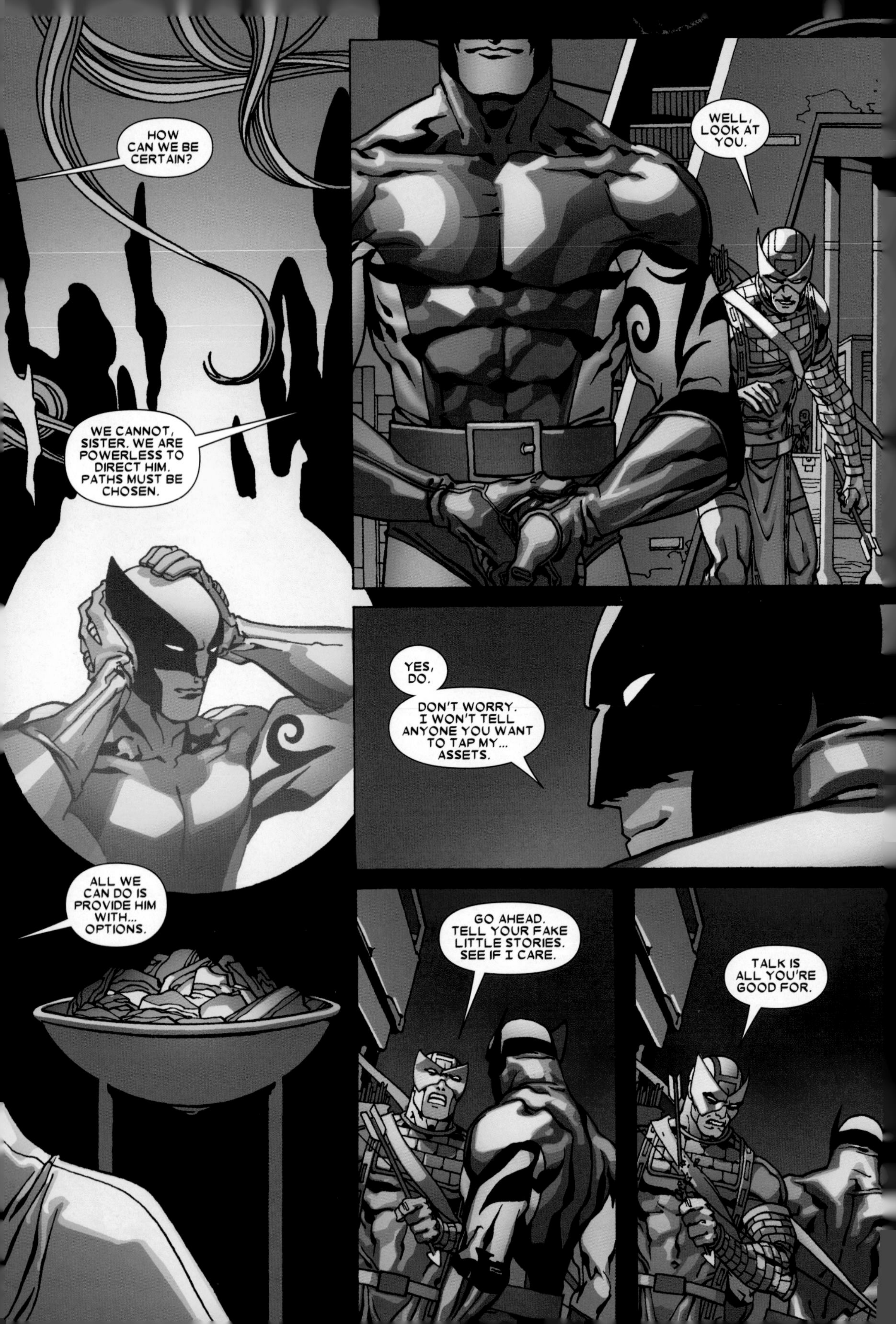
HOW CAN WE BE CERTAIN?
WE CANNOT, SISTER. WE ARE POWERLESS TO DIRECT HIM. PATHS MUST BE CHOSEN.
ALL WE CAN DO IS PROVIDE HIM WITH... OPTIONS.
WELL, LOOK AT YOU.
YES, DO.
DON'T WORRY. I WON'T TELL ANYONE YOU WANT TO TAP MY... ASSETS.
GO AHEAD. TELL YOUR FAKE LITTLE STORIES. SEE IF I CARE.
TALK IS ALL YOU'RE GOOD FOR.

OH, LESTER. YOU KNOW THAT'S NOT TRUE.

LET ME PROVE IT TO YOU.

THIS COULD BE OUR LAST DAY ON EARTH, AFTER ALL.

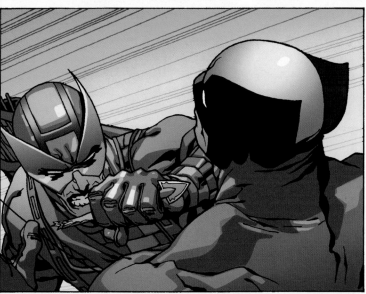

TUT TUT.

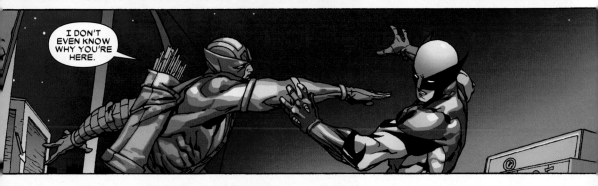

I DON'T EVEN KNOW WHY YOU'RE HERE.

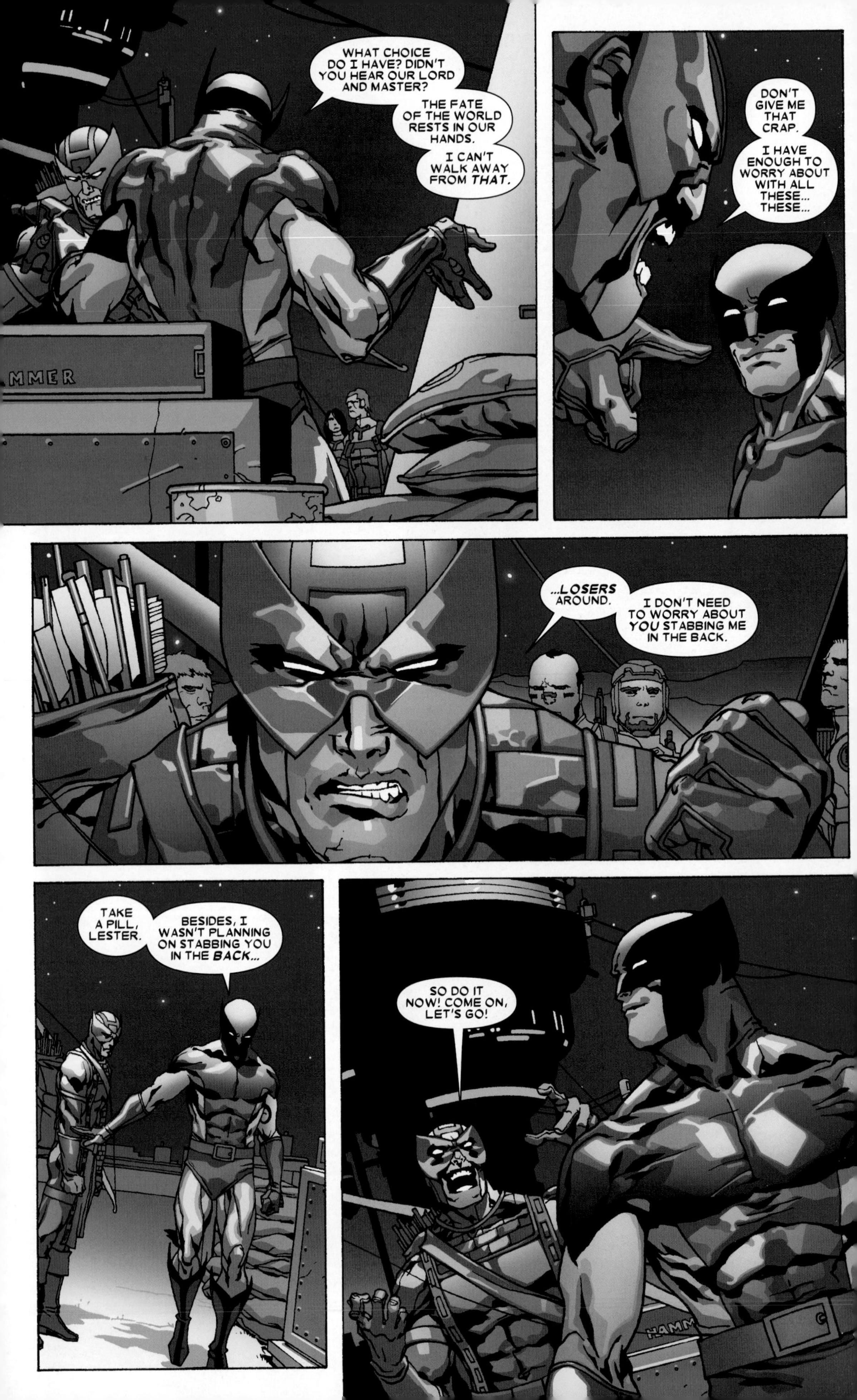
WHAT CHOICE DO I HAVE? DIDN'T YOU HEAR OUR LORD AND MASTER?
THE FATE OF THE WORLD RESTS IN OUR HANDS.
I CAN'T WALK AWAY FROM THAT.
MMER
DON'T GIVE ME THAT CRAP.
I HAVE ENOUGH TO WORRY ABOUT WITH ALL THESE... THESE...
...LOSERS AROUND.
I DON'T NEED TO WORRY ABOUT YOU STABBING ME IN THE BACK.
TAKE A PILL, LESTER.
BESIDES, I WASN'T PLANNING ON STABBING YOU IN THE BACK...
SO DO IT NOW! COME ON, LET'S GO!
HAMM

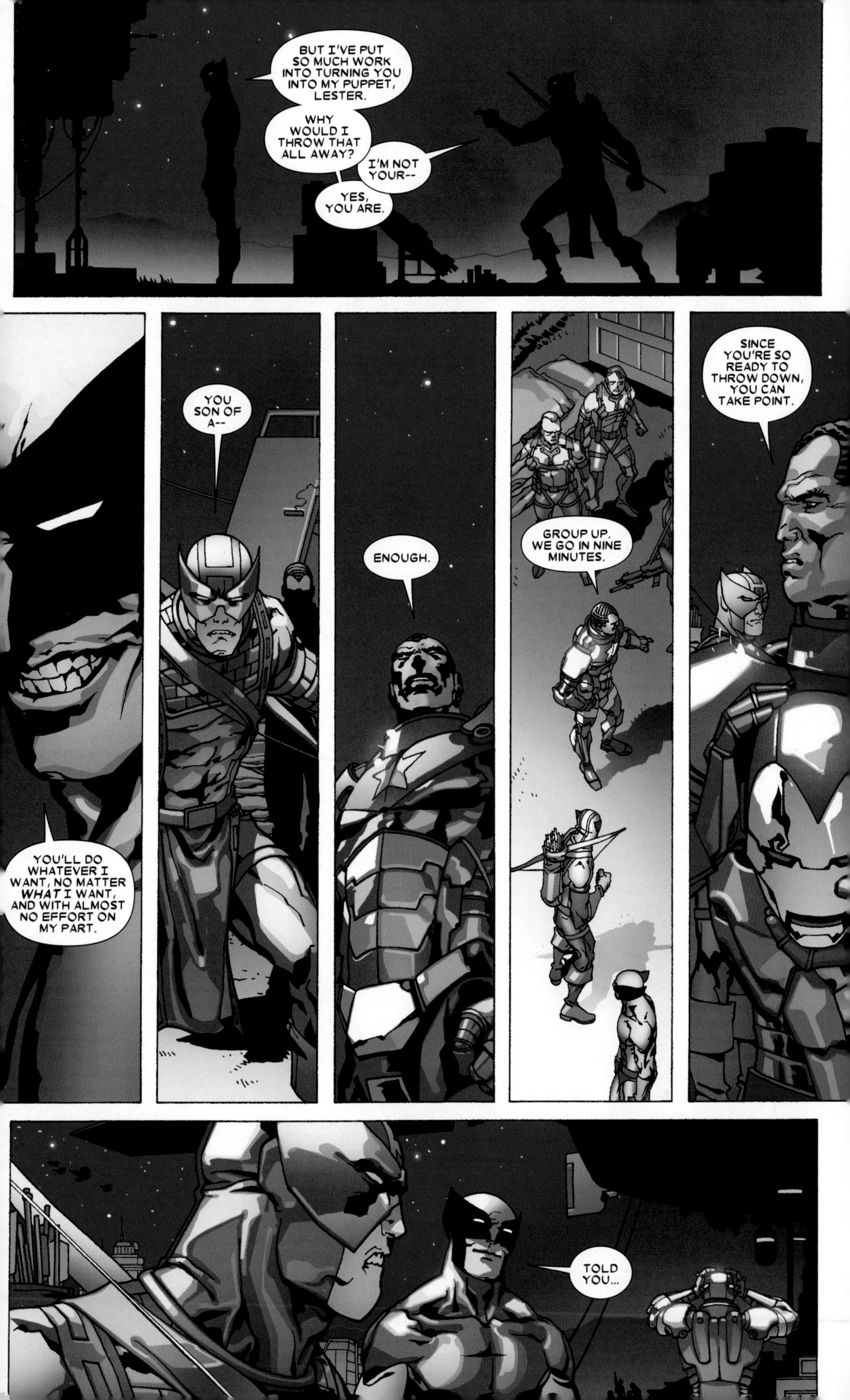
BUT I'VE PUT SO MUCH WORK INTO TURNING YOU INTO MY PUPPET, LESTER.
WHY WOULD I THROW THAT ALL AWAY?
I'M NOT YOUR--
YES, YOU ARE.
YOU'LL DO WHATEVER I WANT, NO MATTER *WHAT* I WANT, AND WITH ALMOST NO EFFORT ON MY PART.
YOU SON OF A--
ENOUGH.
GROUP UP. WE GO IN NINE MINUTES.
SINCE YOU'RE SO READY TO THROW DOWN, YOU CAN TAKE POINT.
TOLD YOU...

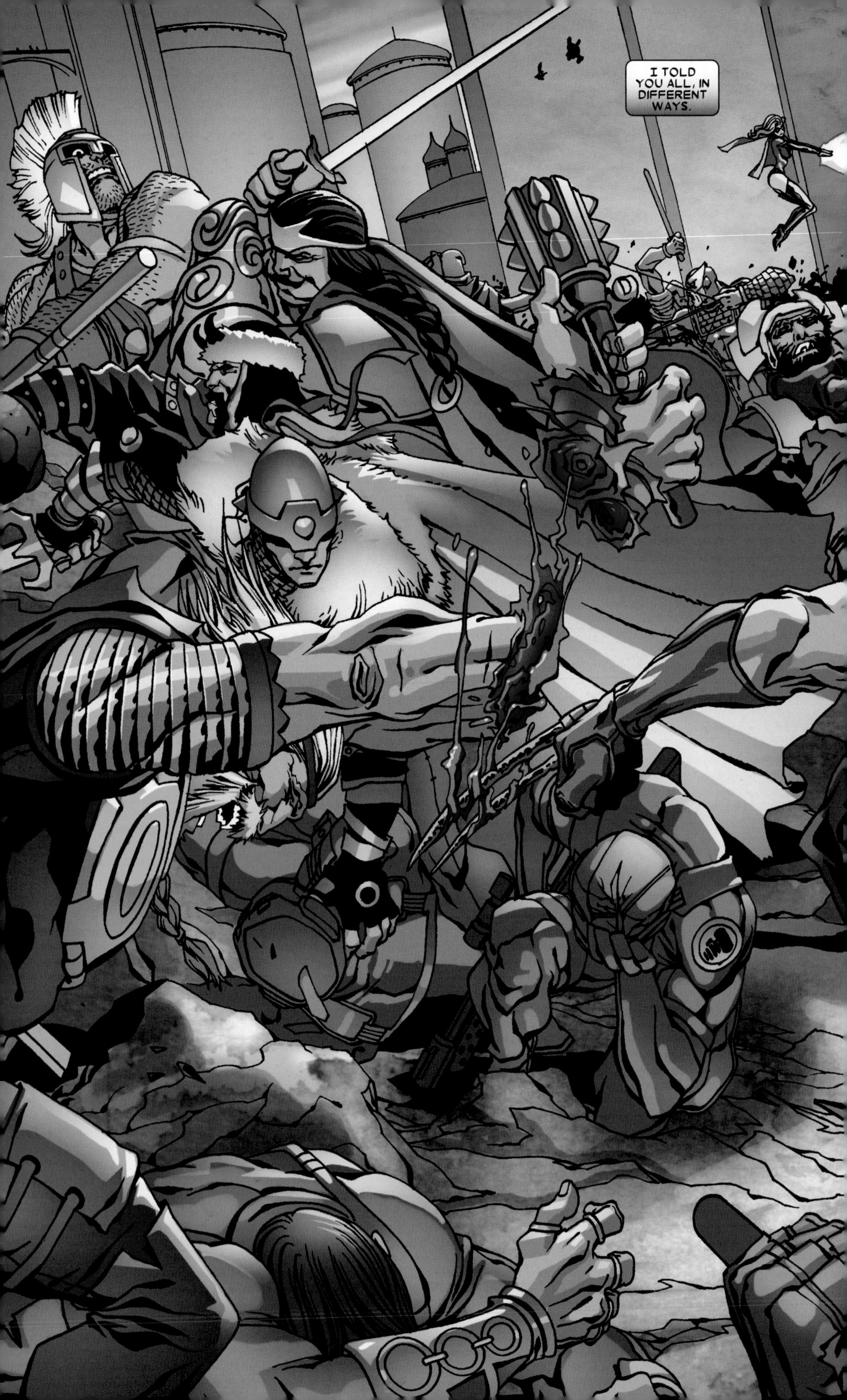
I TOLD YOU ALL, IN DIFFERENT WAYS.

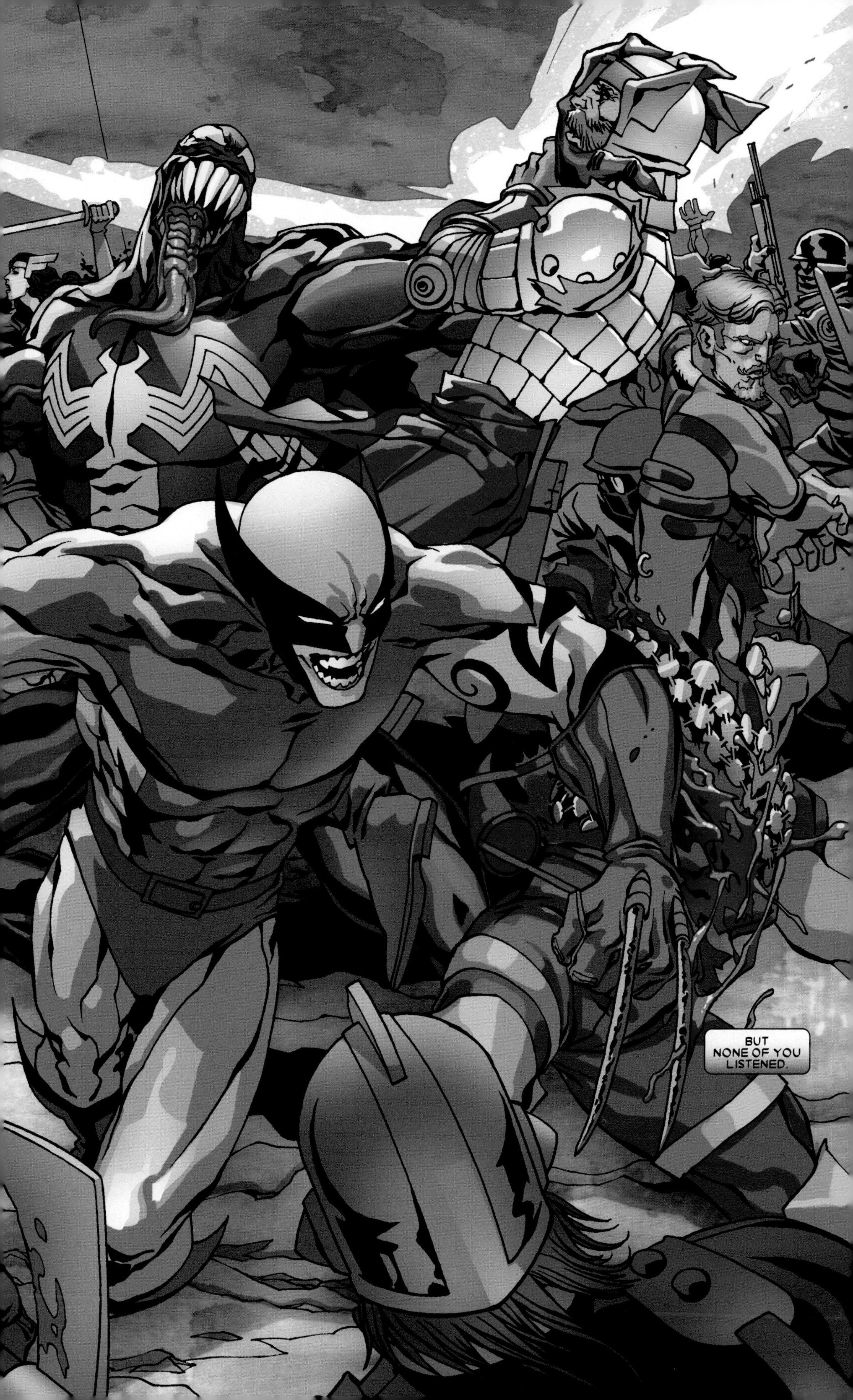
BUT NONE OF YOU LISTENED.

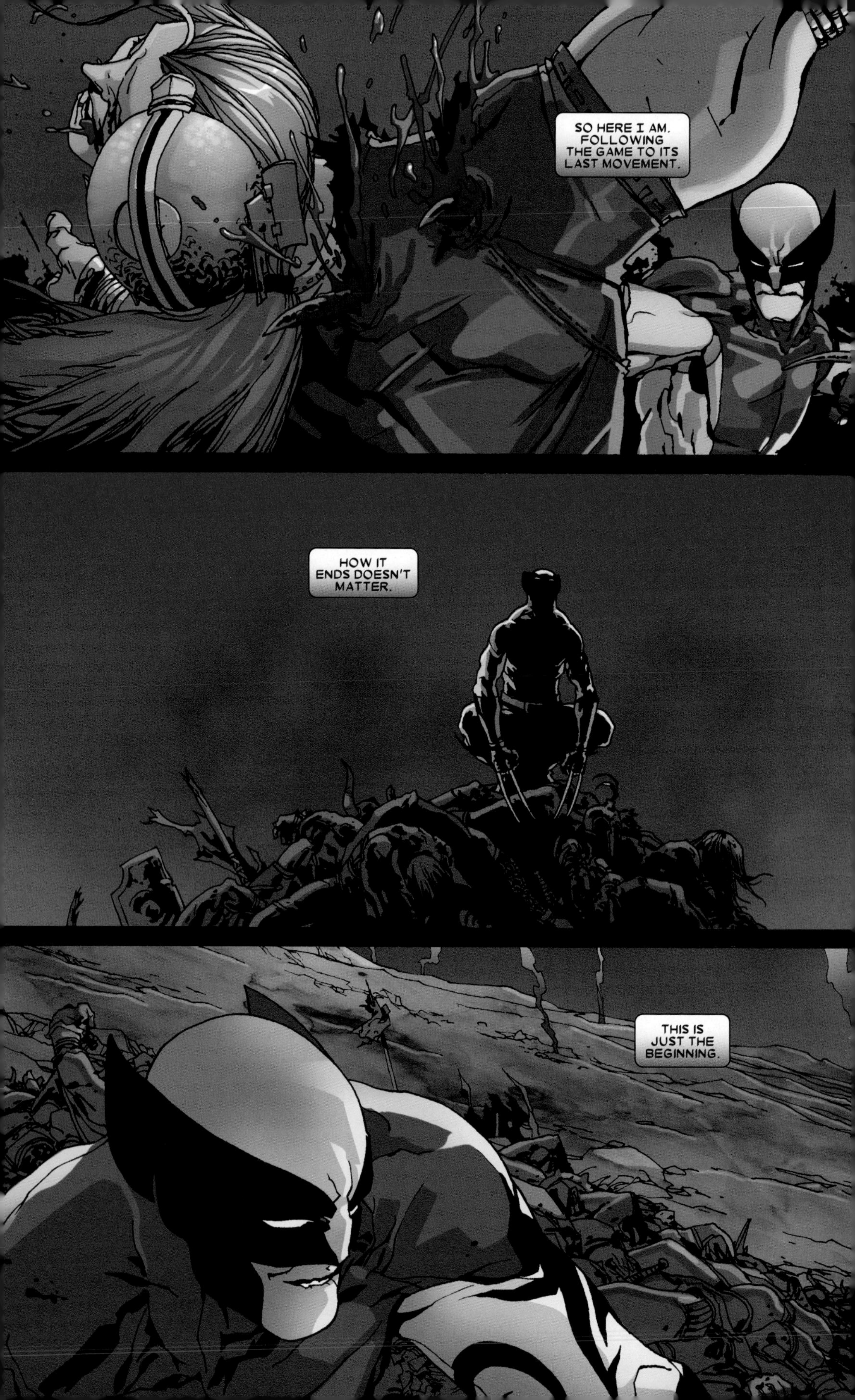
SO HERE I AM. FOLLOWING THE GAME TO ITS LAST MOVEMENT.
HOW IT ENDS DOESN'T MATTER.
THIS IS JUST THE BEGINNING.

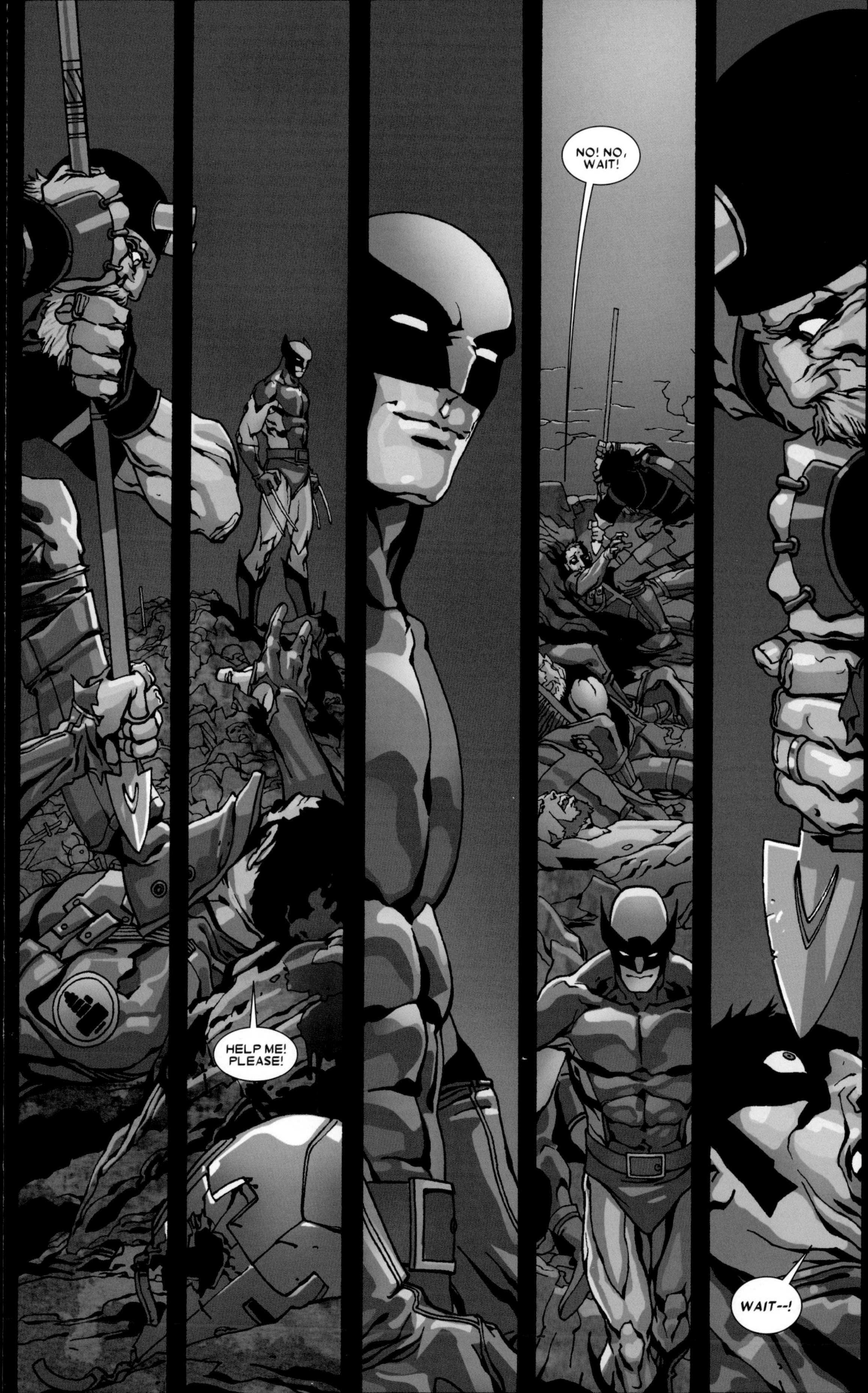
HELP ME! PLEASE!
NO! NO, WAIT!
WAIT--!

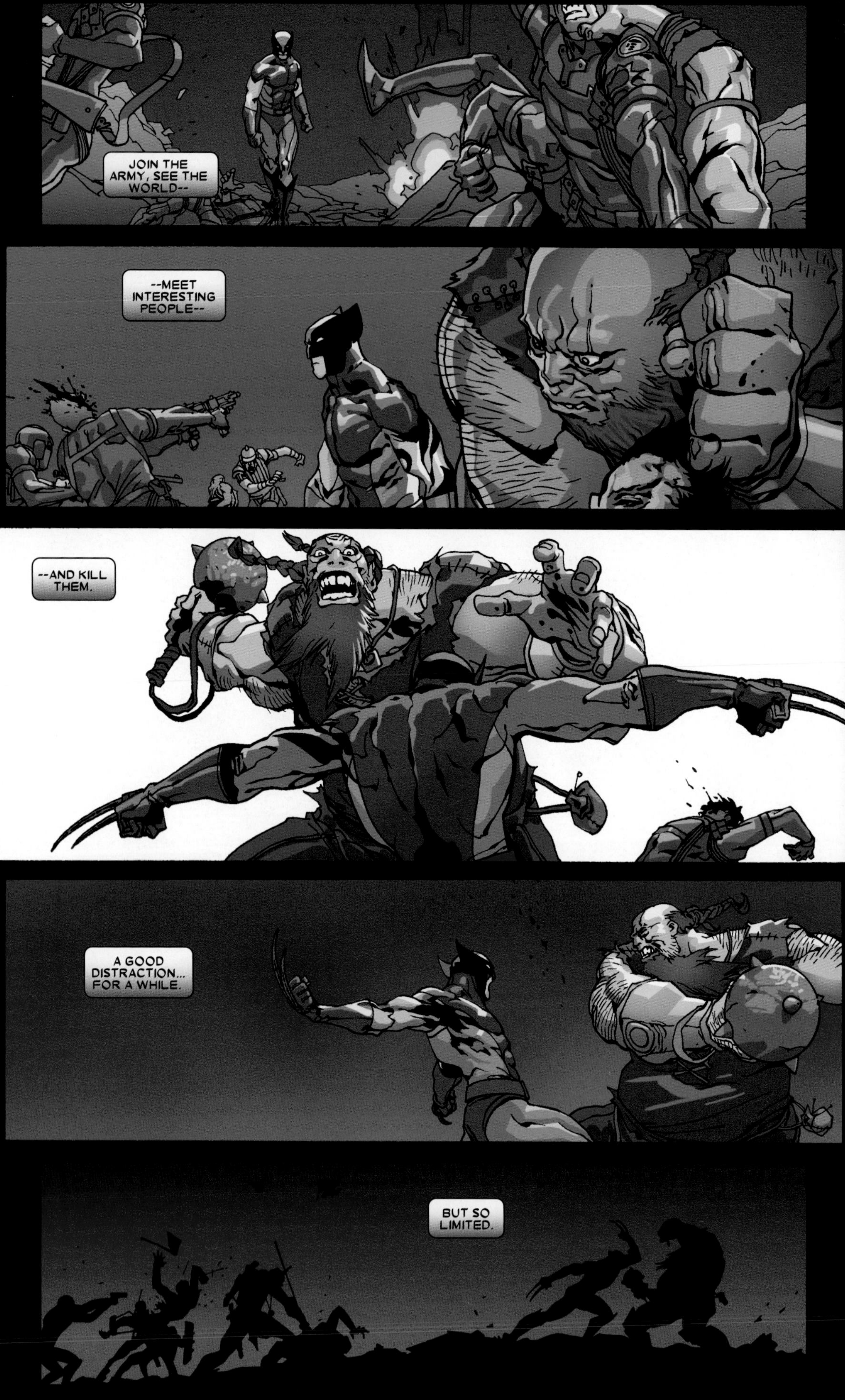
JOIN THE ARMY, SEE THE WORLD--
--MEET INTERESTING PEOPLE--
--AND KILL THEM.
A GOOD DISTRACTION... FOR A WHILE.
BUT SO LIMITED.

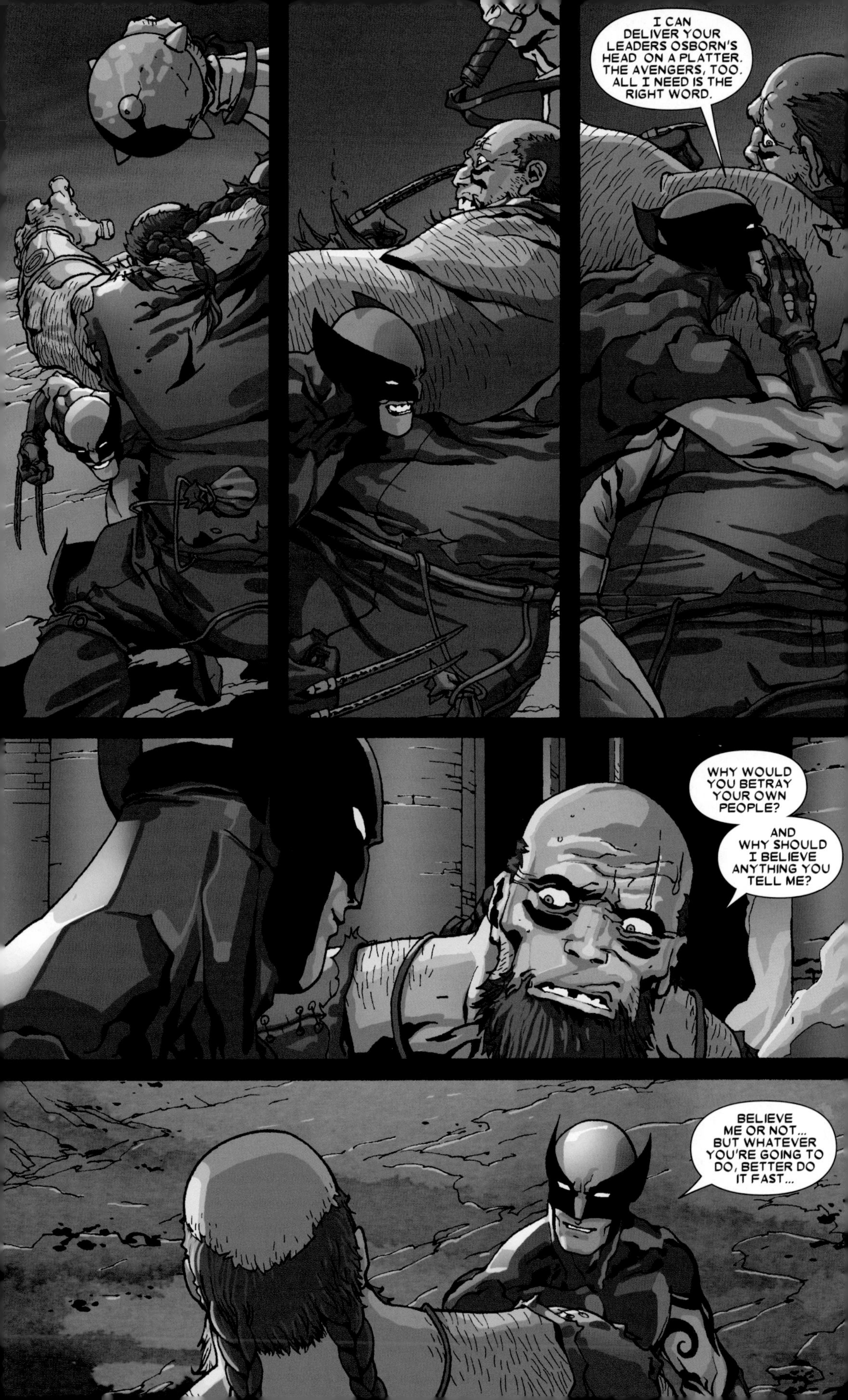
I CAN DELIVER YOUR LEADERS OSBORN'S HEAD ON A PLATTER. THE AVENGERS, TOO. ALL I NEED IS THE RIGHT WORD.
WHY WOULD YOU BETRAY YOUR OWN PEOPLE?
AND WHY SHOULD I BELIEVE ANYTHING YOU TELL ME?
BELIEVE ME OR NOT... BUT WHATEVER YOU'RE GOING TO DO, BETTER DO IT FAST...

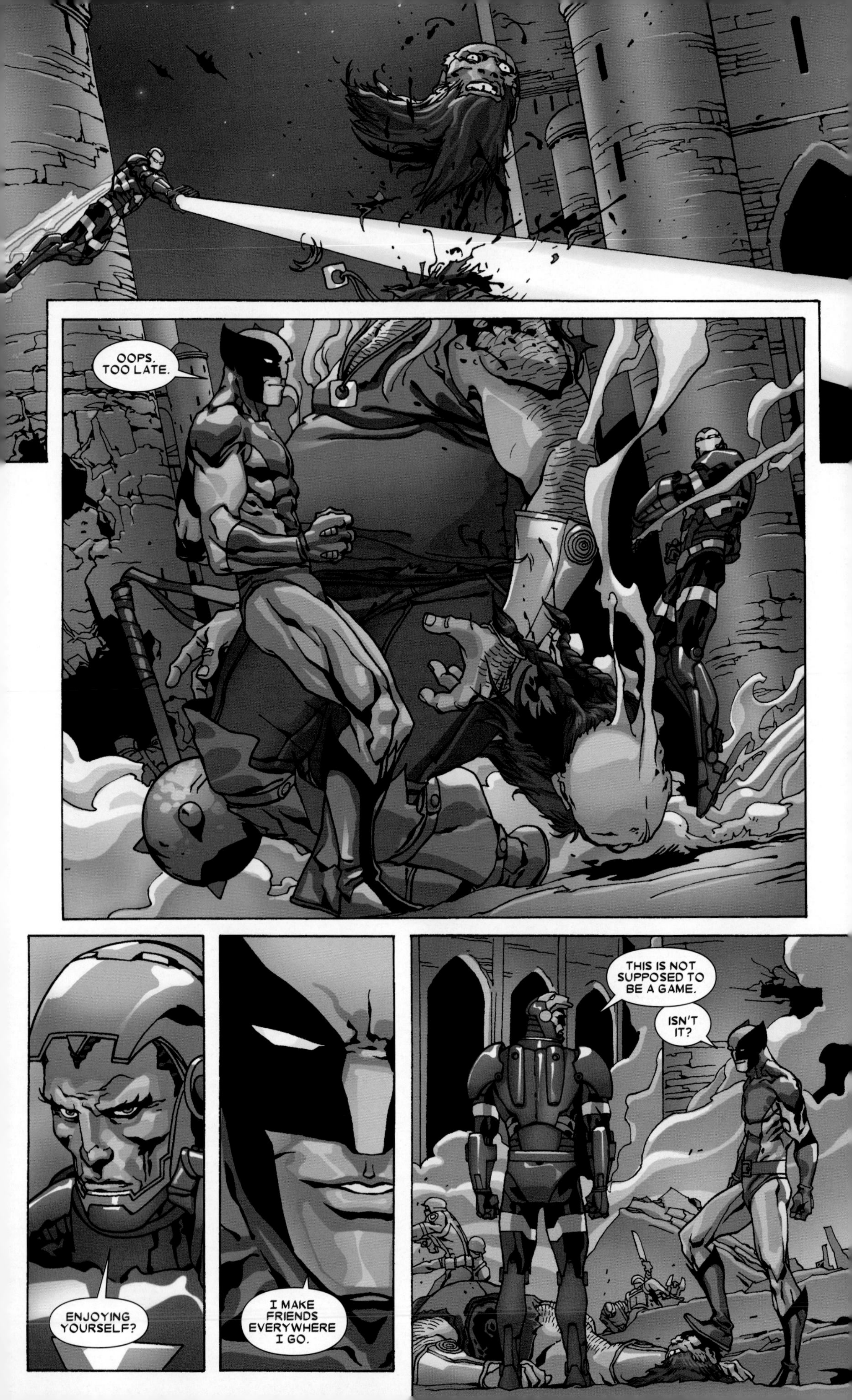
OOPS. TOO LATE.
ENJOYING YOURSELF?
I MAKE FRIENDS EVERYWHERE I GO.
THIS IS NOT SUPPOSED TO BE A GAME.
ISN'T IT?

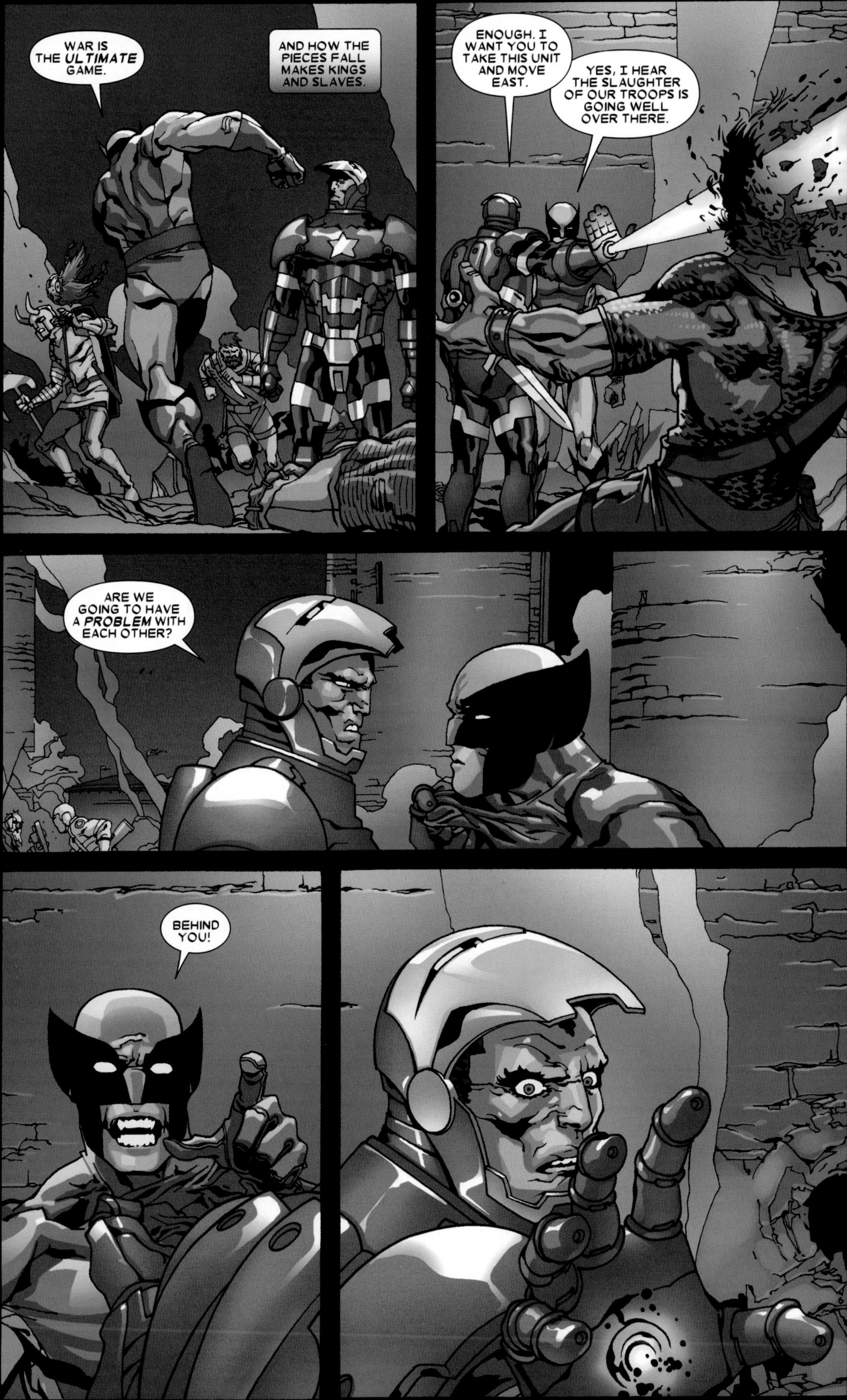

WAR IS THE ULTIMATE GAME.
AND HOW THE PIECES FALL MAKES KINGS AND SLAVES.
ENOUGH. I WANT YOU TO TAKE THIS UNIT AND MOVE EAST.
YES, I HEAR THE SLAUGHTER OF OUR TROOPS IS GOING WELL OVER THERE.
ARE WE GOING TO HAVE A PROBLEM WITH EACH OTHER?
BEHIND YOU!

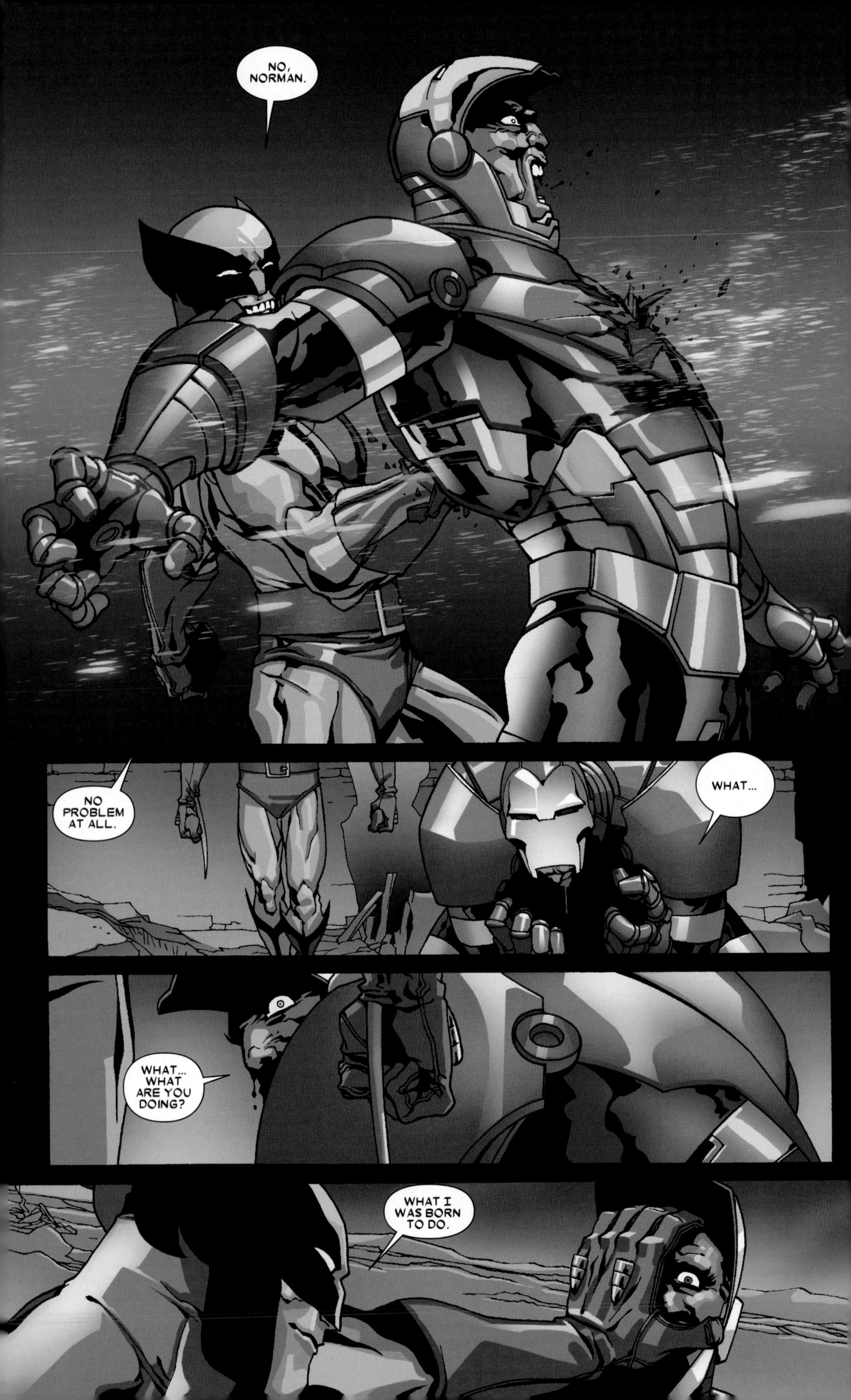
NO, NORMAN.
NO PROBLEM AT ALL.
WHAT...
WHAT... WHAT ARE YOU DOING?
WHAT I WAS BORN TO DO.

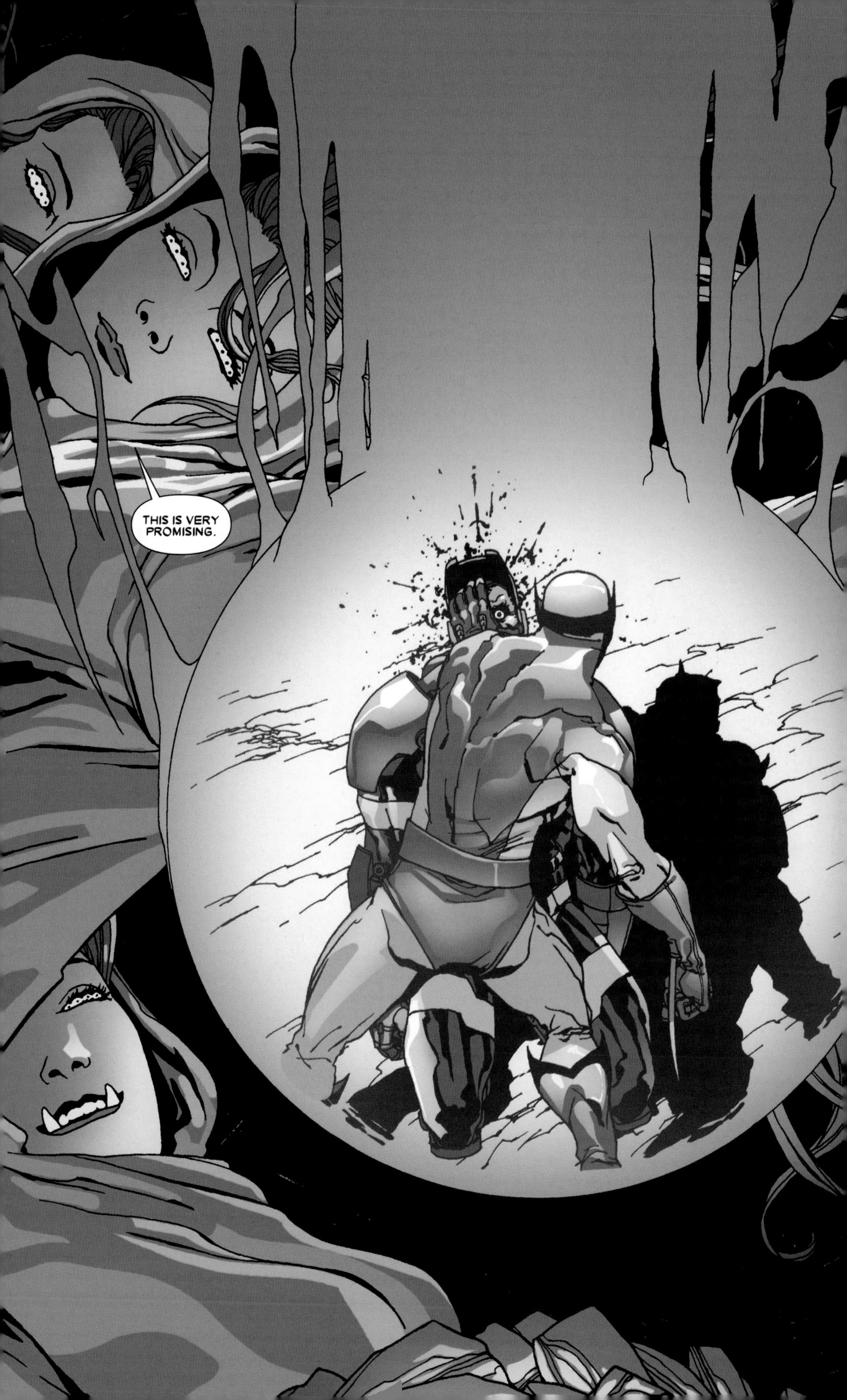
THIS IS VERY PROMISING.

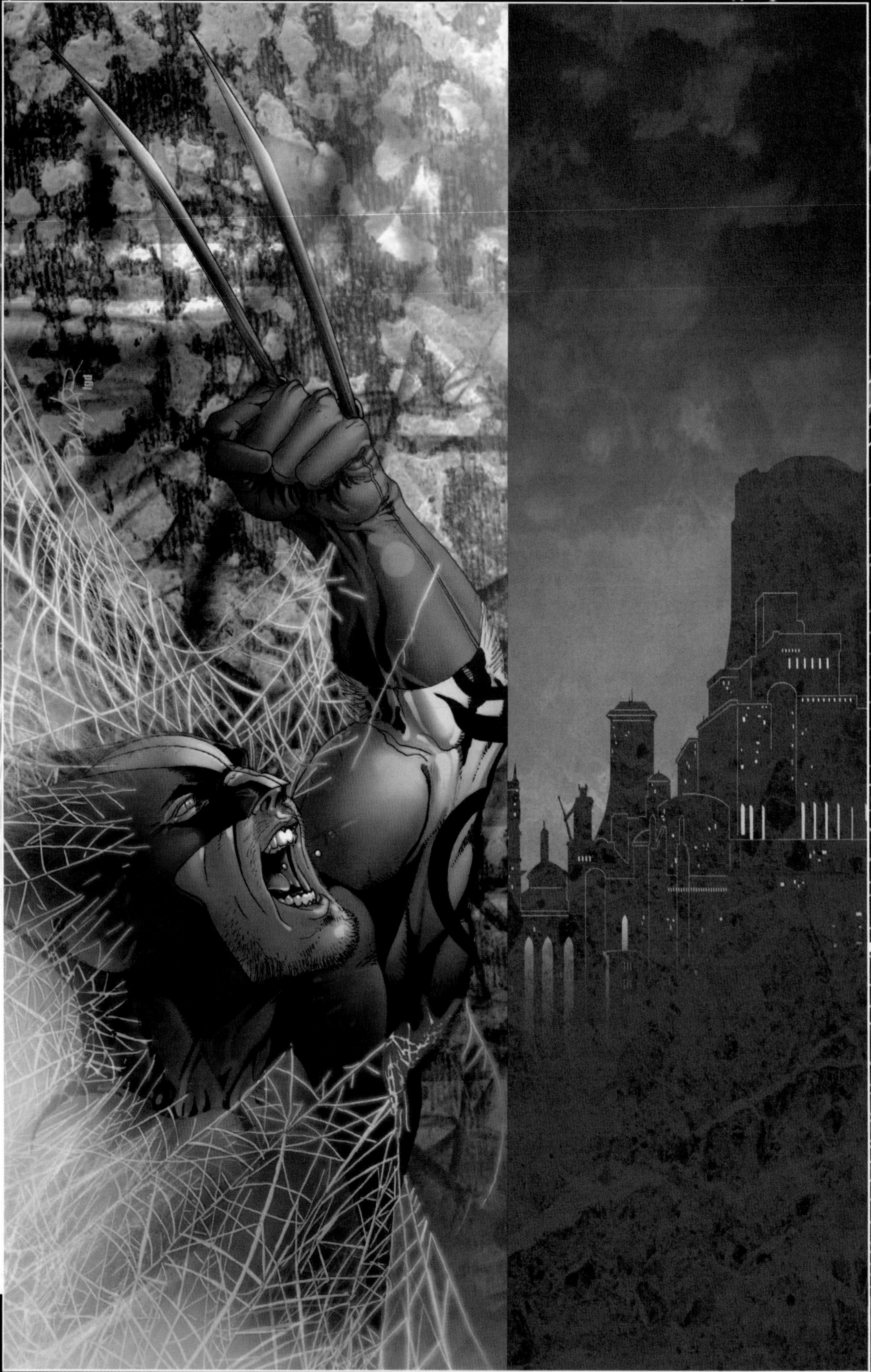

DARK WOLVERINE #83

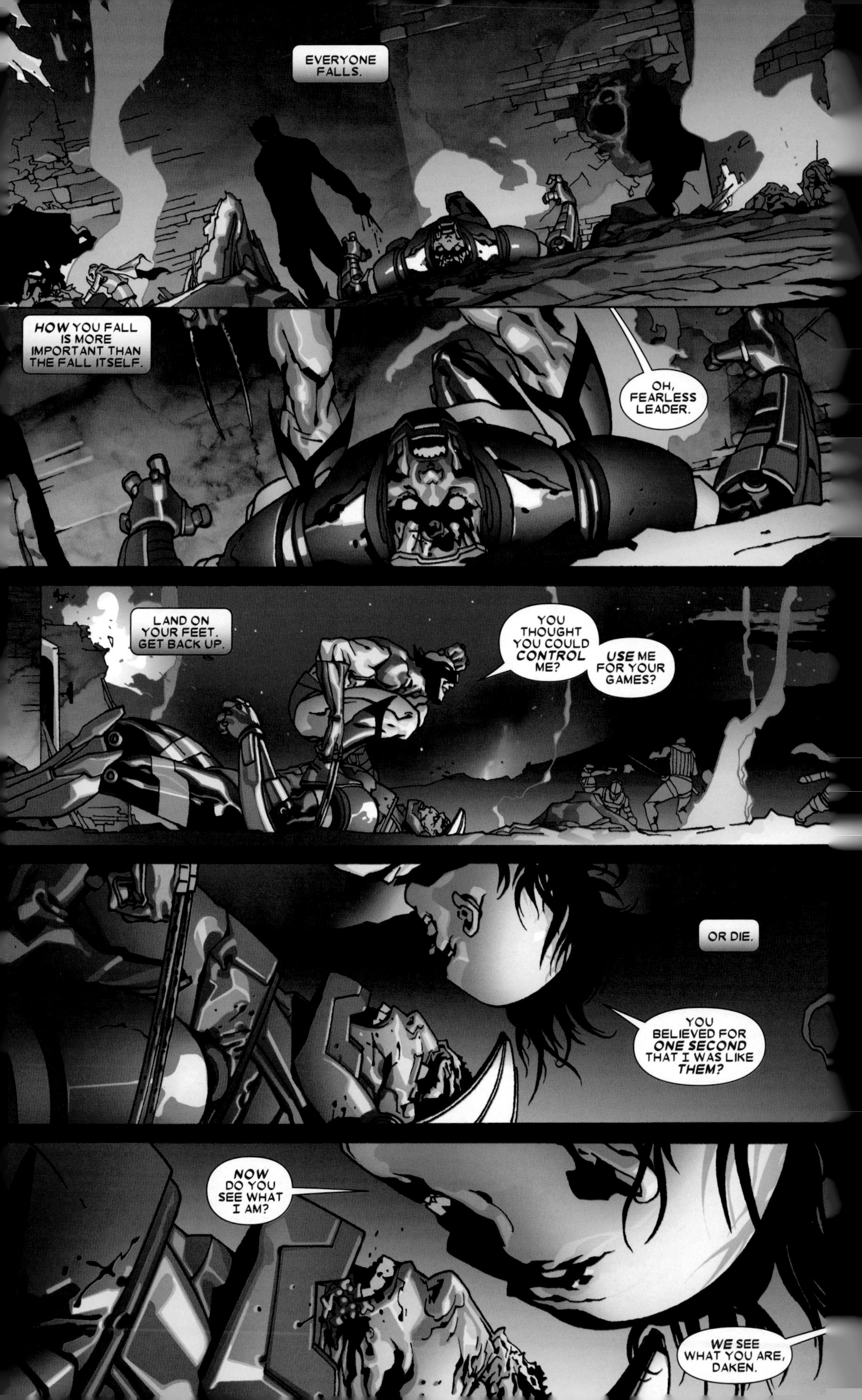
EVERYONE FALLS.
HOW YOU FALL IS MORE IMPORTANT THAN THE FALL ITSELF.
OH, FEARLESS LEADER.
LAND ON YOUR FEET. GET BACK UP.
YOU THOUGHT YOU COULD CONTROL ME?
USE ME FOR YOUR GAMES?
OR DIE.
YOU BELIEVED FOR ONE SECOND THAT I WAS LIKE THEM?
NOW DO YOU SEE WHAT I AM?
WE SEE WHAT YOU ARE, DAKEN.

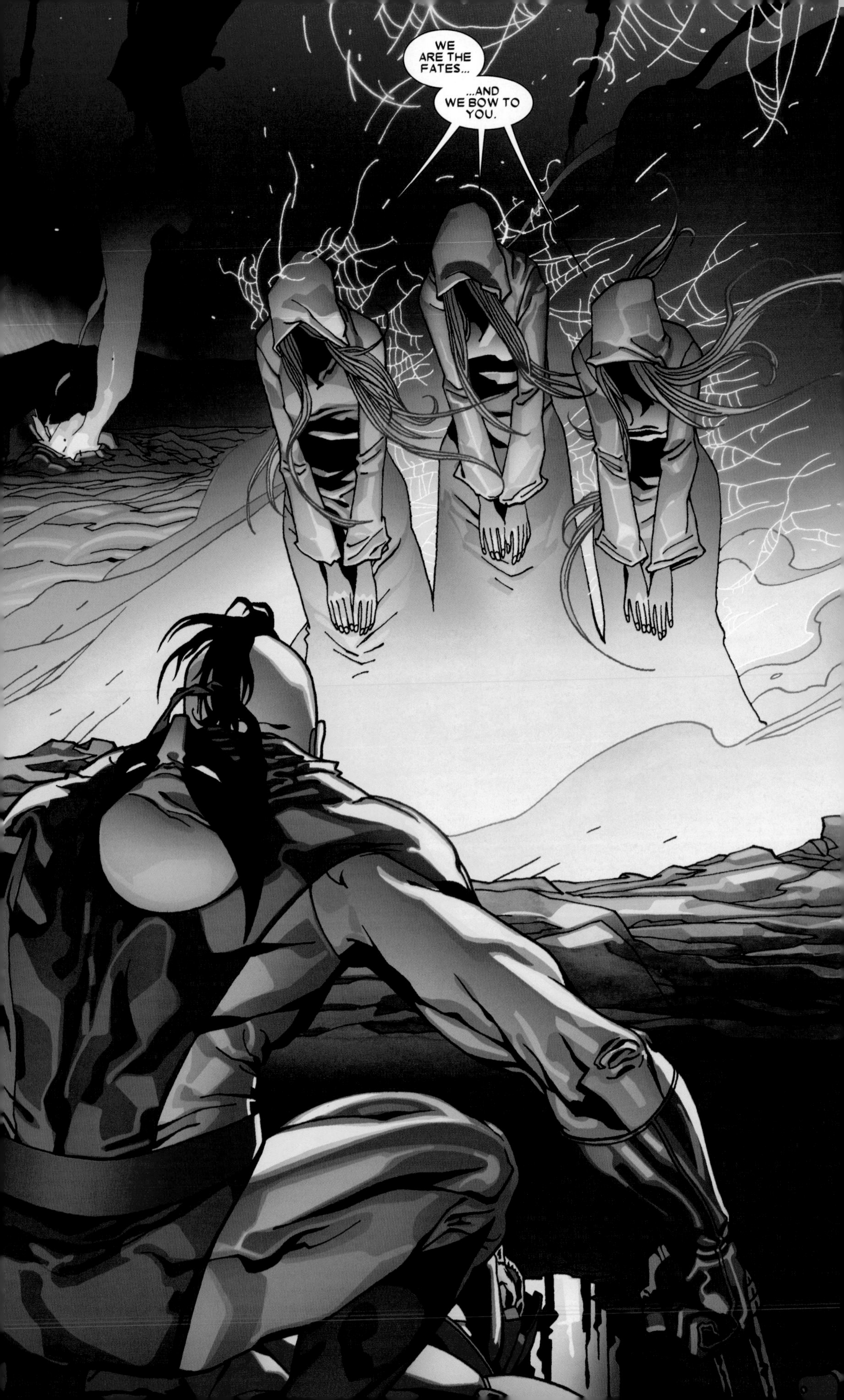
WE ARE THE FATES...
...AND WE BOW TO YOU.

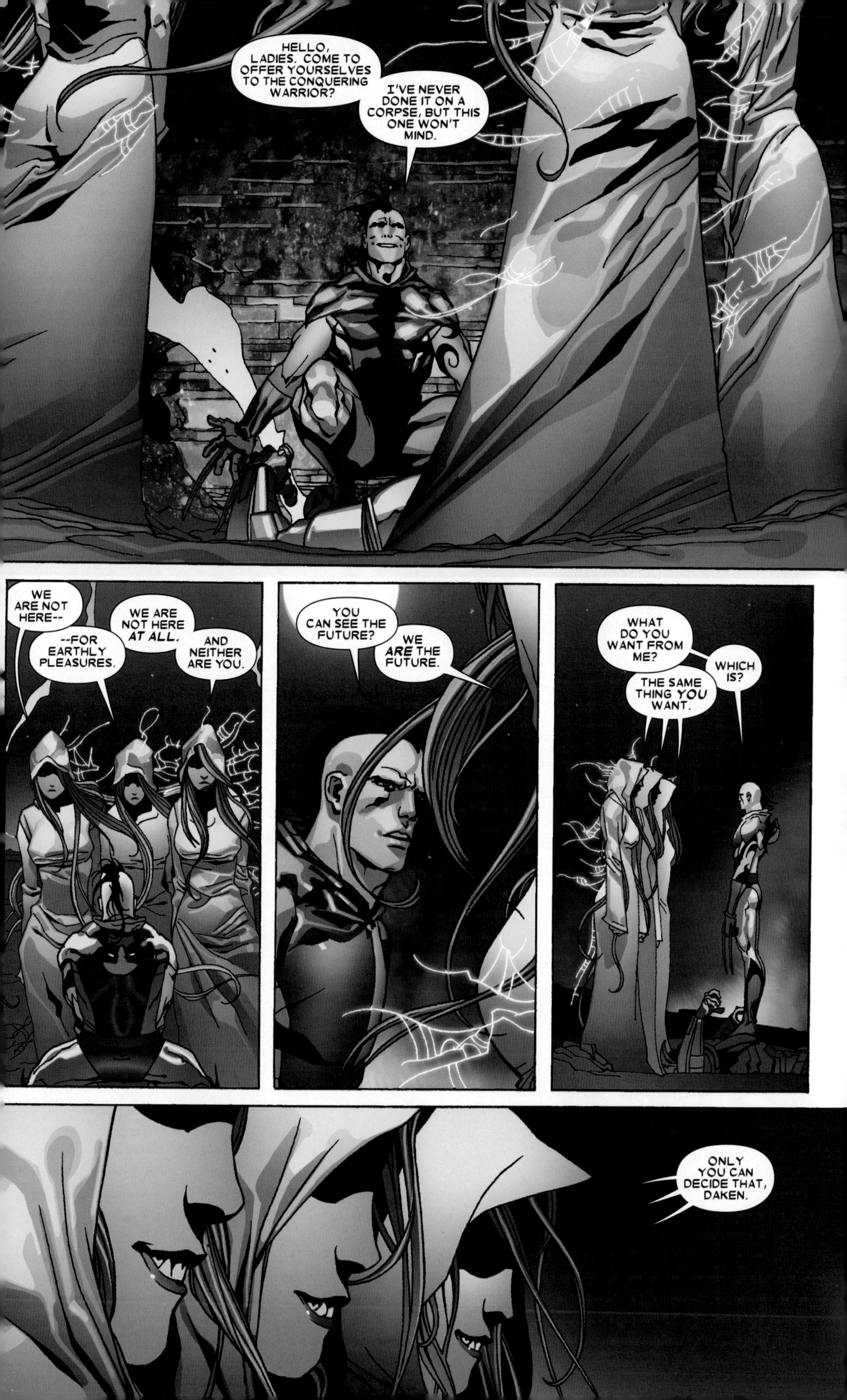
HELLO, LADIES. COME TO OFFER YOURSELVES TO THE CONQUERING WARRIOR?
I'VE NEVER DONE IT ON A CORPSE, BUT THIS ONE WON'T MIND.
WE ARE NOT HERE--
--FOR EARTHLY PLEASURES.
WE ARE NOT HERE AT ALL.
AND NEITHER ARE YOU.
YOU CAN SEE THE FUTURE?
WE ARE THE FUTURE.
WHAT DO YOU WANT FROM ME?
THE SAME THING YOU WANT.
WHICH IS?
ONLY YOU CAN DECIDE THAT, DAKEN.

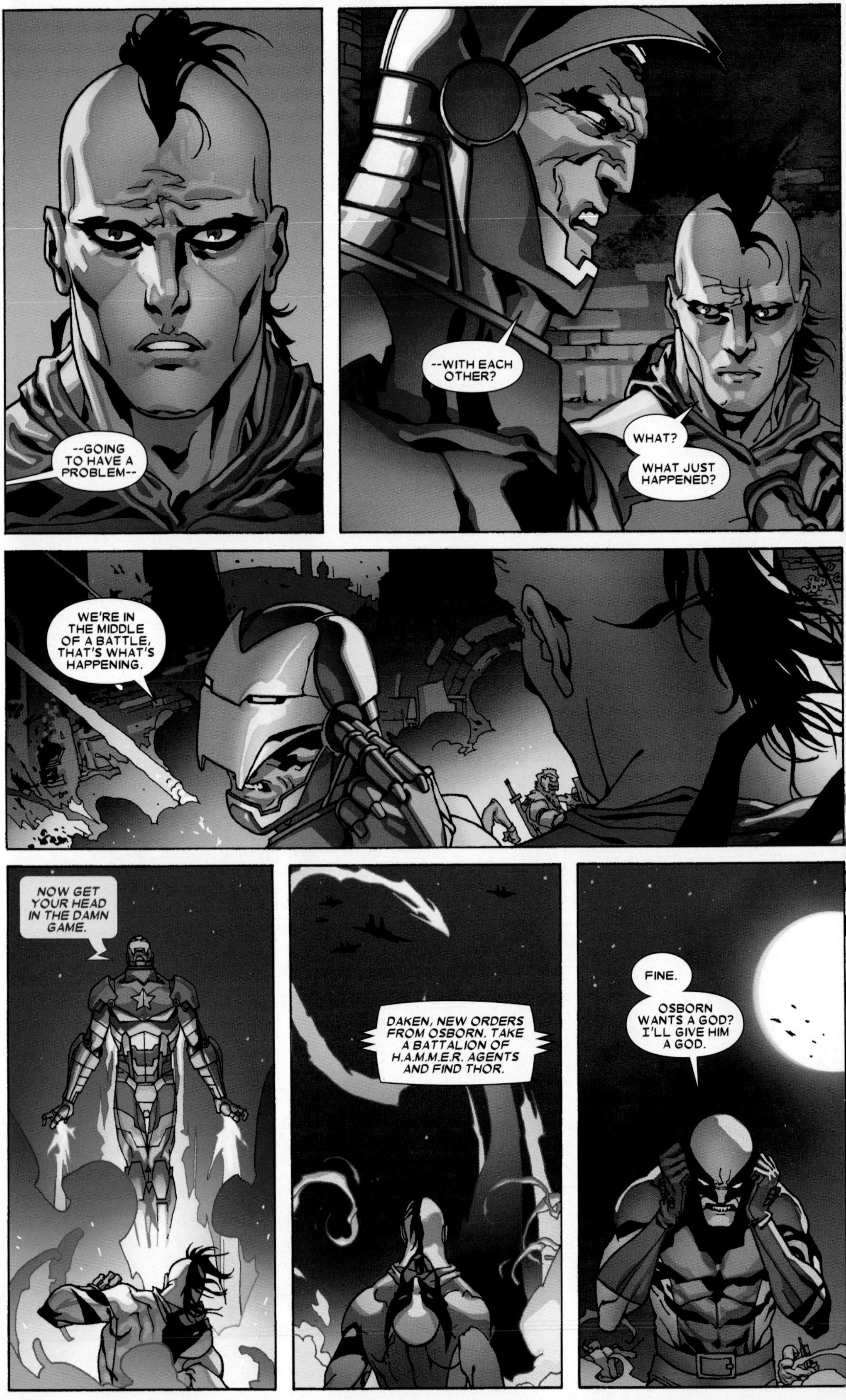
--GOING TO HAVE A PROBLEM--
--WITH EACH OTHER?
WHAT?
WHAT JUST HAPPENED?
WE'RE IN THE MIDDLE OF A BATTLE, THAT'S WHAT'S HAPPENING.
NOW GET YOUR HEAD IN THE DAMN GAME.
DAKEN, NEW ORDERS FROM OSBORN. TAKE A BATTALION OF H.A.M.M.E.R. AGENTS AND FIND THOR.
FINE.
OSBORN WANTS A GOD? I'LL GIVE HIM A GOD.

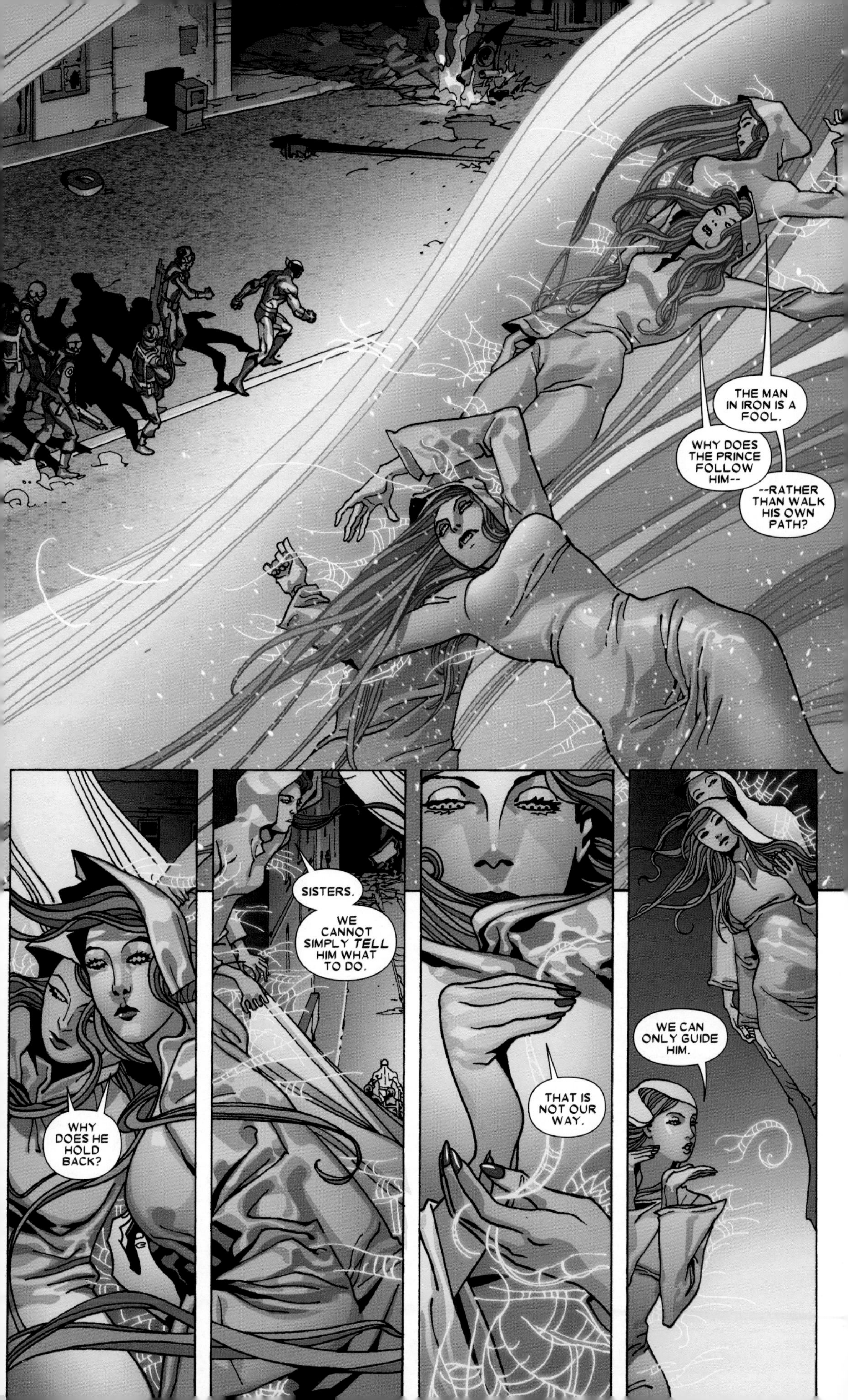
THE MAN IN IRON IS A FOOL.
WHY DOES THE PRINCE FOLLOW HIM--
--RATHER THAN WALK HIS OWN PATH?
WHY DOES HE HOLD BACK?
SISTERS.
WE CANNOT SIMPLY TELL HIM WHAT TO DO.
THAT IS NOT OUR WAY.
WE CAN ONLY GUIDE HIM.

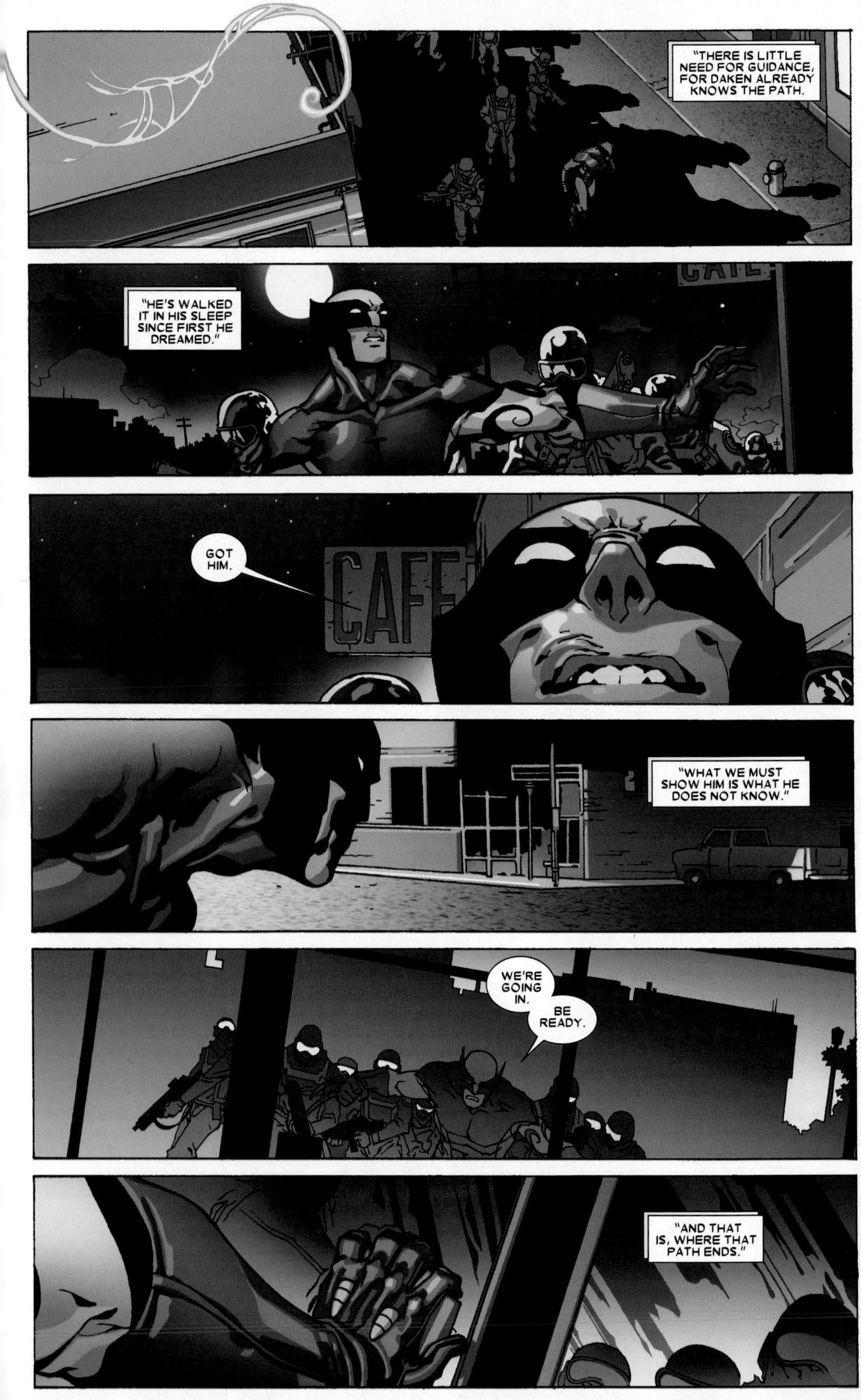
"THERE IS LITTLE NEED FOR GUIDANCE, FOR DAKEN ALREADY KNOWS THE PATH.
"HE'S WALKED IT IN HIS SLEEP SINCE FIRST HE DREAMED."
CAFE
GOT HIM.
CAFE
"WHAT WE MUST SHOW HIM IS WHAT HE DOES NOT KNOW."
WE'RE GOING IN.
BE READY.
"AND THAT IS, WHERE THAT PATH ENDS."

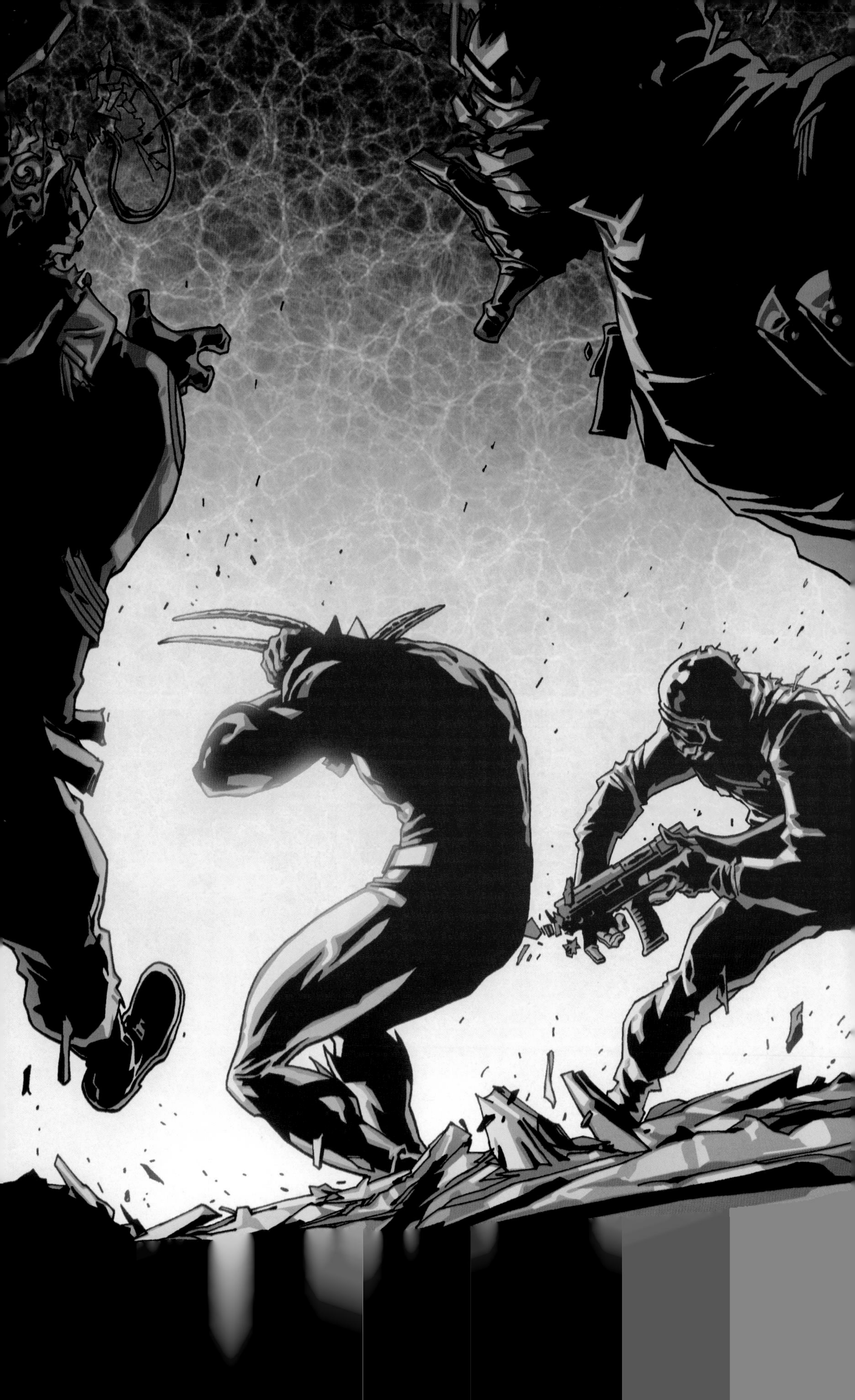

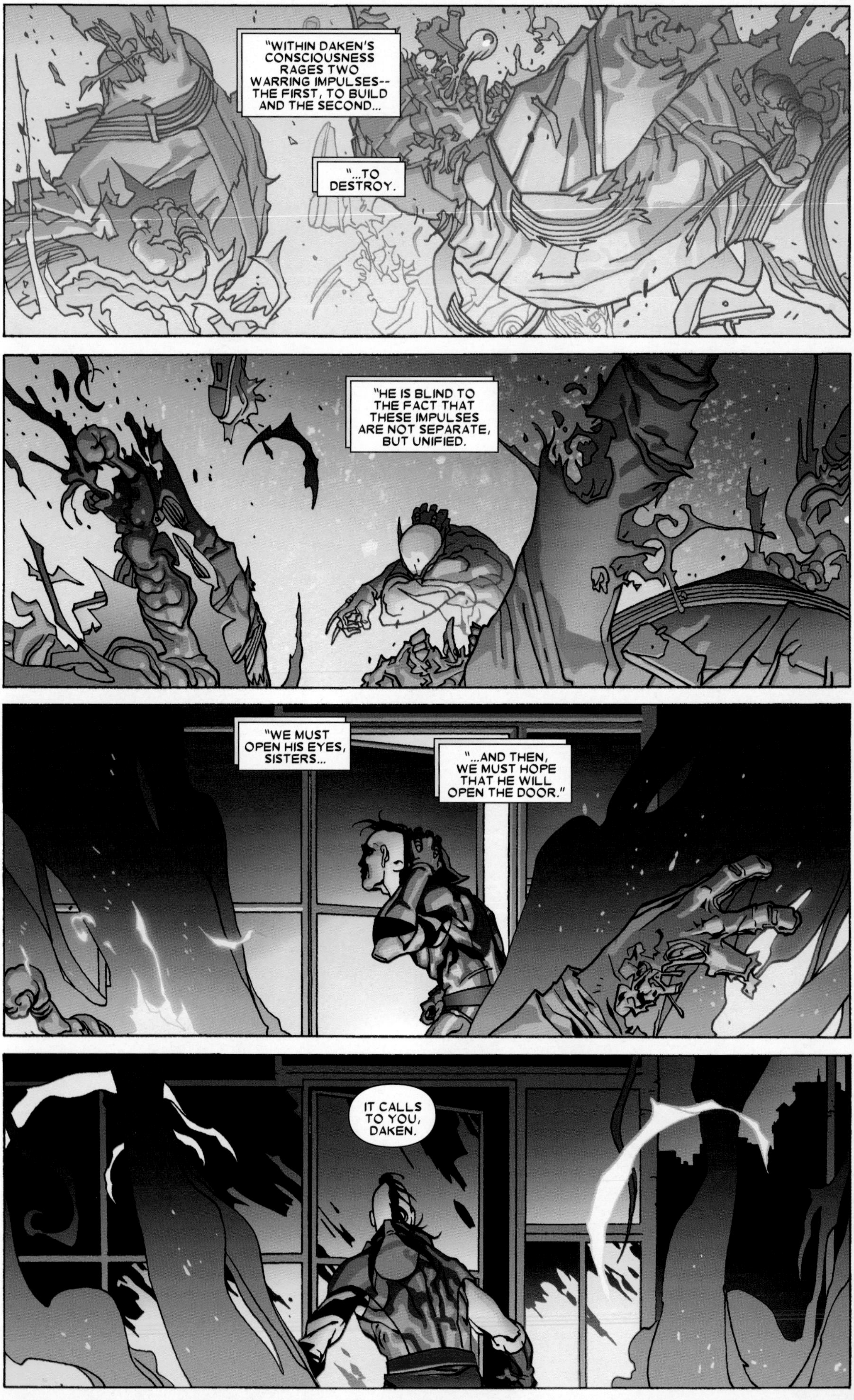
"WITHIN DAKEN'S CONSCIOUSNESS RAGES TWO WARRING IMPULSES-- THE FIRST, TO BUILD AND THE SECOND...
"...TO DESTROY.
"HE IS BLIND TO THE FACT THAT THESE IMPULSES ARE NOT SEPARATE, BUT UNIFIED.
"WE MUST OPEN HIS EYES, SISTERS...
"...AND THEN, WE MUST HOPE THAT HE WILL OPEN THE DOOR."
IT CALLS TO YOU, DAKEN.

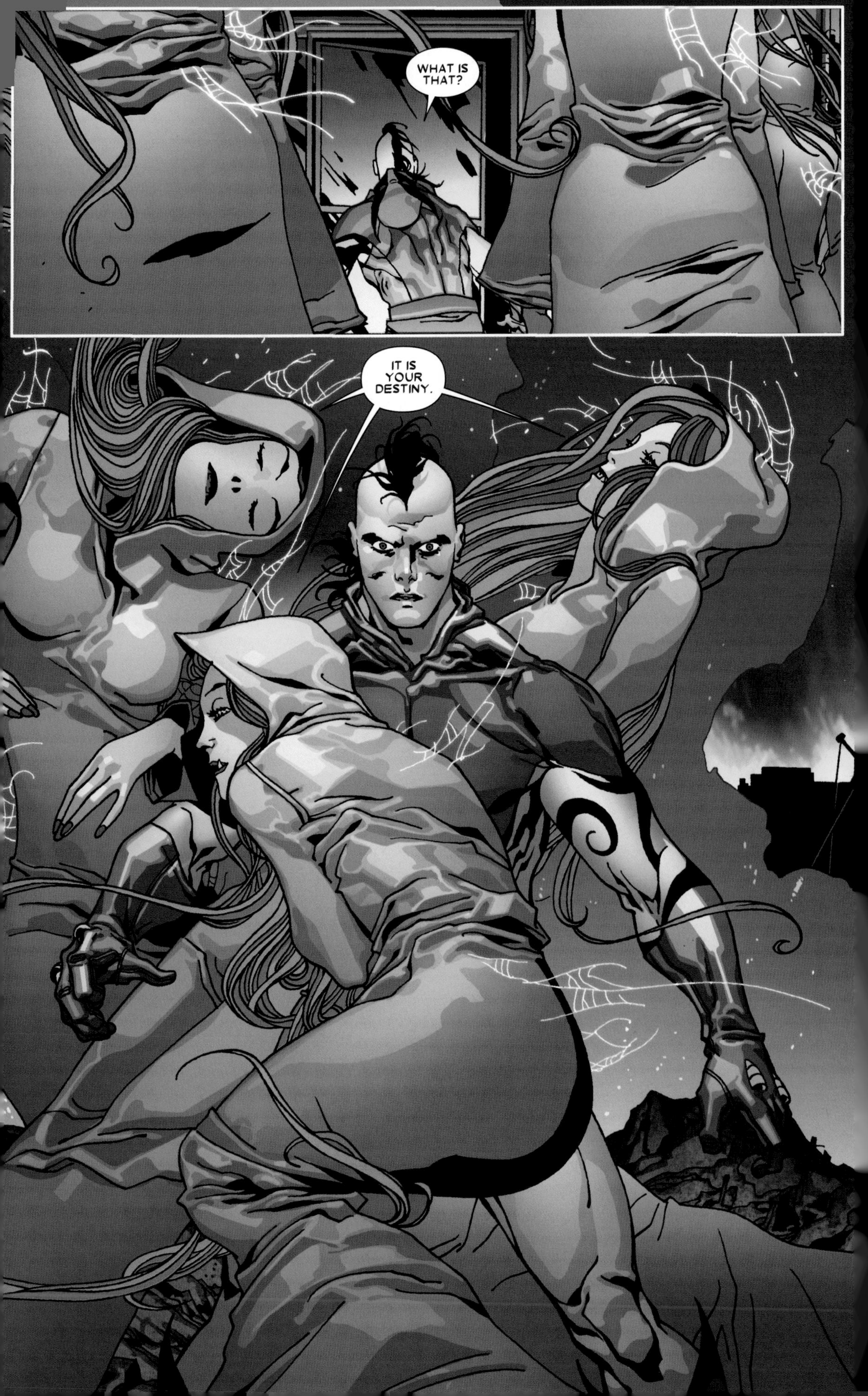
WHAT IS THAT?
IT IS YOUR DESTINY.

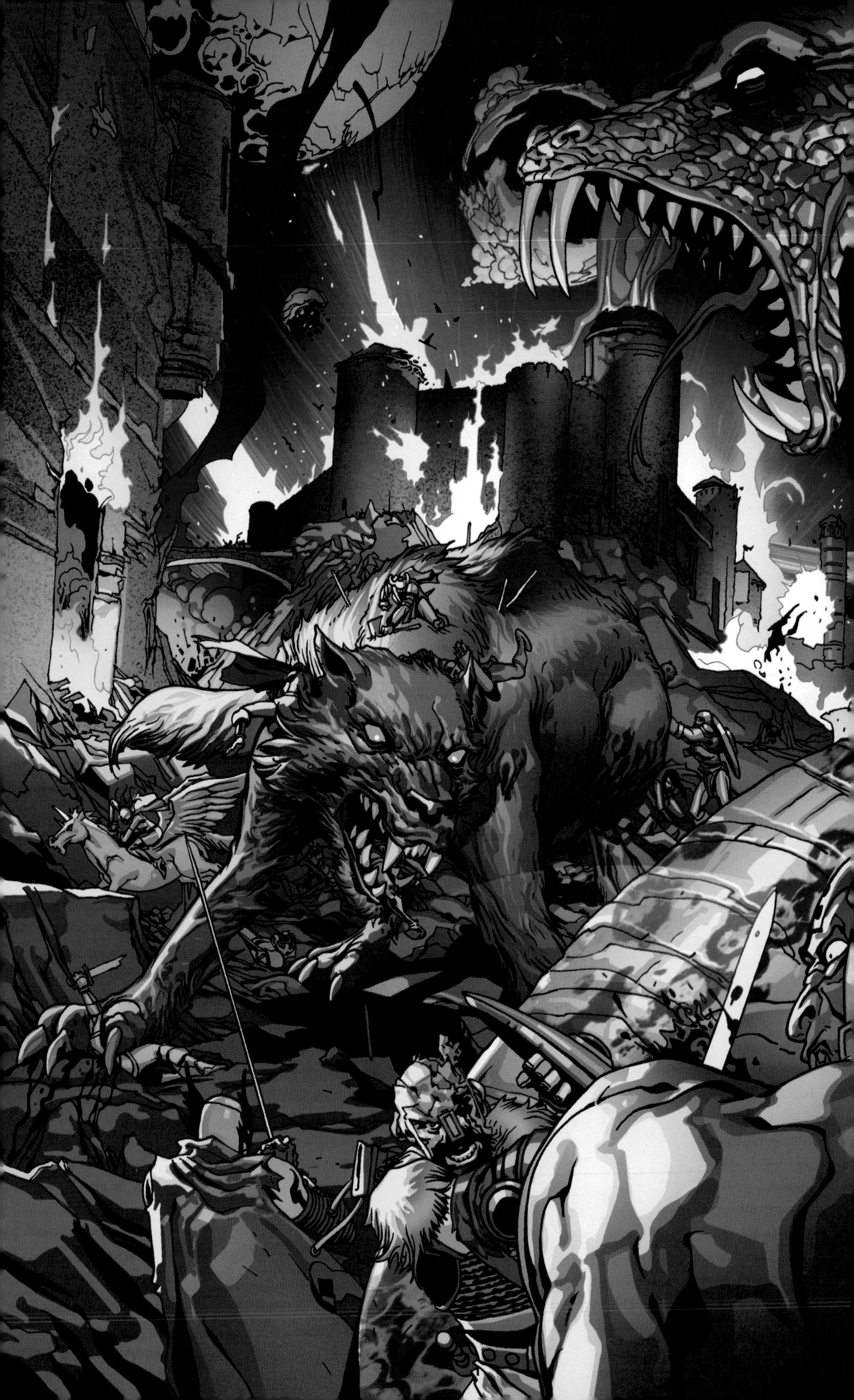

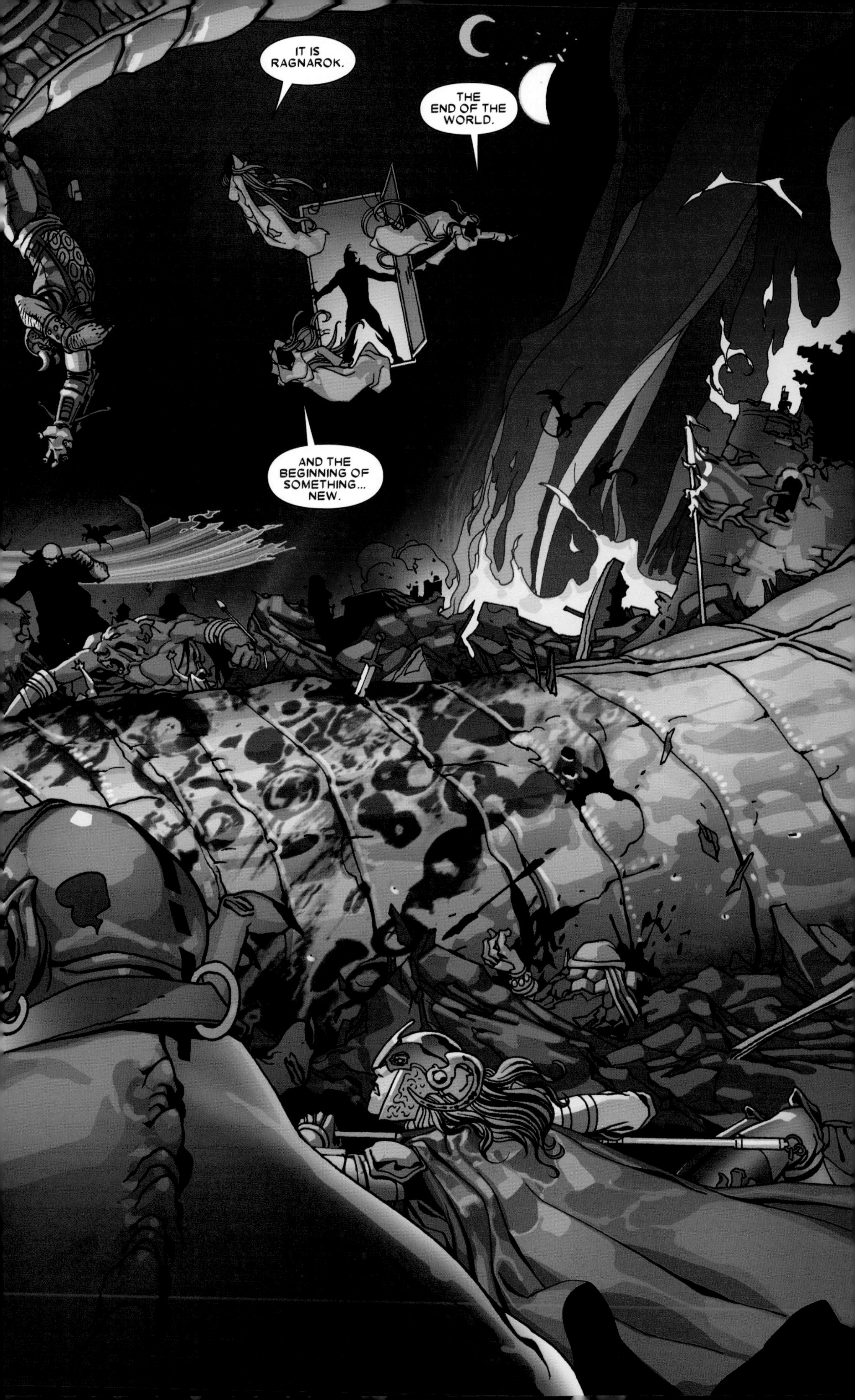
IT IS RAGNAROK.
THE END OF THE WORLD.
AND THE BEGINNING OF SOMETHING... NEW.

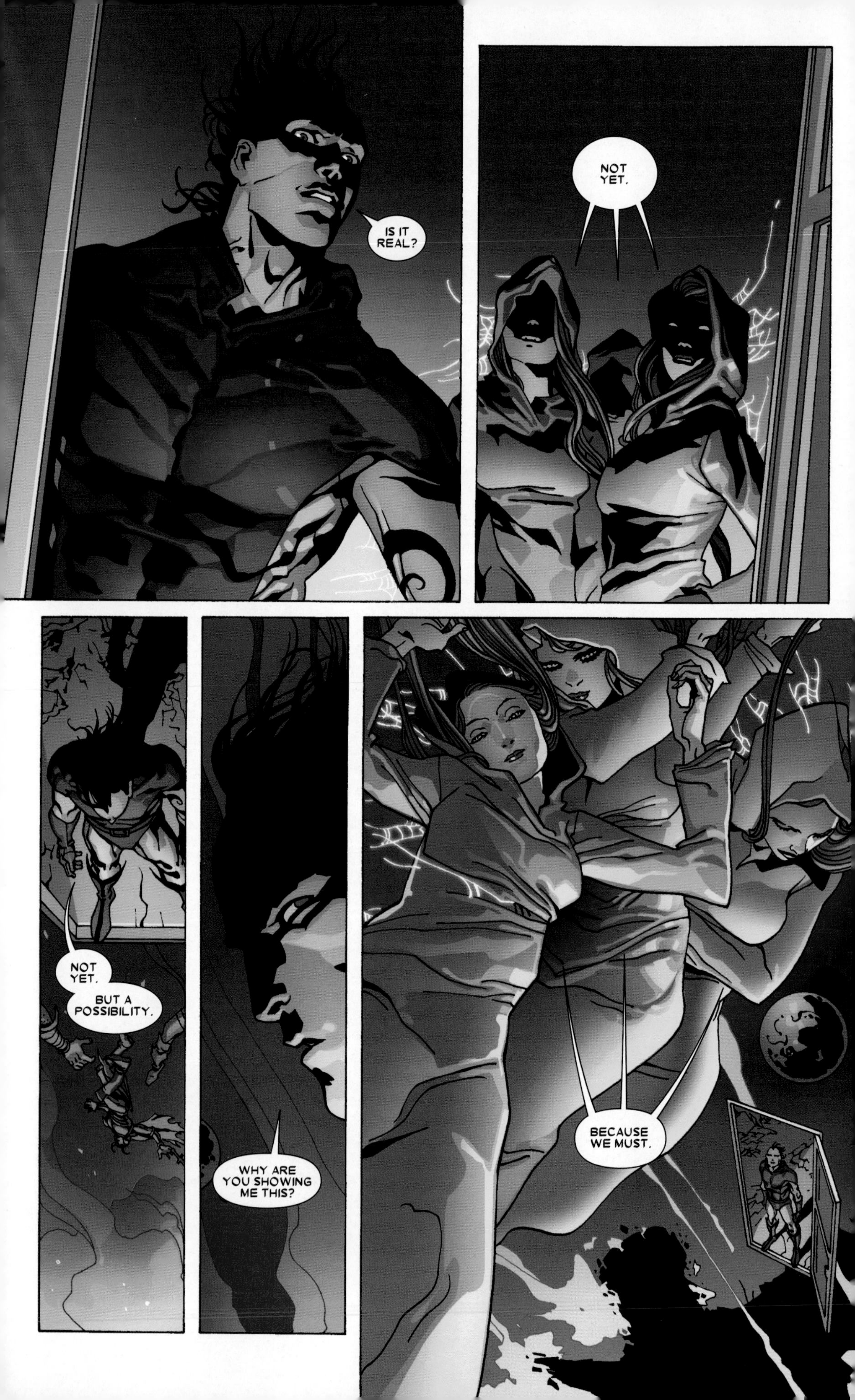
IS IT REAL?
NOT YET.
NOT YET.
BUT A POSSIBILITY.
WHY ARE YOU SHOWING ME THIS?
BECAUSE WE MUST.

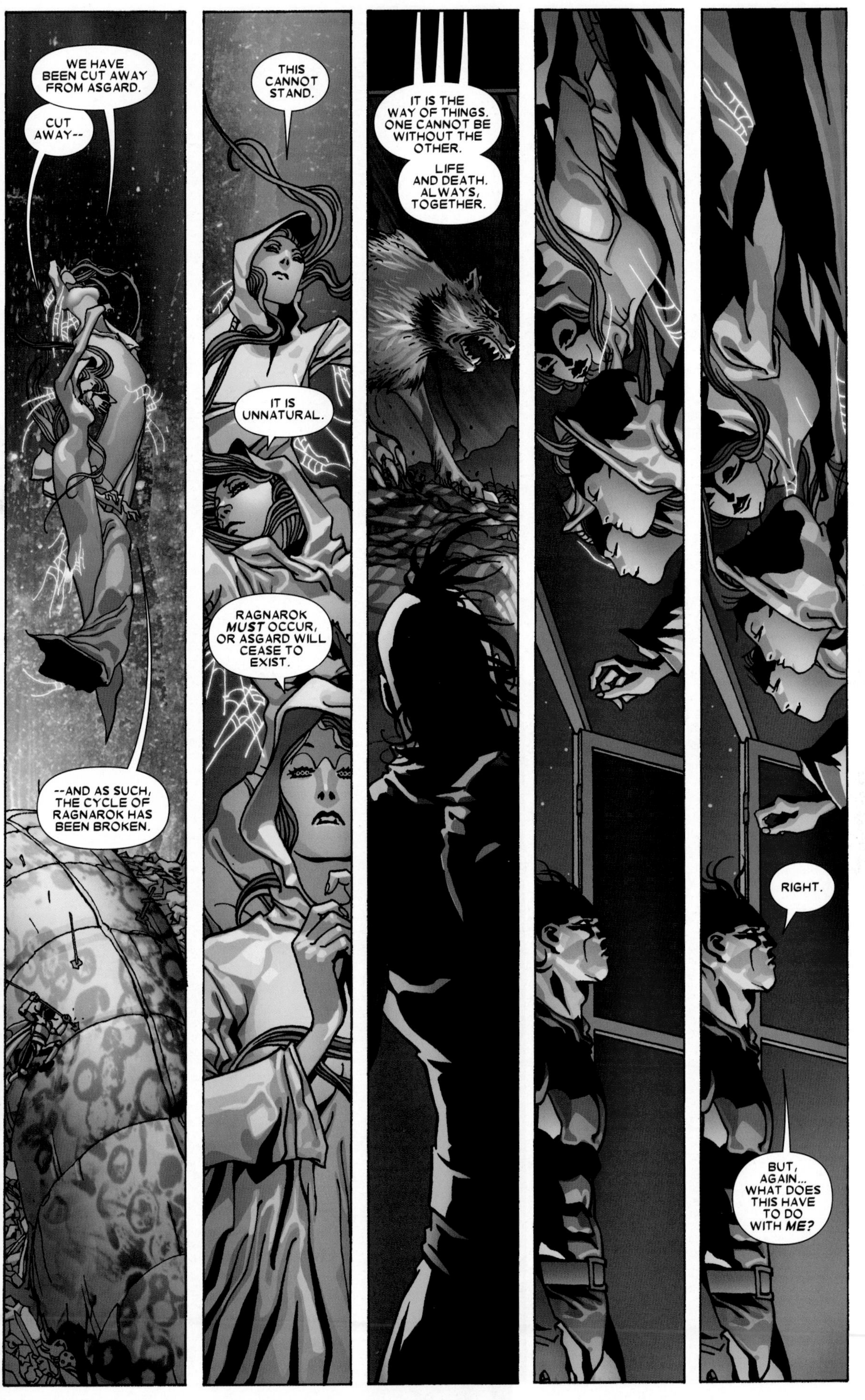

WE HAVE BEEN CUT AWAY FROM ASGARD.
CUT AWAY--
--AND AS SUCH, THE CYCLE OF RAGNAROK HAS BEEN BROKEN.
THIS CANNOT STAND.
IT IS UNNATURAL.
RAGNAROK *MUST* OCCUR, OR ASGARD WILL CEASE TO EXIST.
IT IS THE WAY OF THINGS. ONE CANNOT BE WITHOUT THE OTHER.
LIFE AND DEATH. ALWAYS, TOGETHER.
RIGHT.
BUT, AGAIN... WHAT DOES THIS HAVE TO DO WITH *ME*?

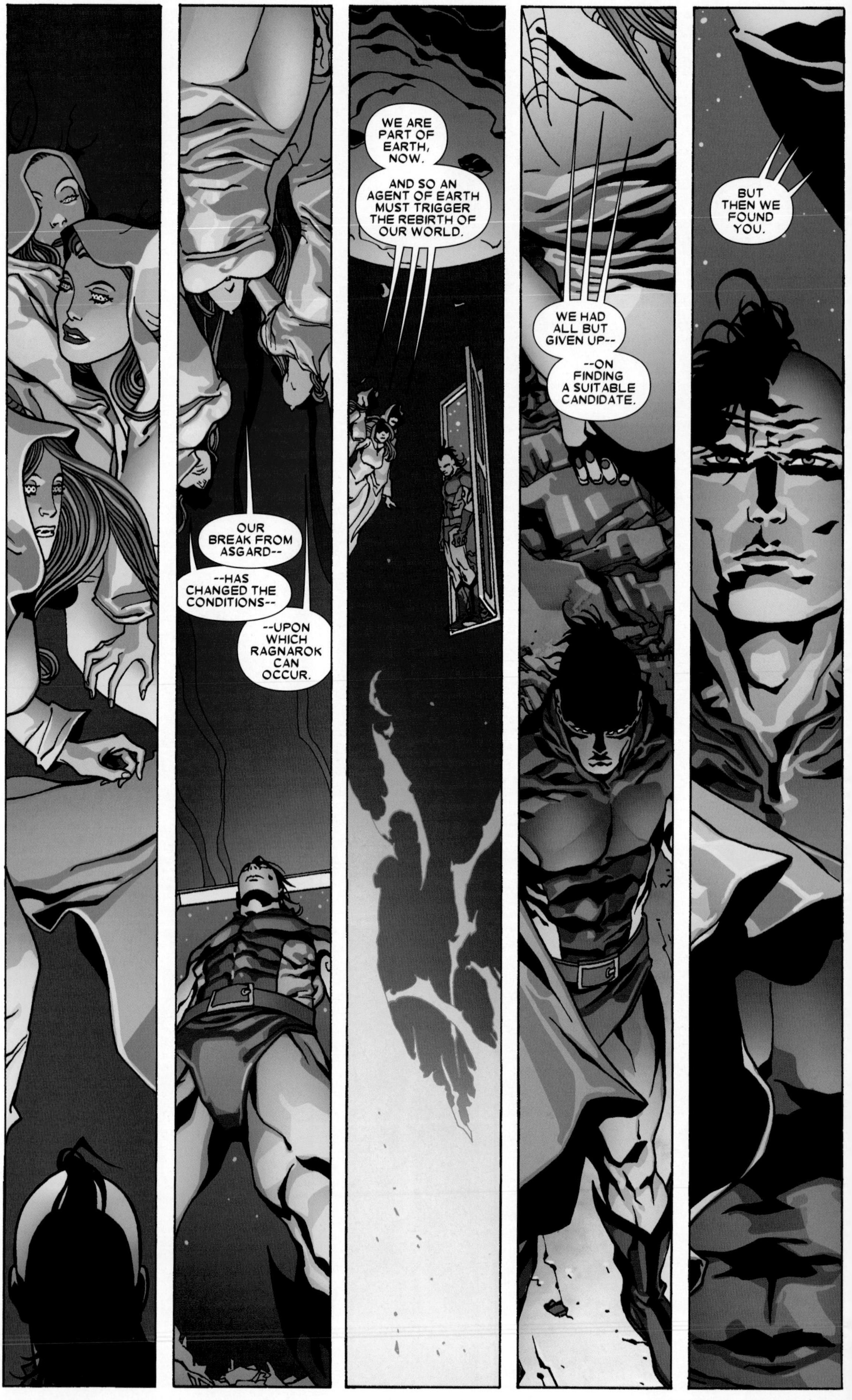
OUR BREAK FROM ASGARD--
--HAS CHANGED THE CONDITIONS--
--UPON WHICH RAGNAROK CAN OCCUR.
WE ARE PART OF EARTH, NOW.
AND SO AN AGENT OF EARTH MUST TRIGGER THE REBIRTH OF OUR WORLD.
WE HAD ALL BUT GIVEN UP--
--ON FINDING A SUITABLE CANDIDATE.
BUT THEN WE FOUND YOU.

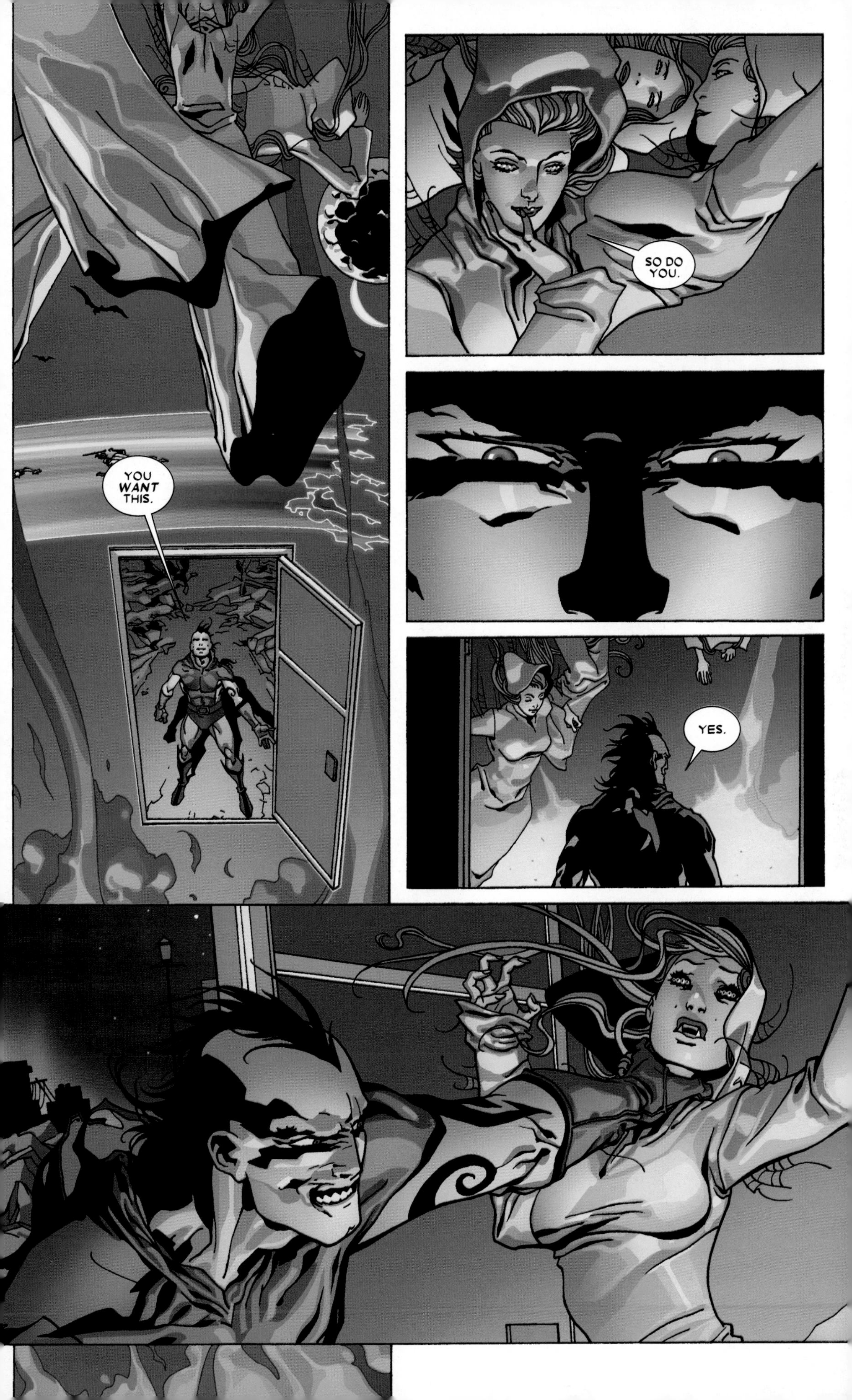

YOU WANT THIS.
SO DO YOU.
YES.

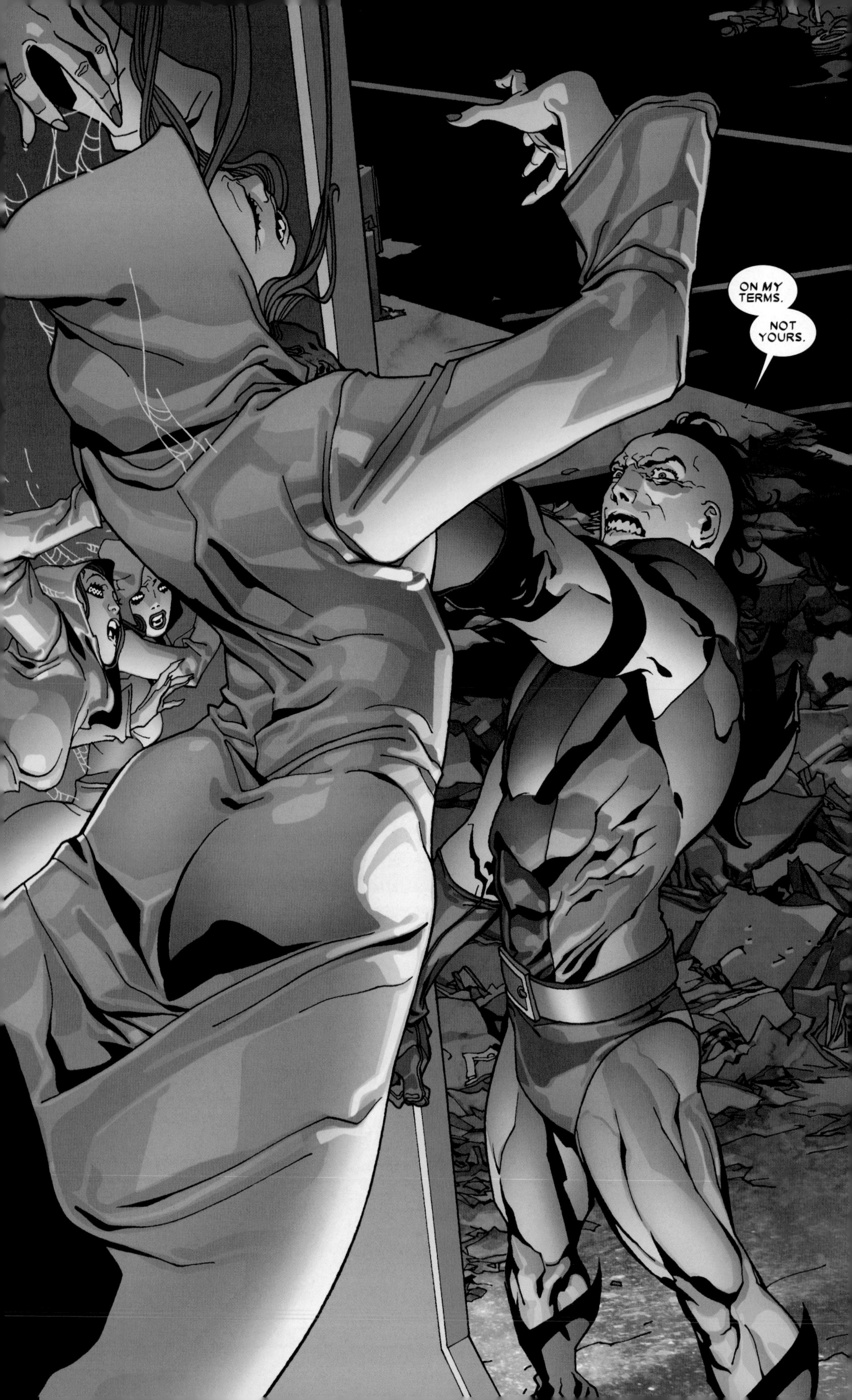
ON MY TERMS.
NOT YOURS.

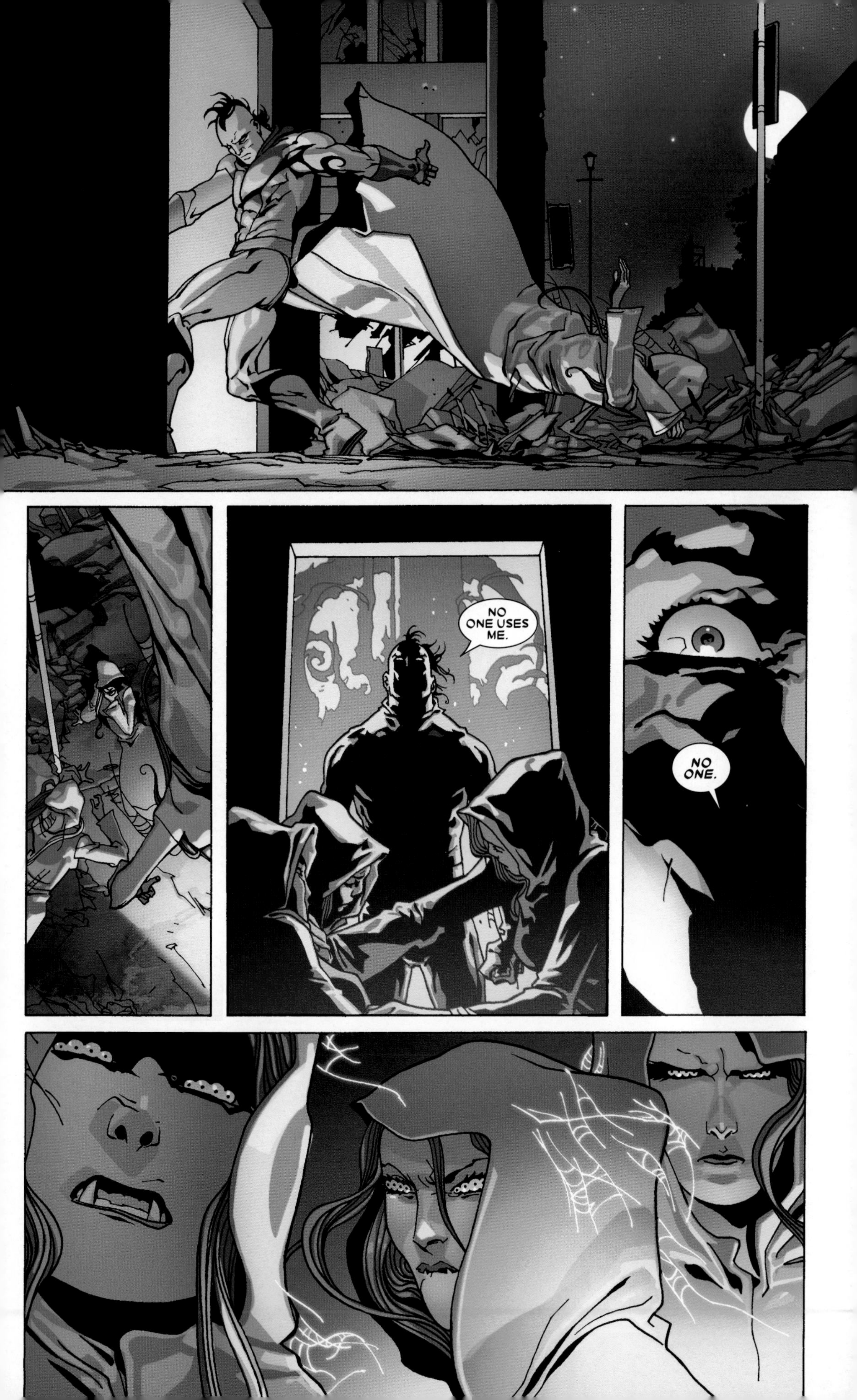
NO ONE USES ME.
NO ONE.

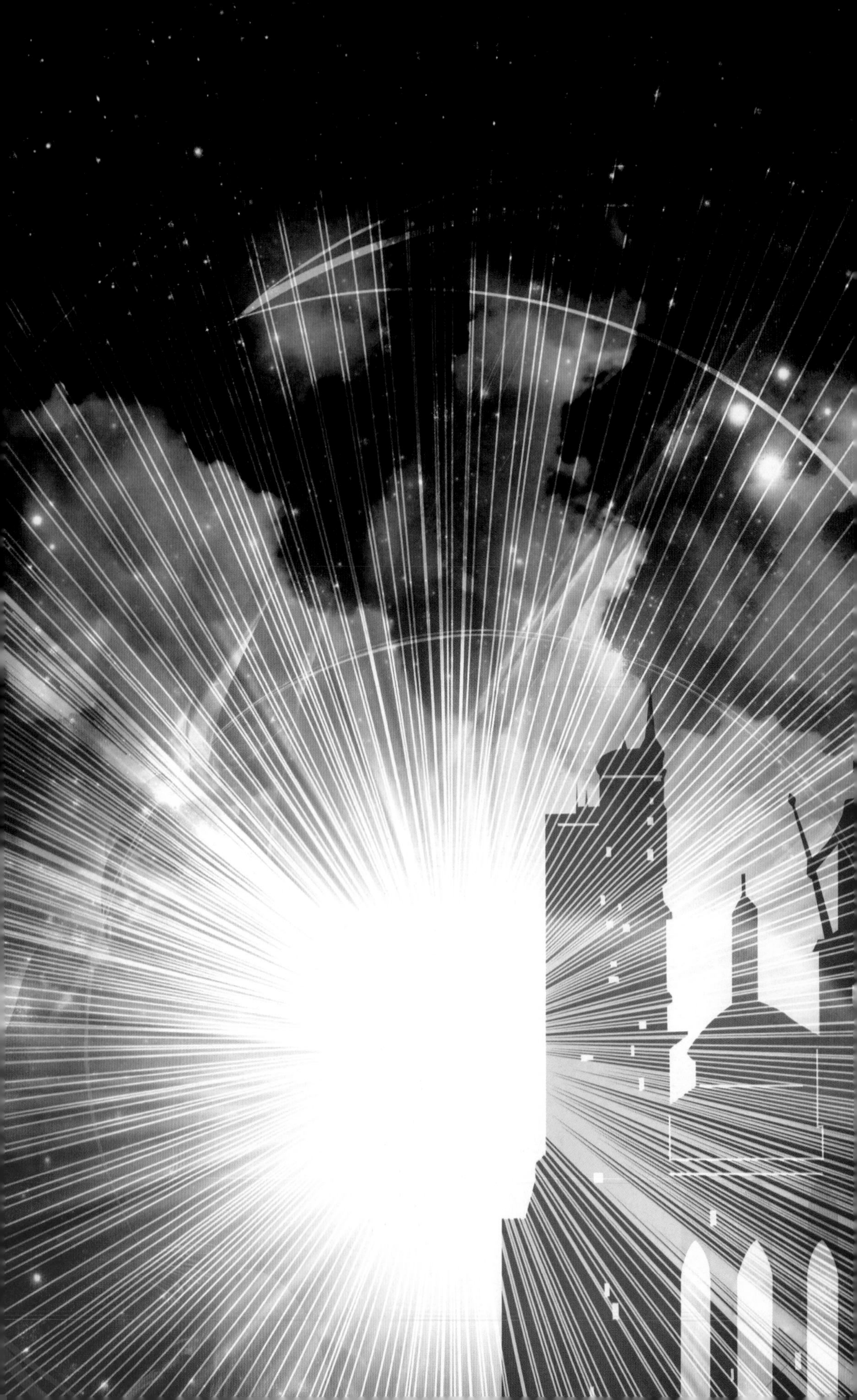

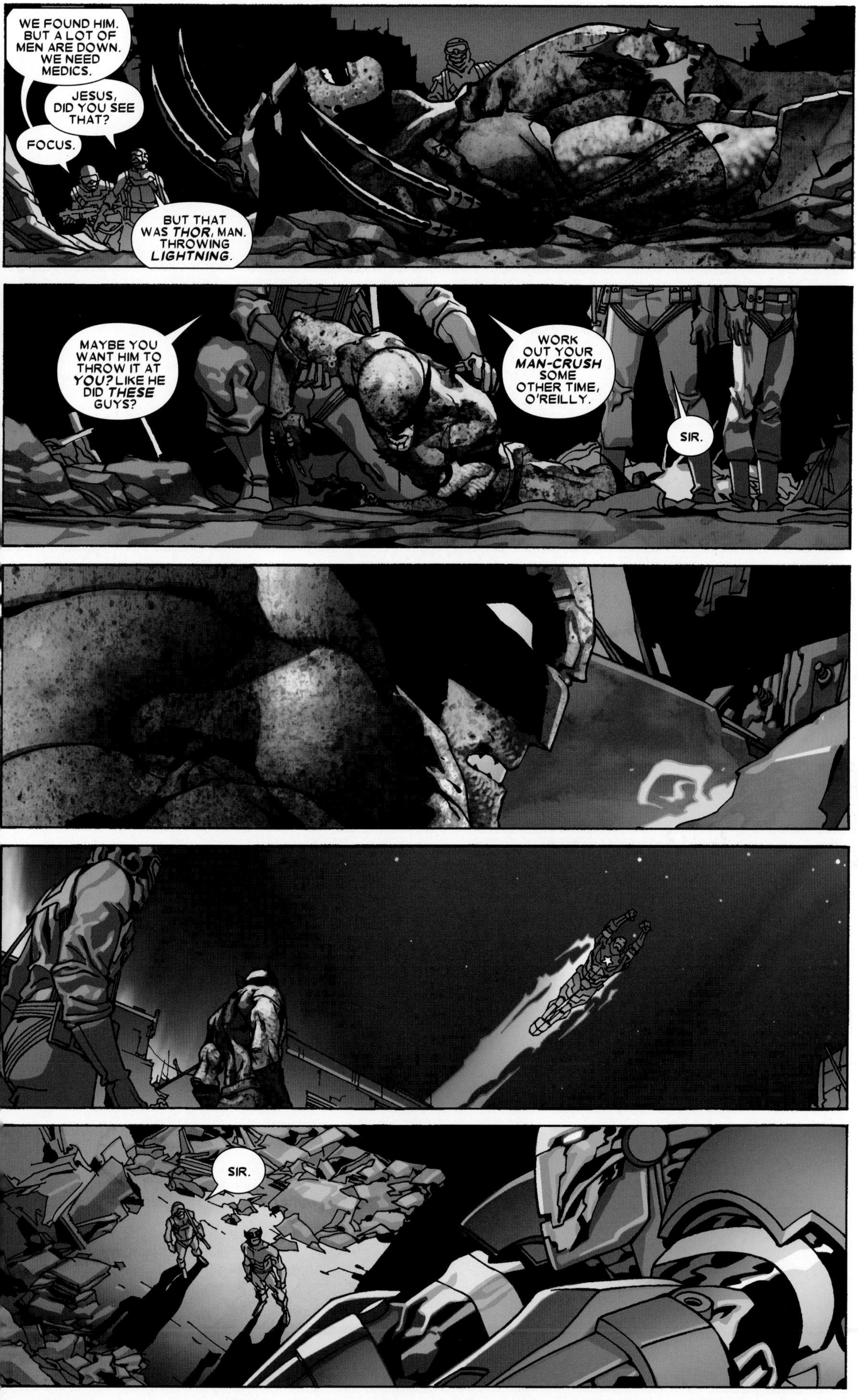
WE FOUND HIM. BUT A LOT OF MEN ARE DOWN. WE NEED MEDICS.
JESUS, DID YOU SEE THAT?
FOCUS.
BUT THAT WAS THOR, MAN. THROWING LIGHTNING.
MAYBE YOU WANT HIM TO THROW IT AT YOU? LIKE HE DID THESE GUYS?
WORK OUT YOUR MAN-CRUSH SOME OTHER TIME, O'REILLY.
SIR.
SIR.

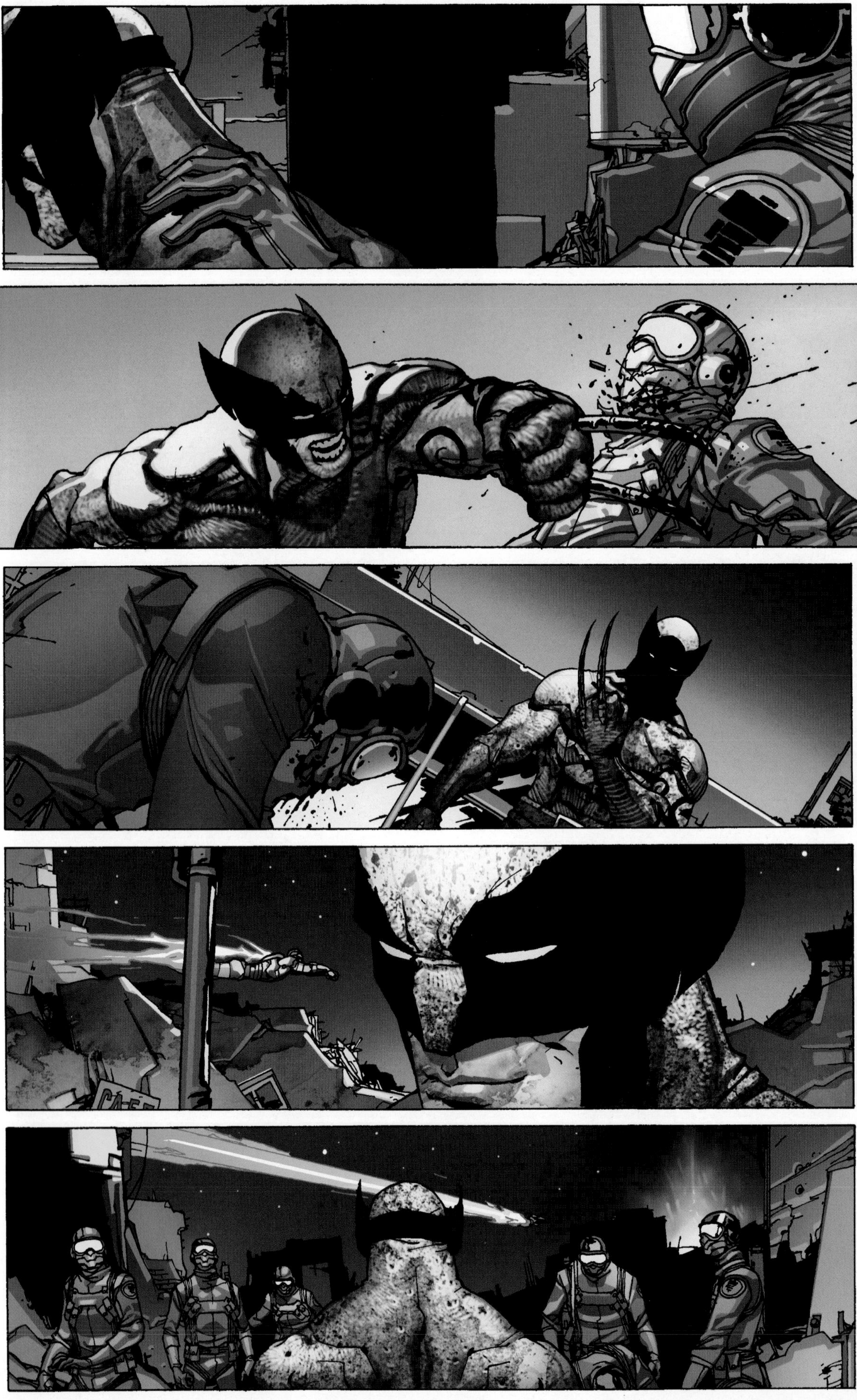

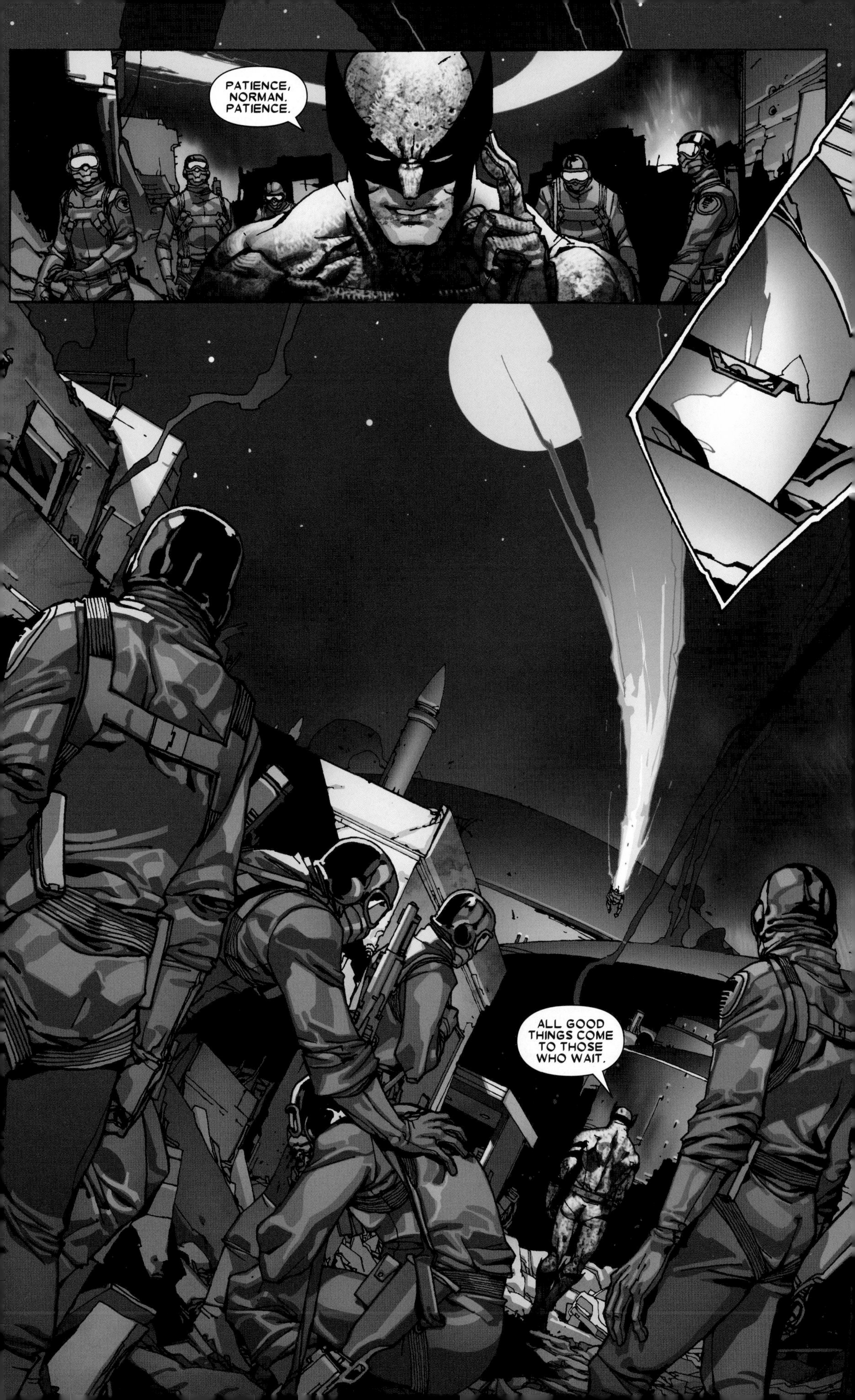
PATIENCE, NORMAN. PATIENCE.
ALL GOOD THINGS COME TO THOSE WHO WAIT.

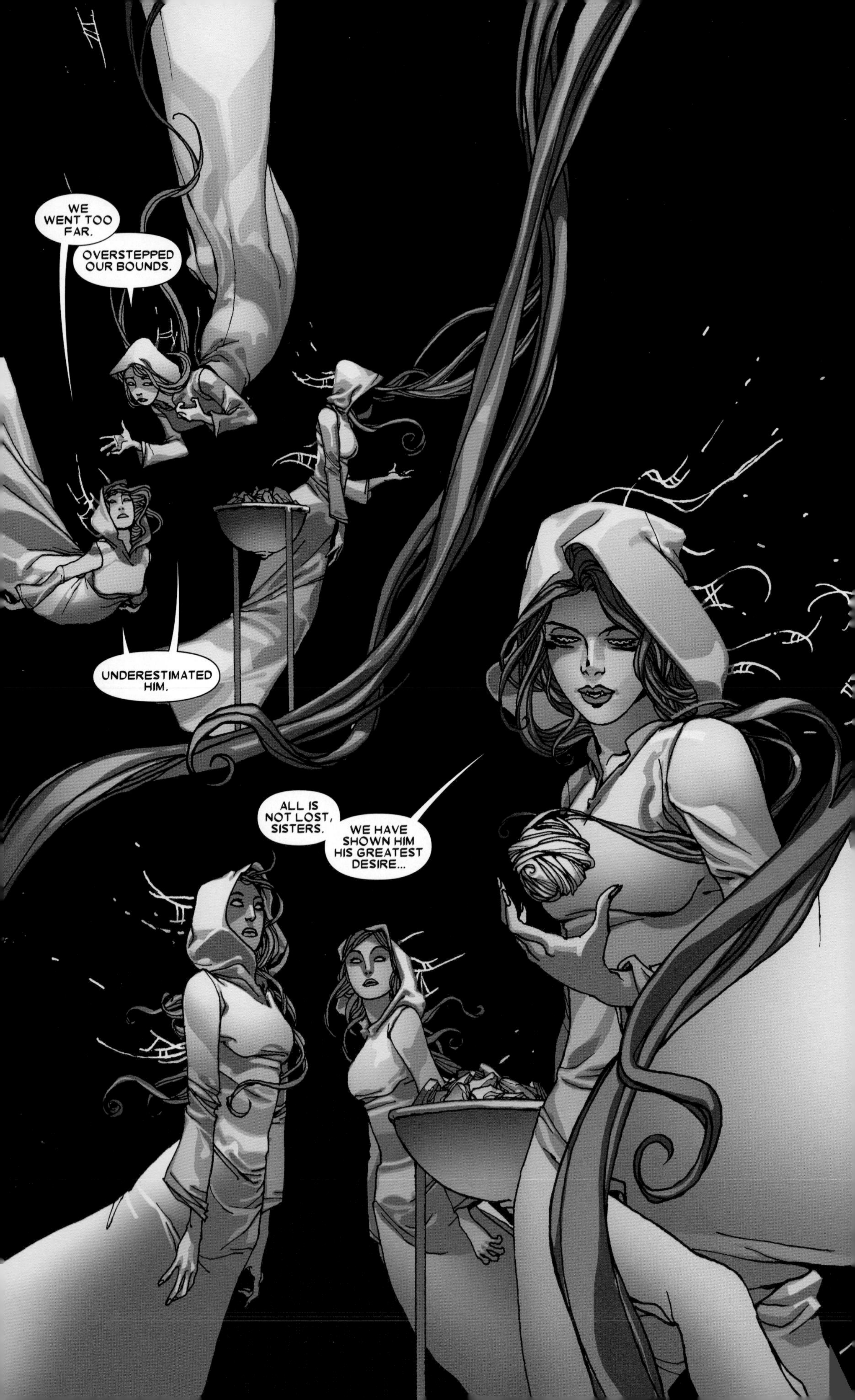
WE WENT TOO FAR.
OVERSTEPPED OUR BOUNDS.
UNDERESTIMATED HIM.
ALL IS NOT LOST, SISTERS.
WE HAVE SHOWN HIM HIS GREATEST DESIRE...

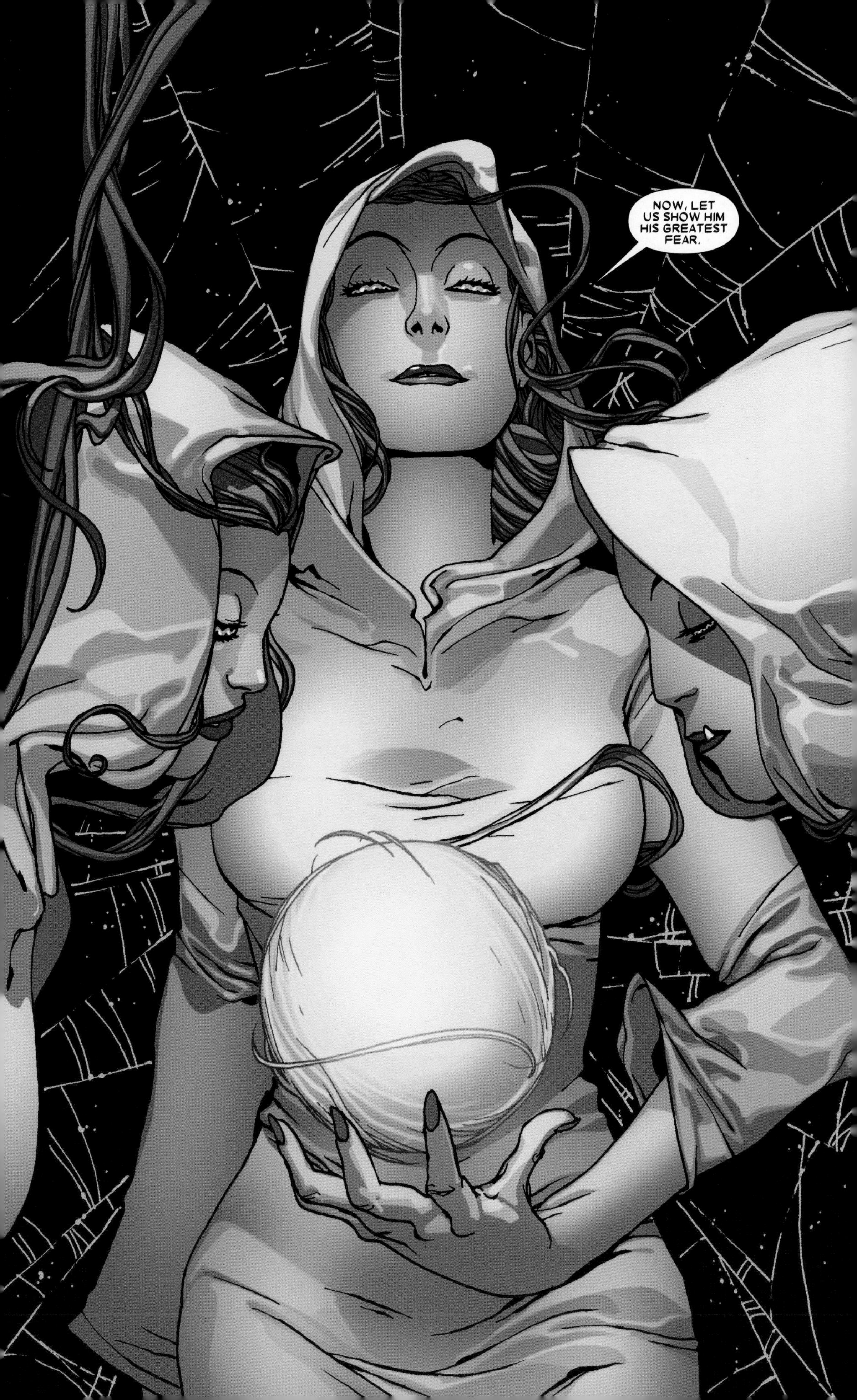
NOW, LET US SHOW HIM HIS GREATEST FEAR.

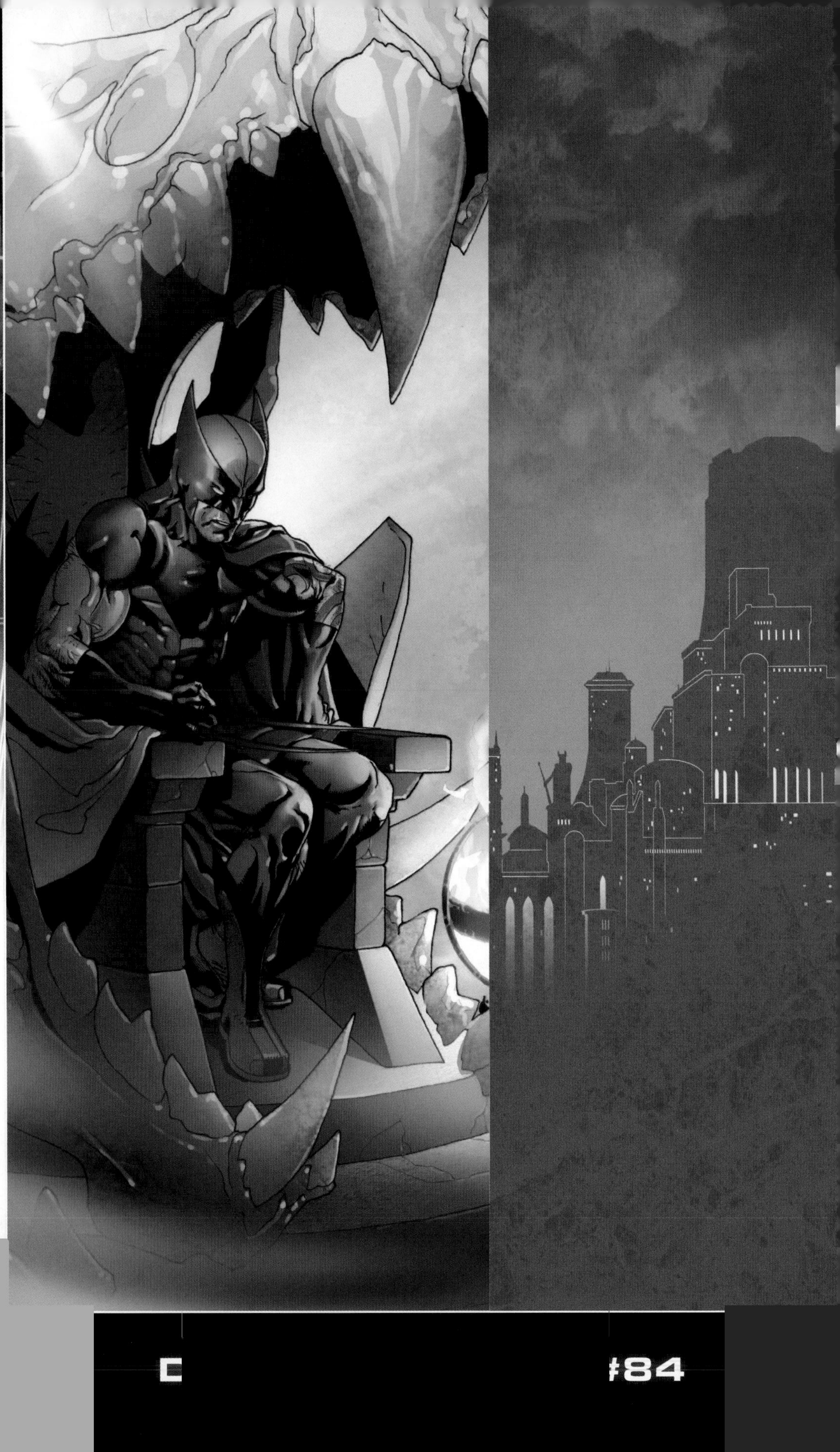
#84

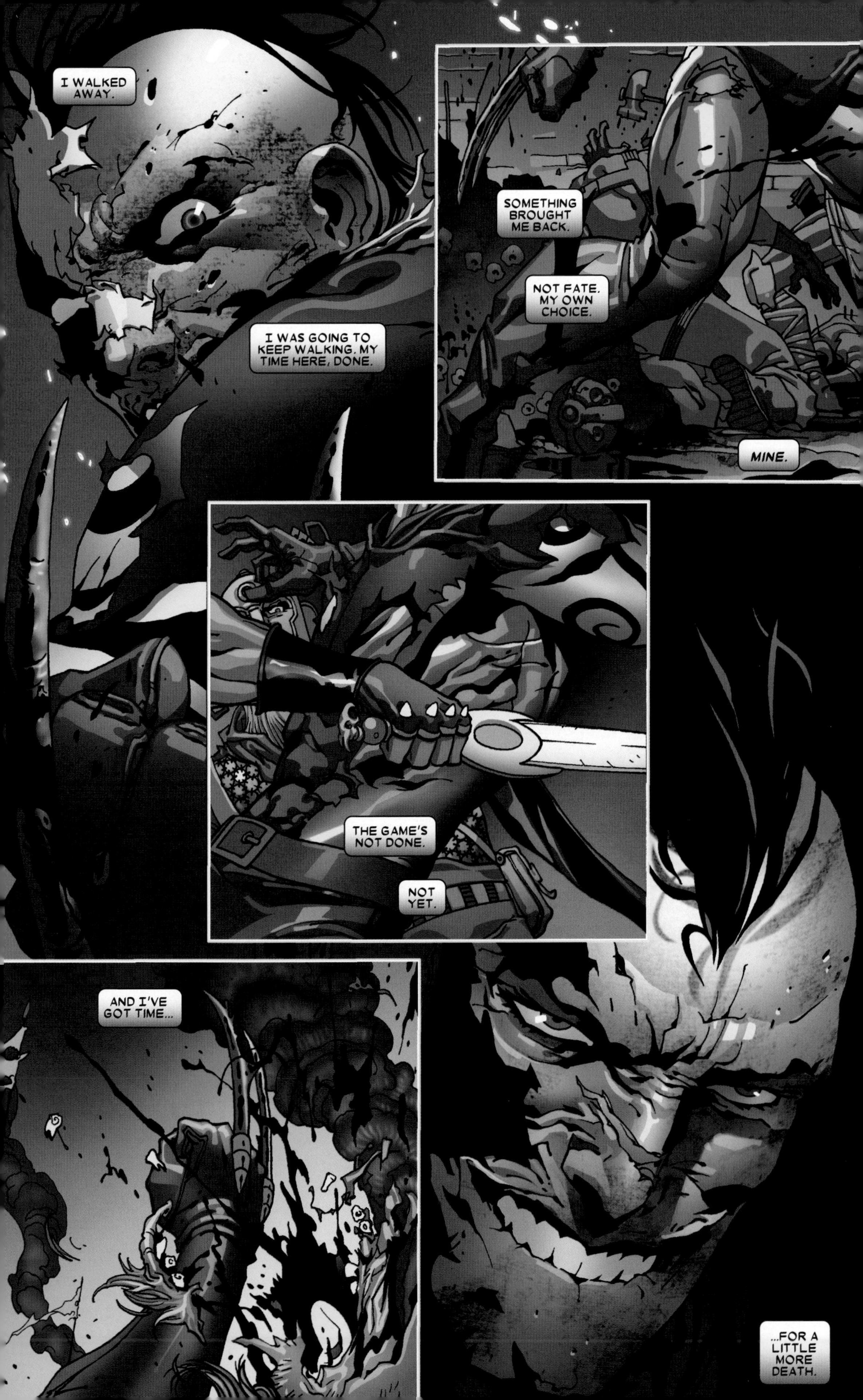
I WALKED AWAY.
I WAS GOING TO KEEP WALKING. MY TIME HERE, DONE.
SOMETHING BROUGHT ME BACK.
NOT FATE. MY OWN CHOICE.
MINE.
THE GAME'S NOT DONE.
NOT YET.
AND I'VE GOT TIME...
...FOR A LITTLE MORE DEATH.

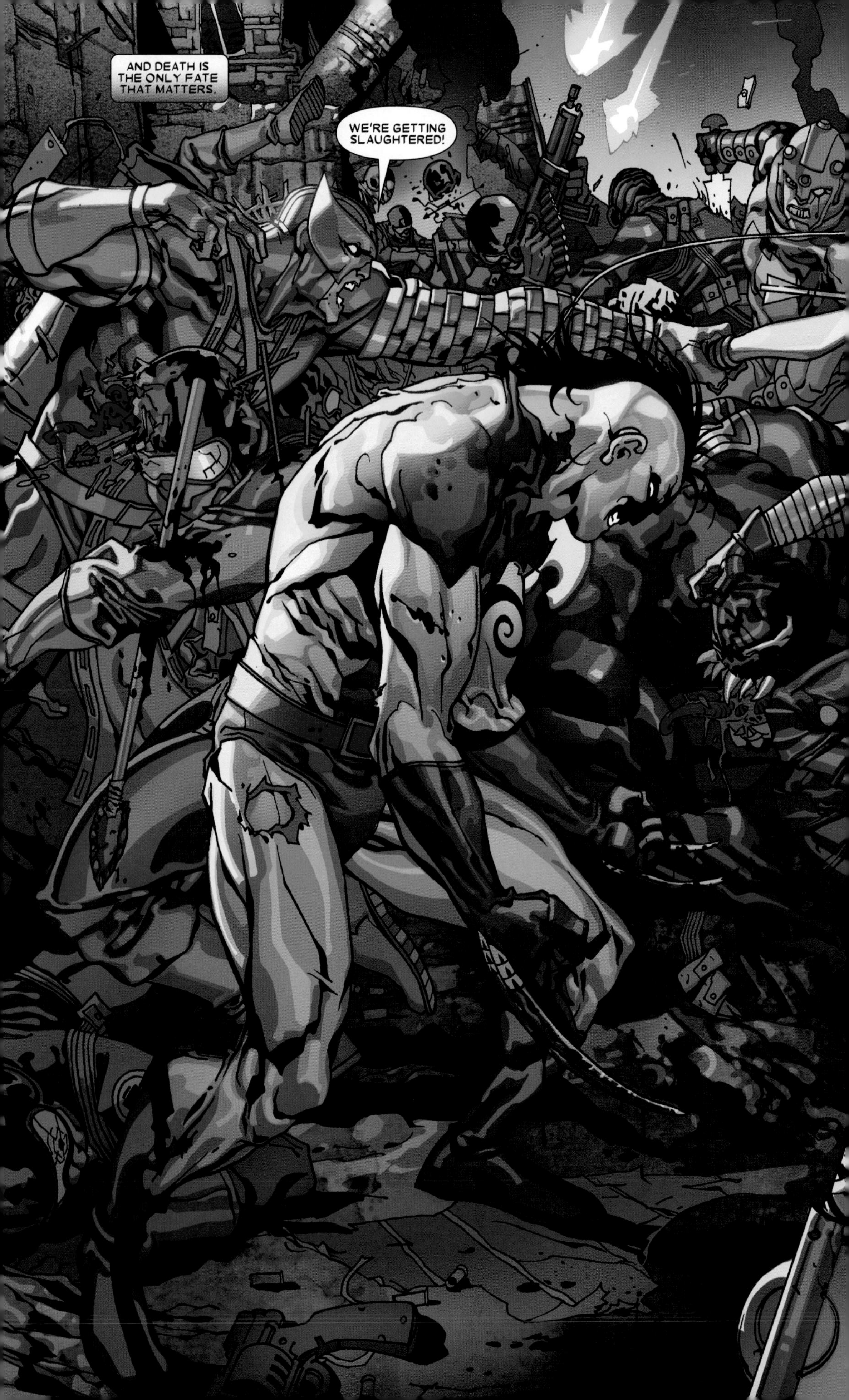
AND DEATH IS THE ONLY FATE THAT MATTERS.
WE'RE GETTING SLAUGHTERED!

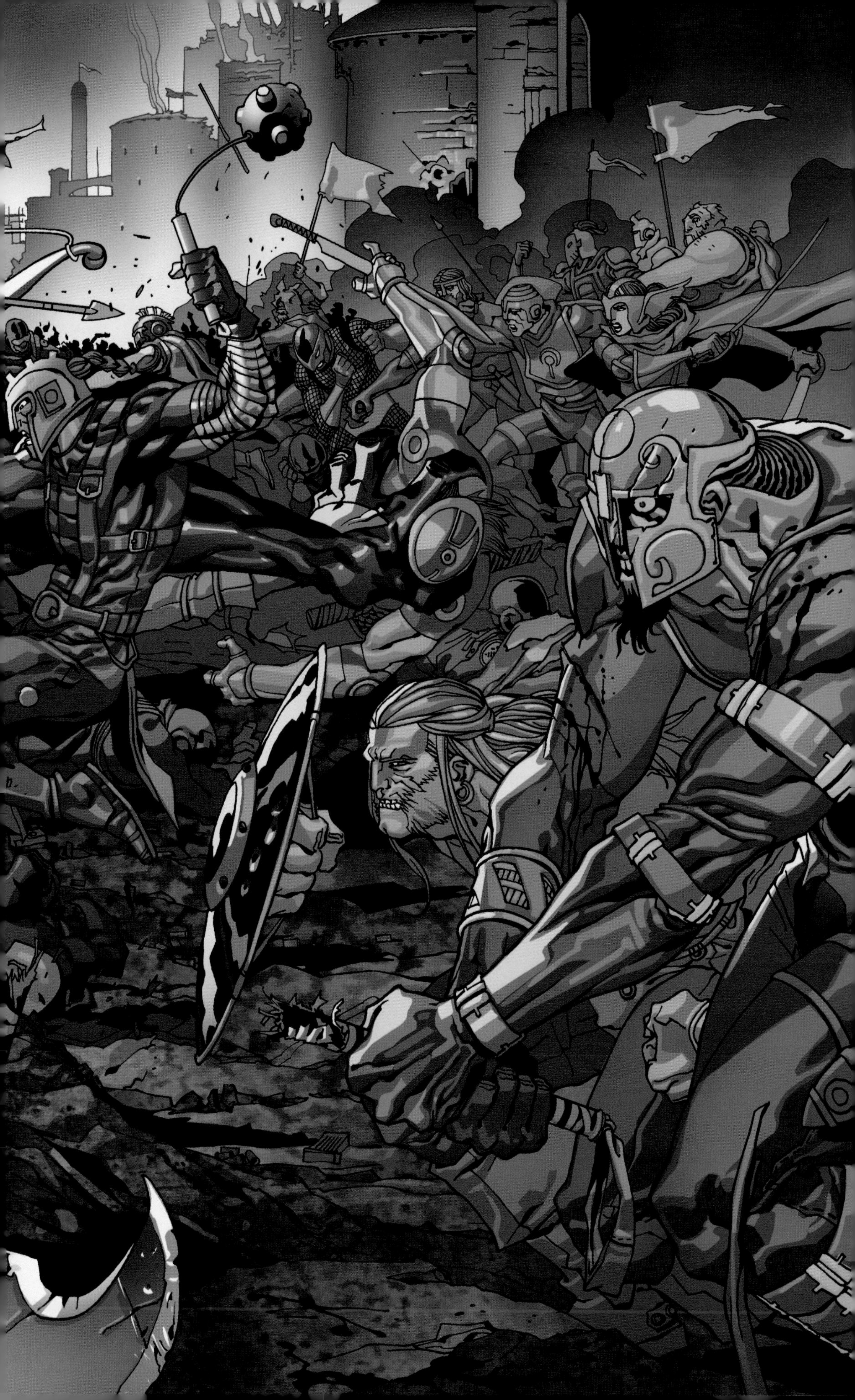

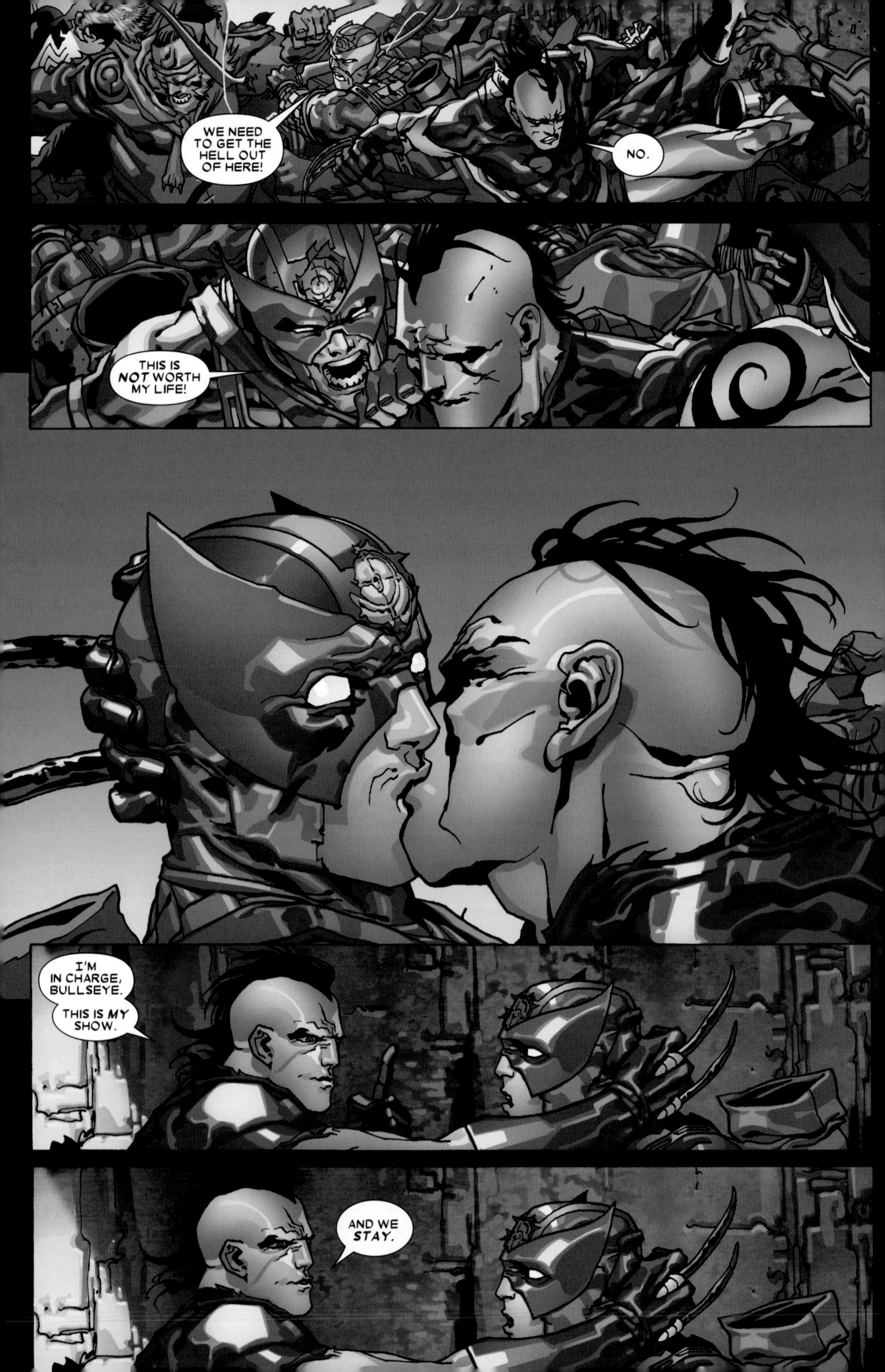
WE NEED TO GET THE HELL OUT OF HERE!
NO.
THIS IS NOT WORTH MY LIFE!
I'M IN CHARGE, BULLSEYE.
THIS IS MY SHOW.
AND WE STAY.

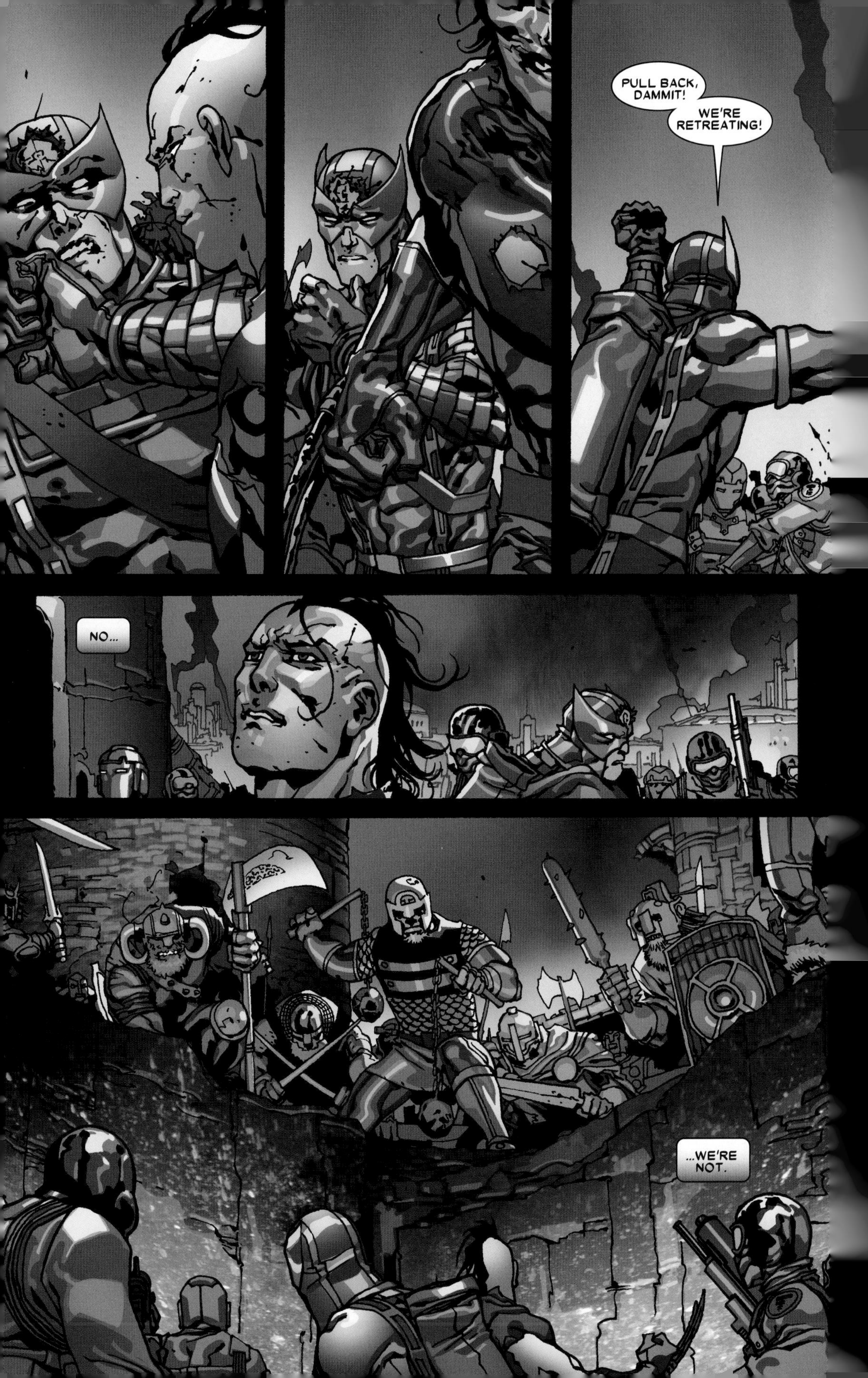
PULL BACK, DAMMIT!
WE'RE RETREATING!
NO...
...WE'RE NOT.

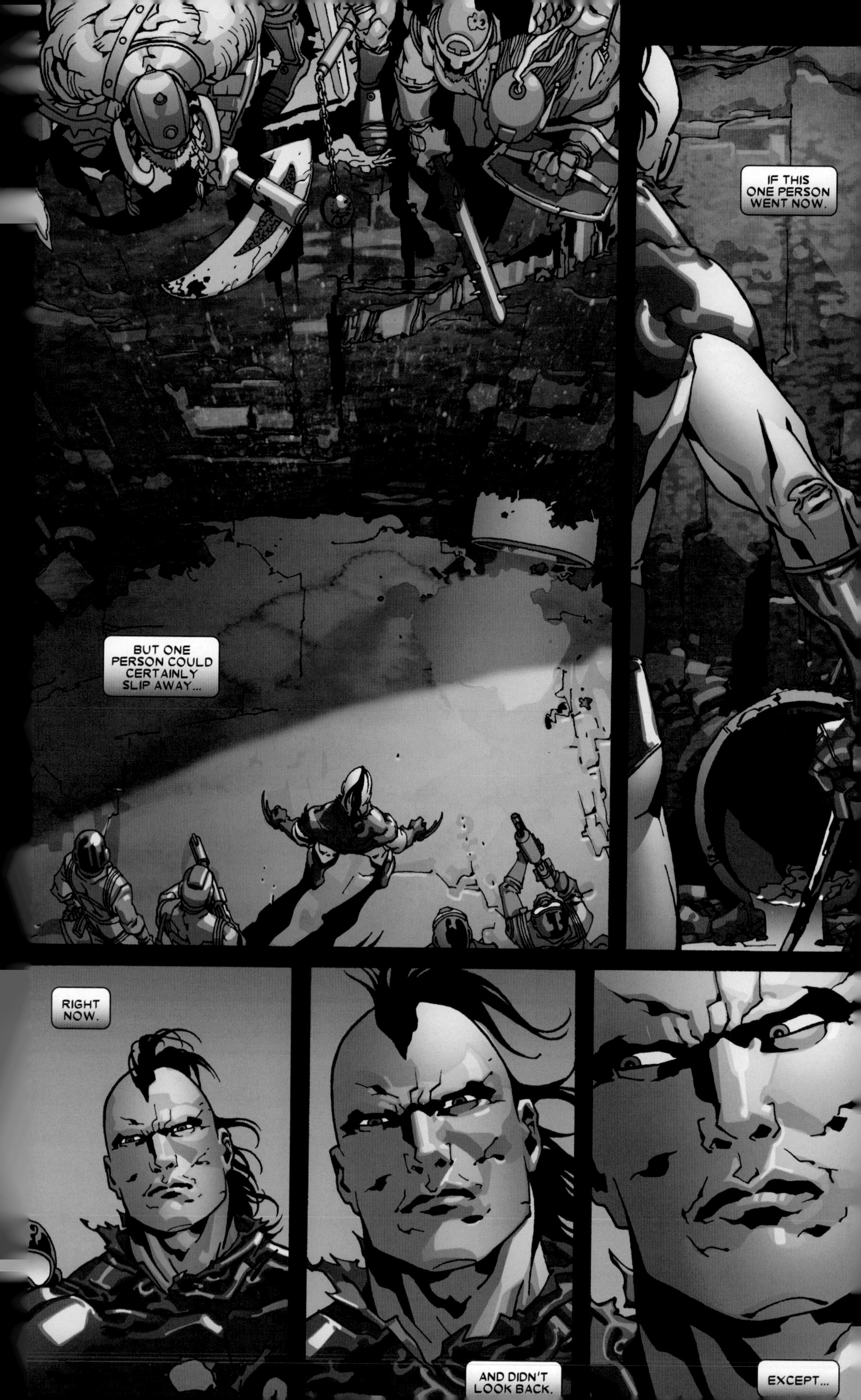
IF THIS
ONE PERSON
WENT NOW.
BUT ONE
PERSON COULD
CERTAINLY
SLIP AWAY...
RIGHT
NOW.
AND DIDN'T
LOOK BACK.
EXCEPT...

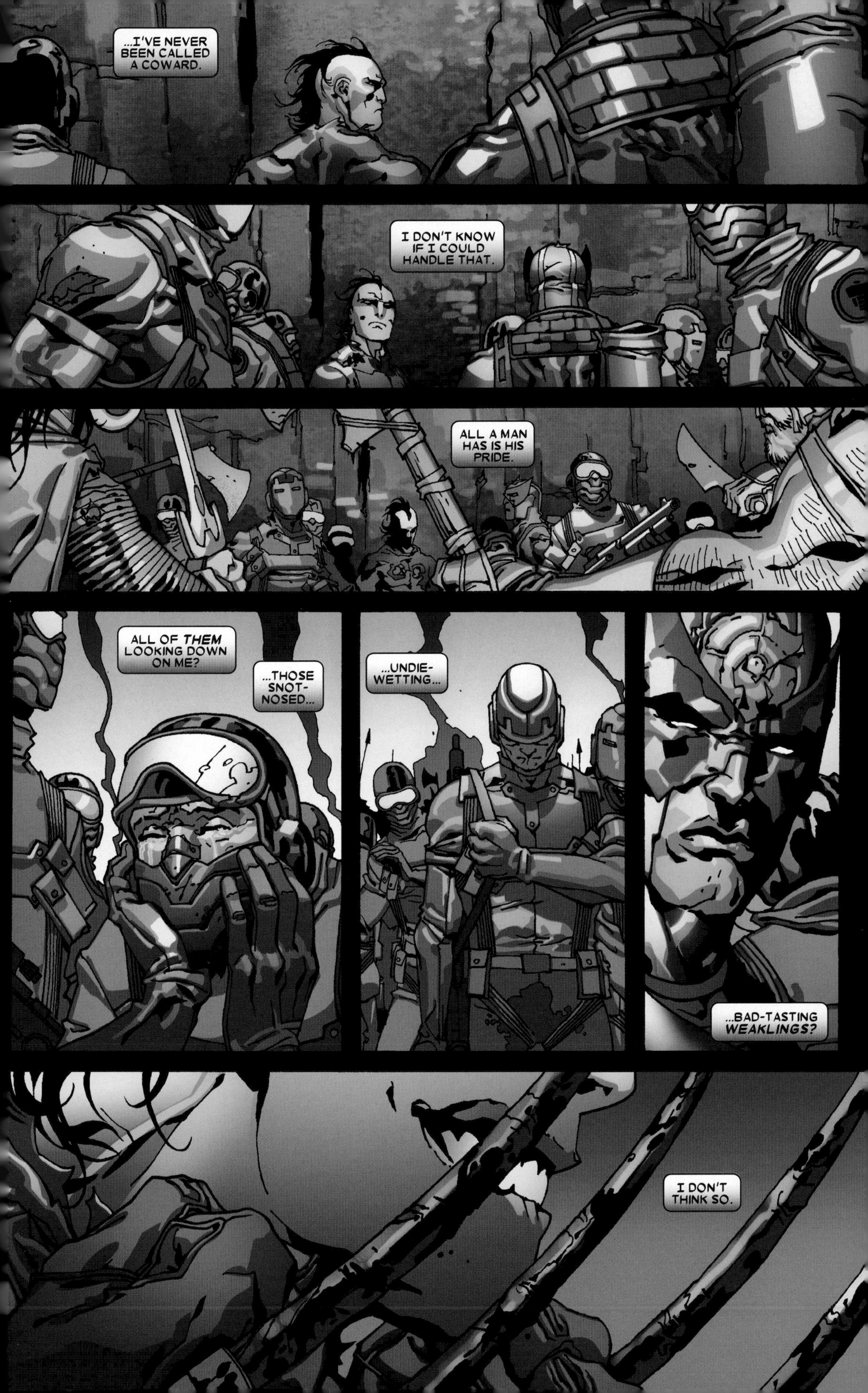
...I'VE NEVER BEEN CALLED A COWARD.
I DON'T KNOW IF I COULD HANDLE THAT.
ALL A MAN HAS IS HIS PRIDE.
ALL OF *THEM* LOOKING DOWN ON ME?
...THOSE SNOT-NOSED...
...UNDIE-WETTING...
...BAD-TASTING *WEAKLINGS?*
I DON'T THINK SO.

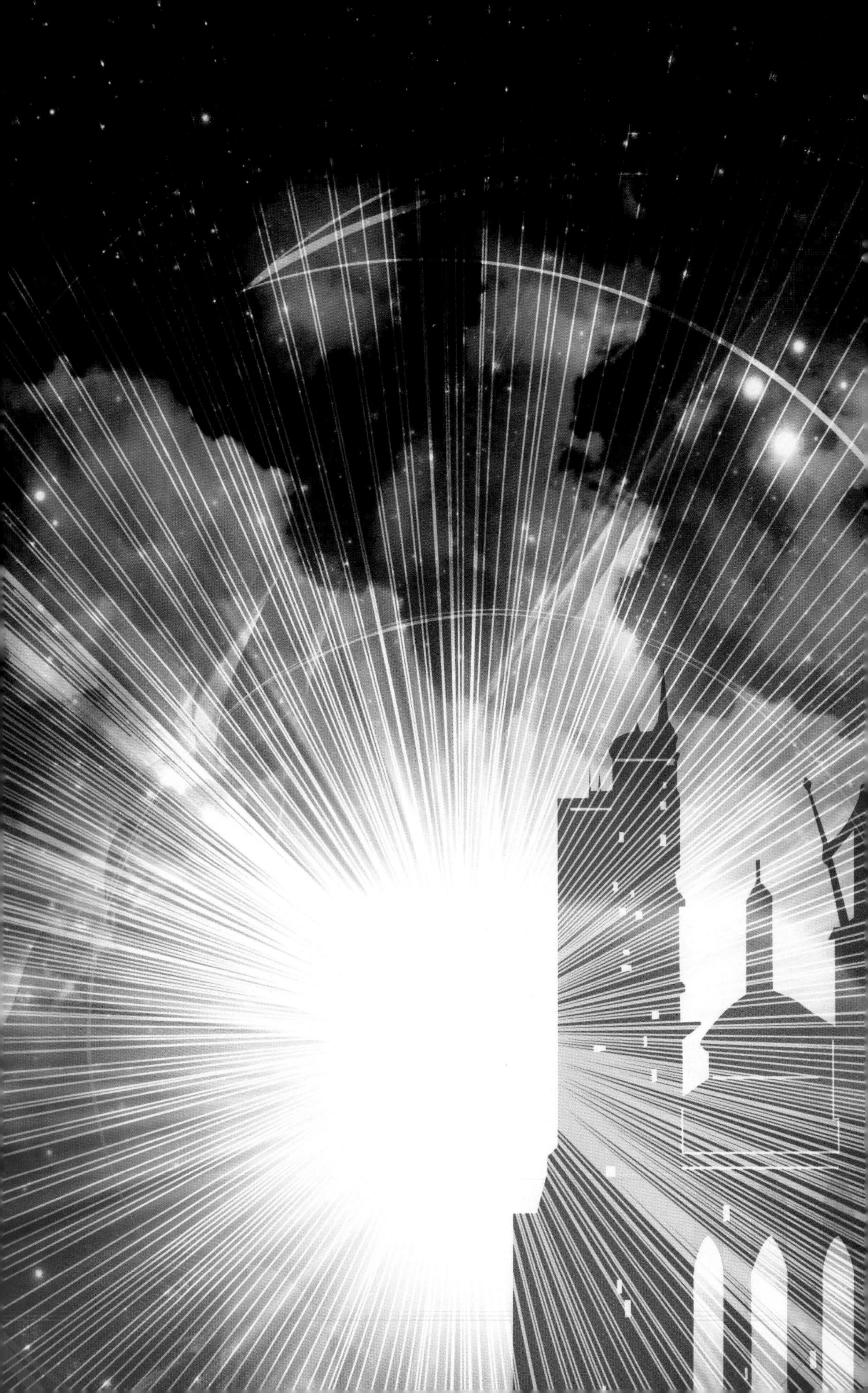

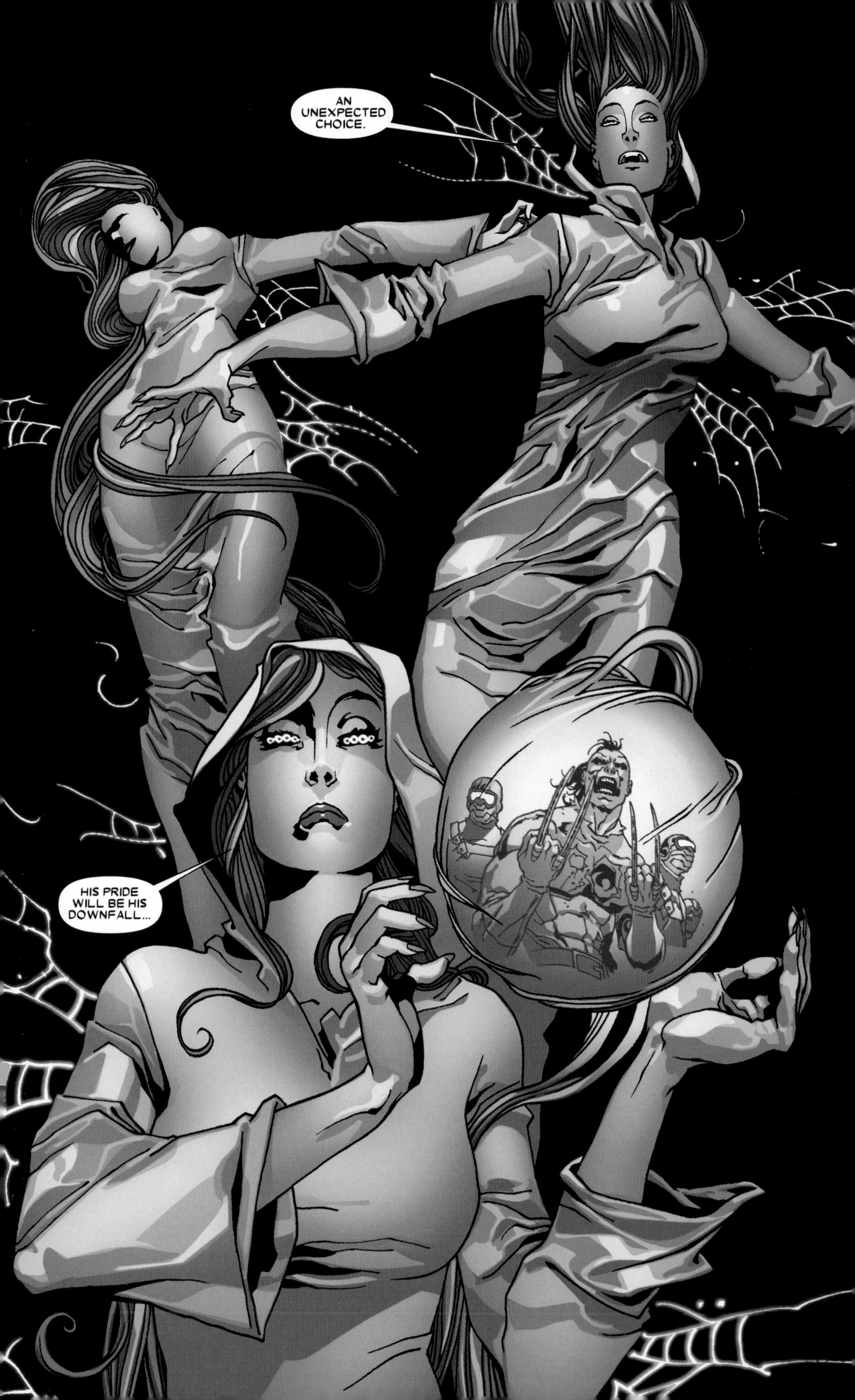
AN UNEXPECTED CHOICE.
HIS PRIDE WILL BE HIS DOWNFALL...

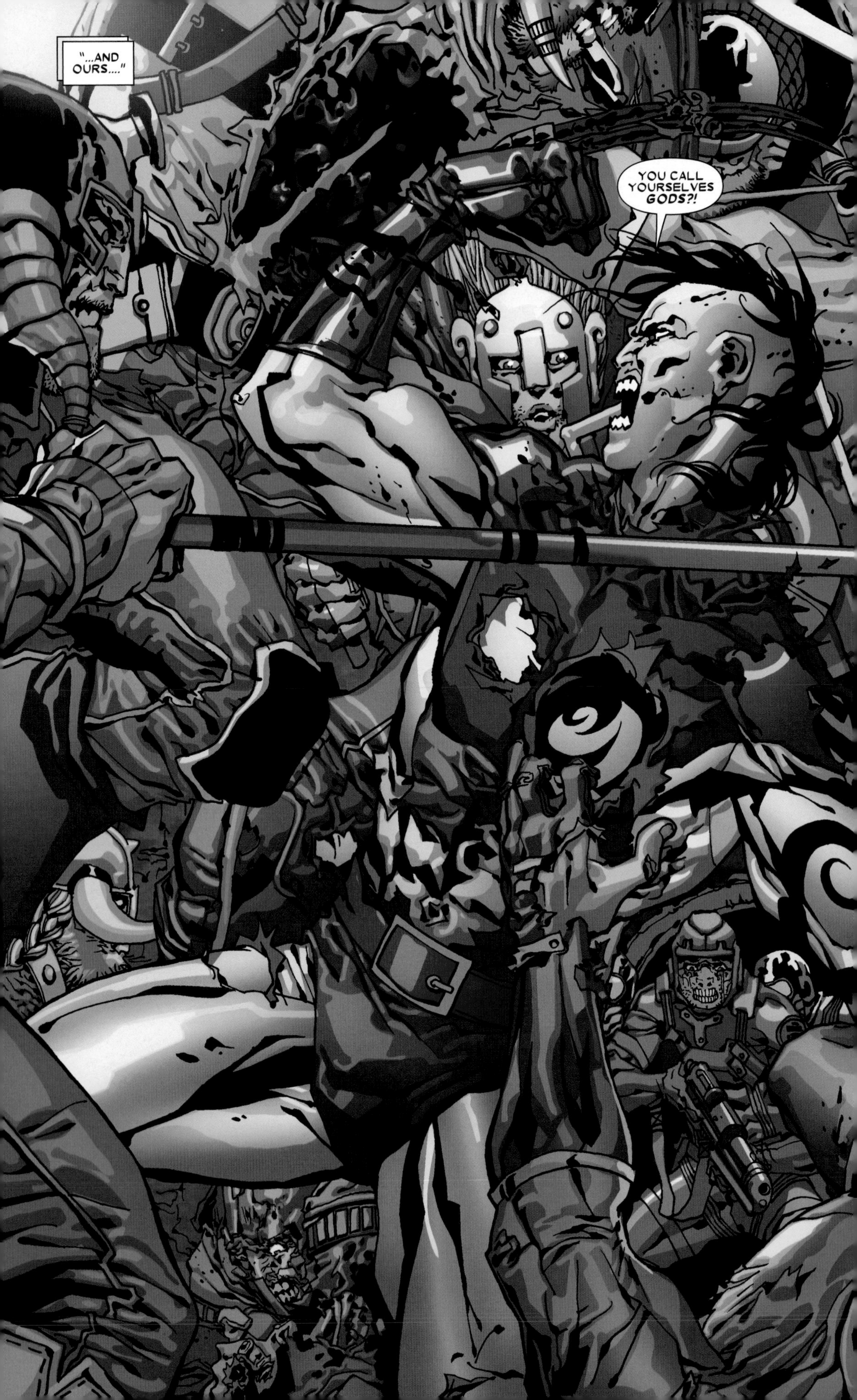
"...AND OURS...."
YOU CALL YOURSELVES GODS?!

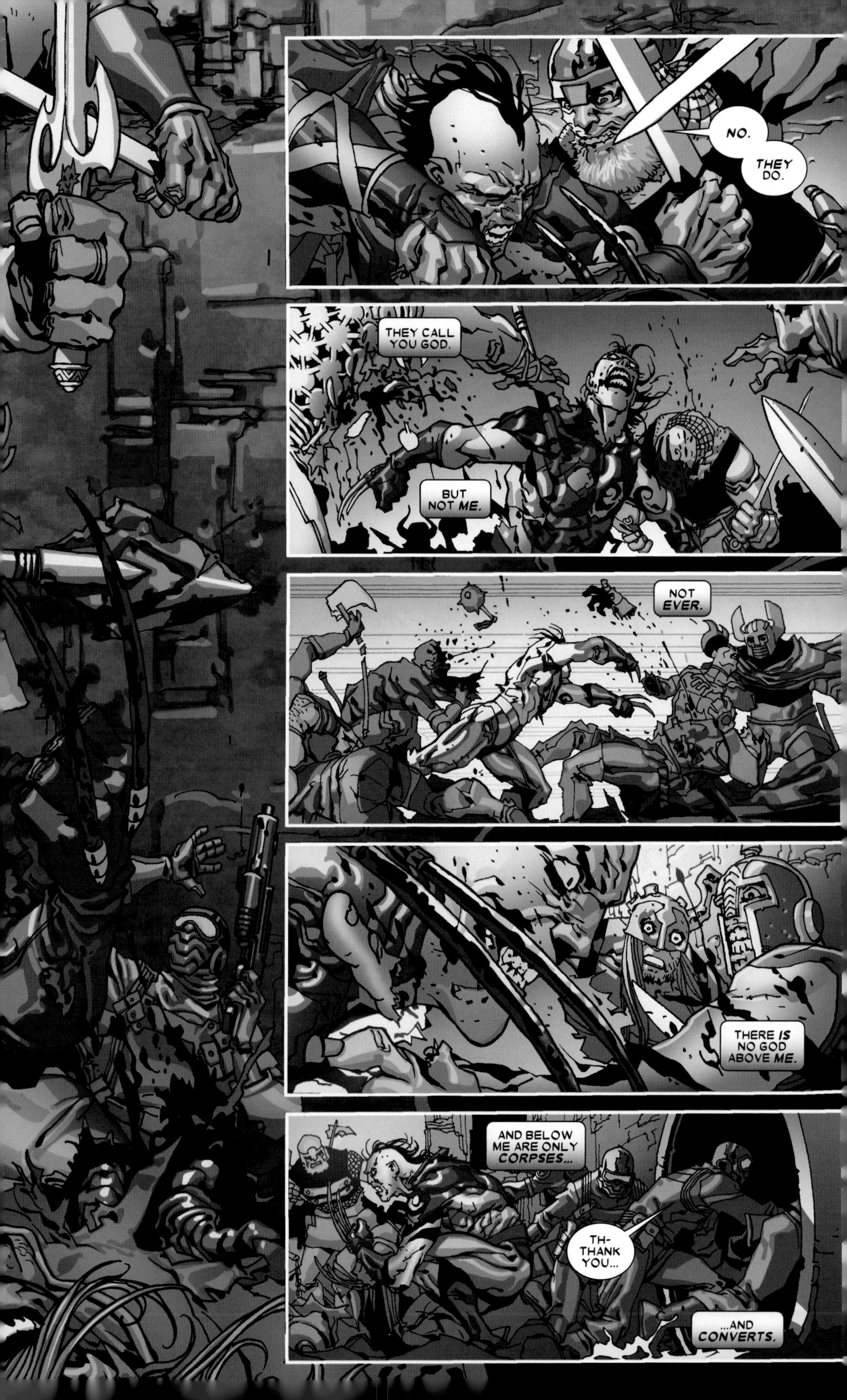
NO. THEY DO.
THEY CALL YOU GOD.
BUT NOT ME.
NOT EVER.
THERE IS NO GOD ABOVE ME.
AND BELOW ME ARE ONLY CORPSES...
TH- THANK YOU...
...AND CONVERTS.

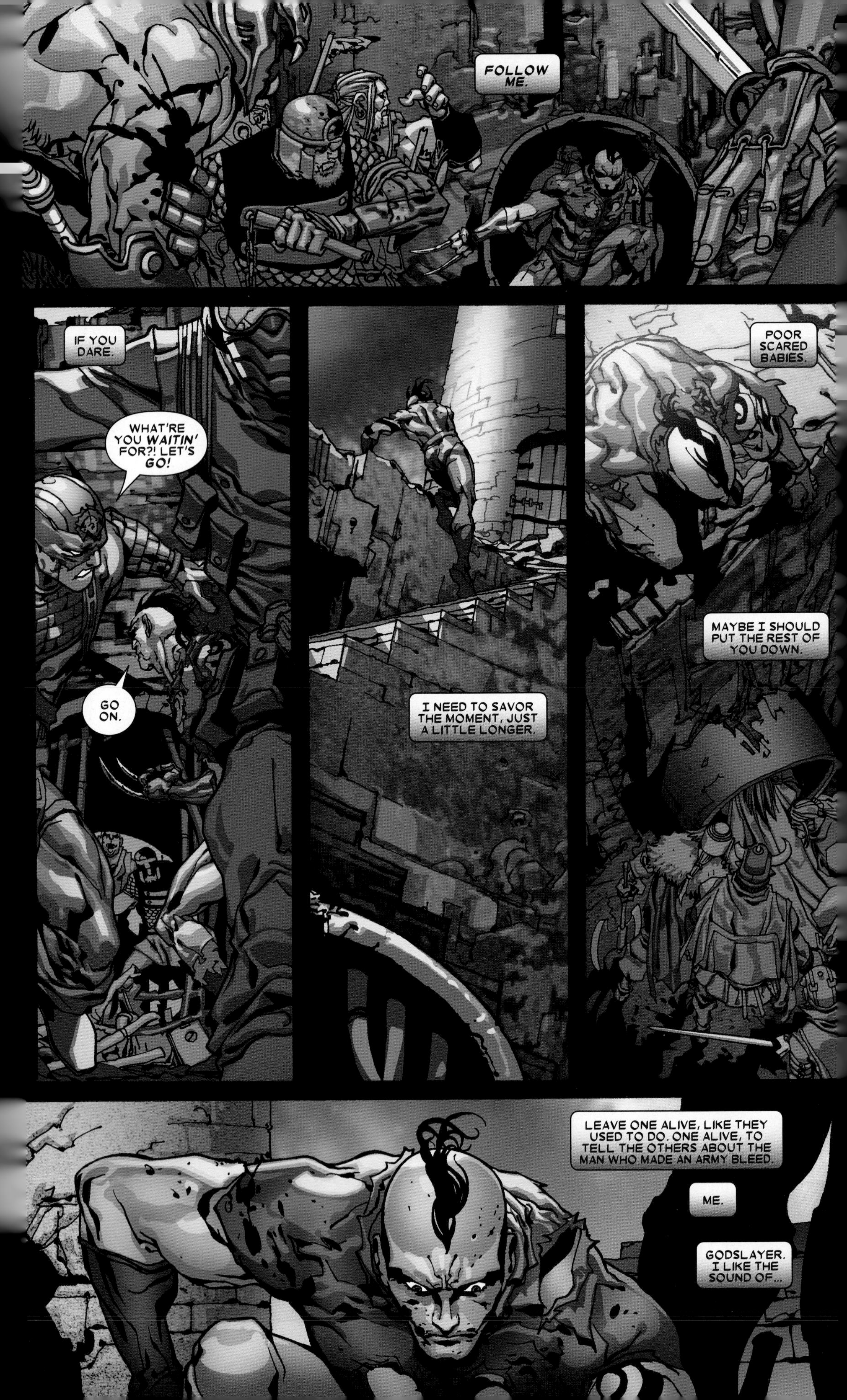
FOLLOW ME.
IF YOU DARE.
WHAT'RE YOU WAITIN' FOR?! LET'S GO!
GO ON.
I NEED TO SAVOR THE MOMENT, JUST A LITTLE LONGER.
POOR SCARED BABIES.
MAYBE I SHOULD PUT THE REST OF YOU DOWN.
LEAVE ONE ALIVE, LIKE THEY USED TO DO. ONE ALIVE, TO TELL THE OTHERS ABOUT THE MAN WHO MADE AN ARMY BLEED.
ME.
GODSLAYER. I LIKE THE SOUND OF...

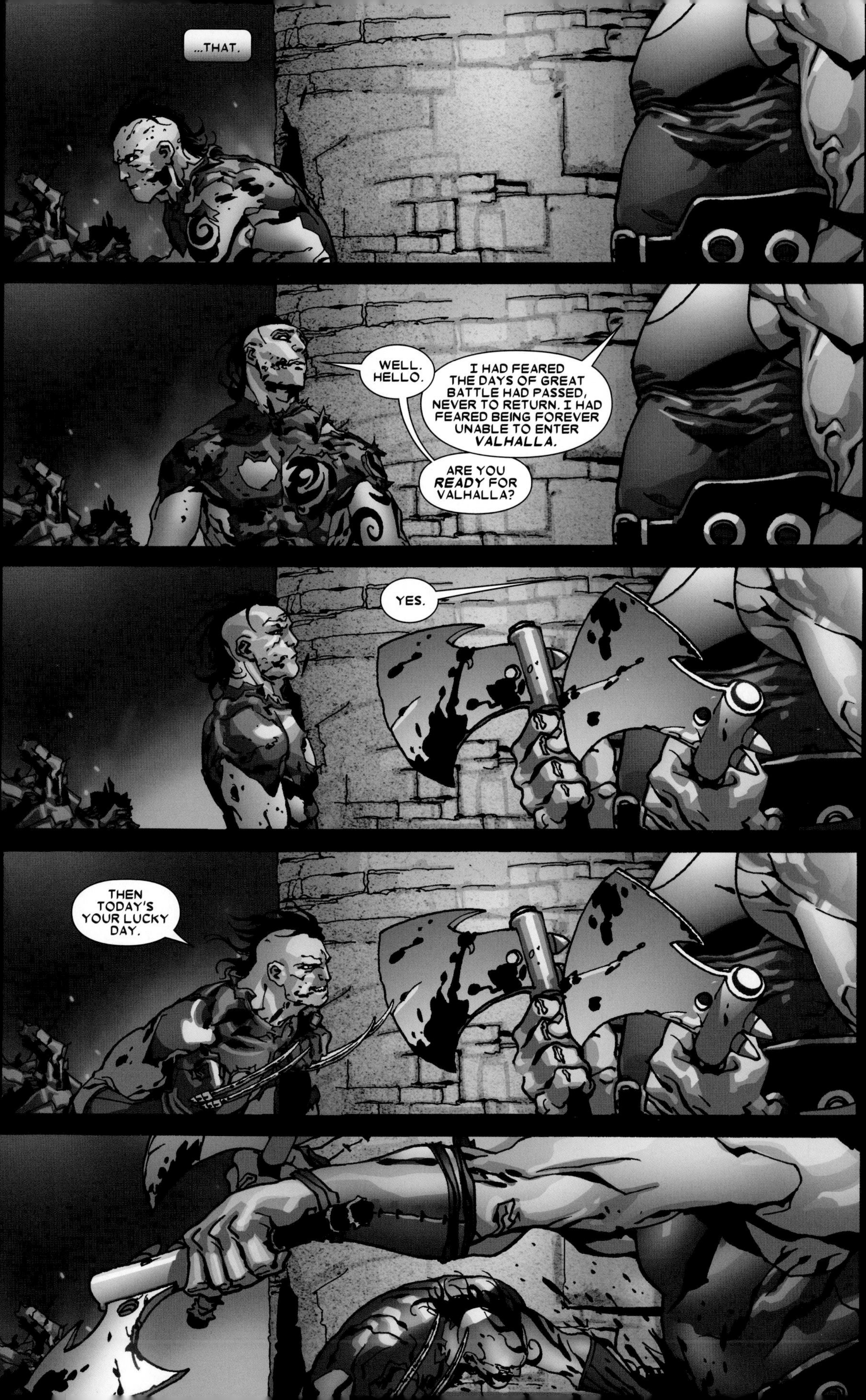
...THAT.
WELL. HELLO.
I HAD FEARED THE DAYS OF GREAT BATTLE HAD PASSED, NEVER TO RETURN. I HAD FEARED BEING FOREVER UNABLE TO ENTER VALHALLA.
ARE YOU READY FOR VALHALLA?
YES.
THEN TODAY'S YOUR LUCKY DAY.

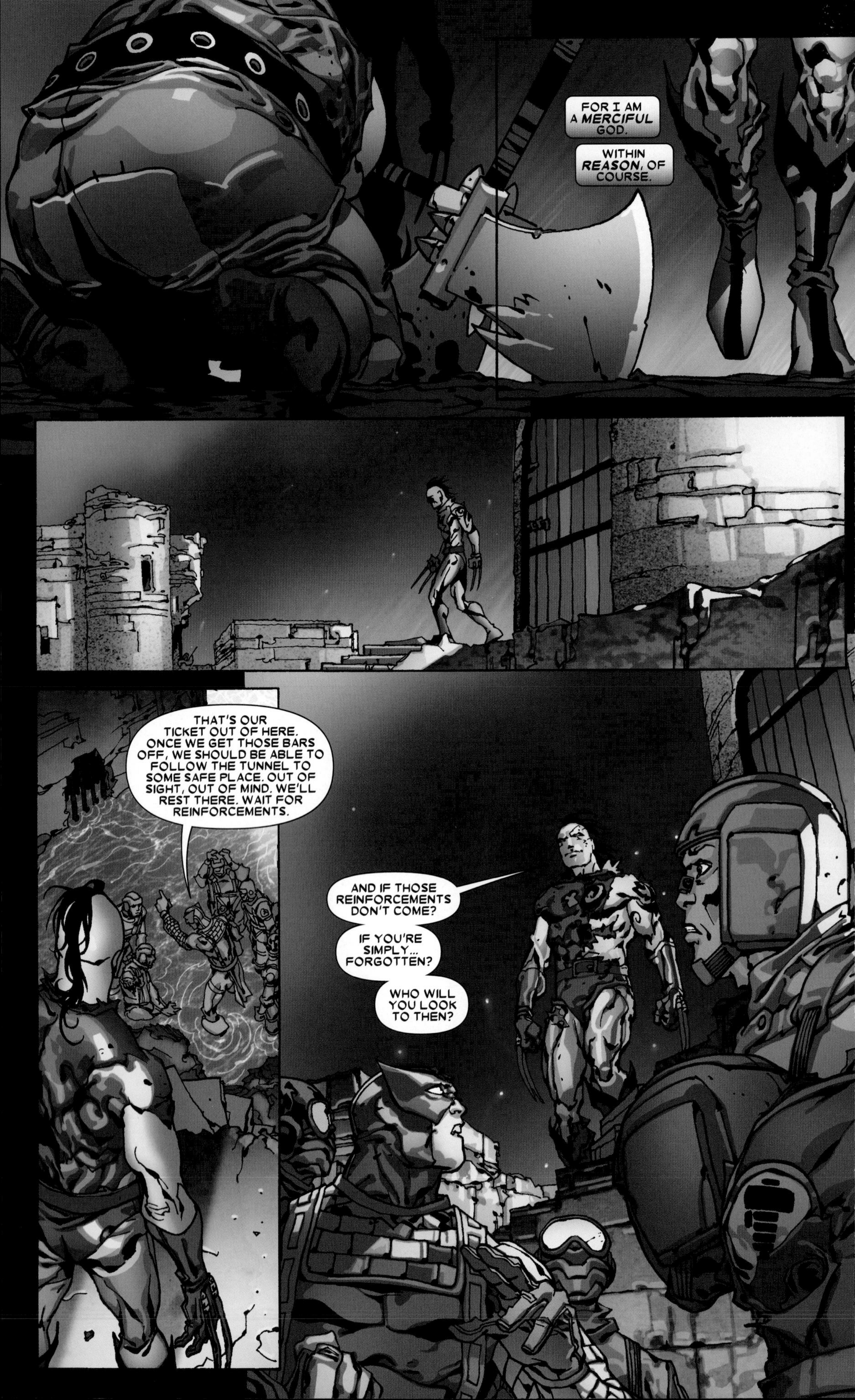
FOR I AM A MERCIFUL GOD.
WITHIN REASON, OF COURSE.
THAT'S OUR TICKET OUT OF HERE. ONCE WE GET THOSE BARS OFF, WE SHOULD BE ABLE TO FOLLOW THE TUNNEL TO SOME SAFE PLACE. OUT OF SIGHT, OUT OF MIND. WE'LL REST THERE. WAIT FOR REINFORCEMENTS.
AND IF THOSE REINFORCEMENTS DON'T COME?
IF YOU'RE SIMPLY... FORGOTTEN?
WHO WILL YOU LOOK TO THEN?

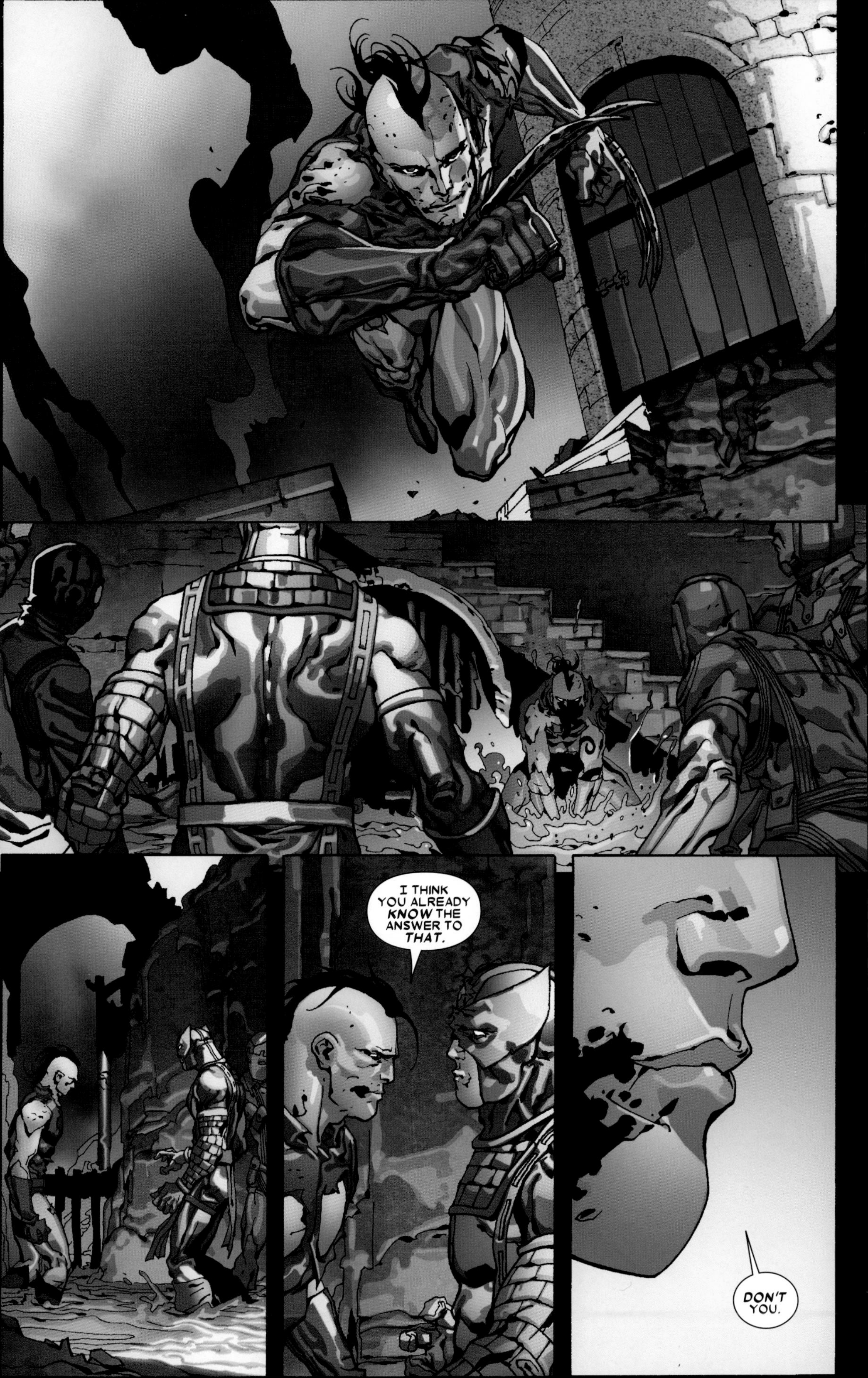
I THINK YOU ALREADY *KNOW* THE ANSWER TO *THAT*.
DON'T YOU.

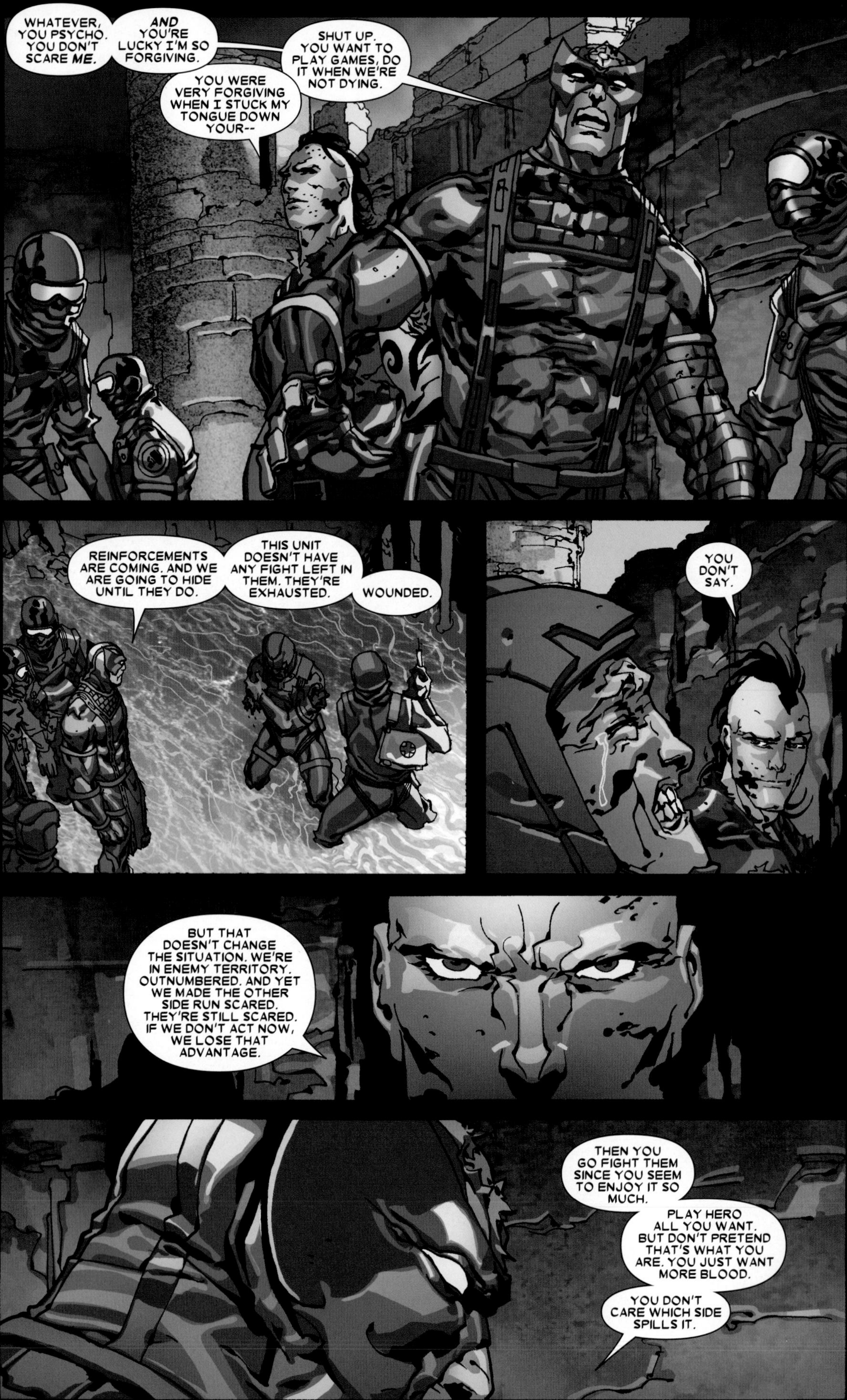
WHATEVER, YOU PSYCHO. YOU DON'T SCARE ME.
AND YOU'RE LUCKY I'M SO FORGIVING.
YOU WERE VERY FORGIVING WHEN I STUCK MY TONGUE DOWN YOUR--
SHUT UP. YOU WANT TO PLAY GAMES, DO IT WHEN WE'RE NOT DYING.
REINFORCEMENTS ARE COMING. AND WE ARE GOING TO HIDE UNTIL THEY DO.
THIS UNIT DOESN'T HAVE ANY FIGHT LEFT IN THEM. THEY'RE EXHAUSTED.
WOUNDED.
YOU DON'T SAY.
BUT THAT DOESN'T CHANGE THE SITUATION. WE'RE IN ENEMY TERRITORY. OUTNUMBERED. AND YET WE MADE THE OTHER SIDE RUN SCARED. THEY'RE STILL SCARED. IF WE DON'T ACT NOW, WE LOSE THAT ADVANTAGE.
THEN YOU GO FIGHT THEM SINCE YOU SEEM TO ENJOY IT SO MUCH.
PLAY HERO ALL YOU WANT. BUT DON'T PRETEND THAT'S WHAT YOU ARE. YOU JUST WANT MORE BLOOD.
YOU DON'T CARE WHICH SIDE SPILLS IT.

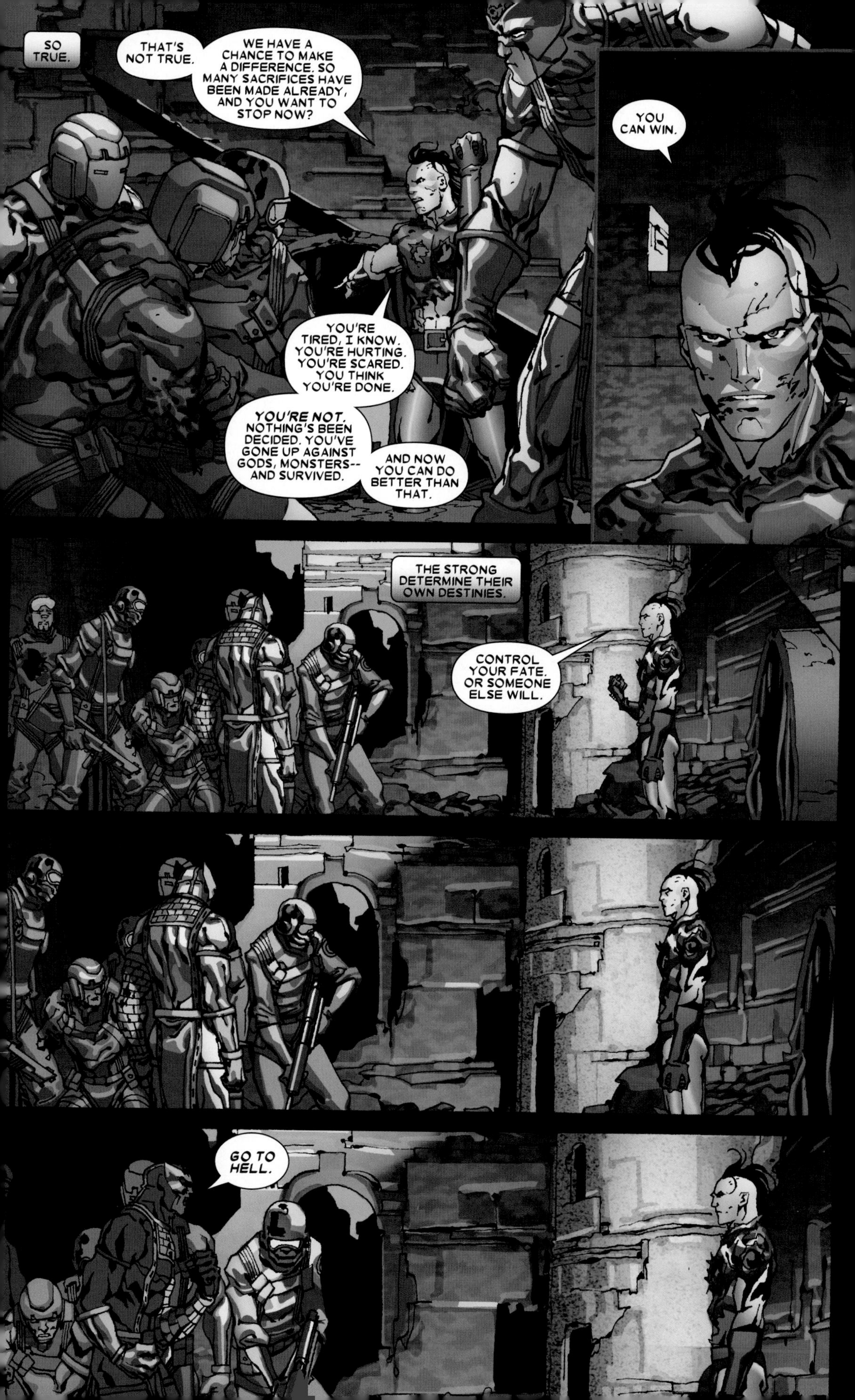
SO TRUE.
THAT'S NOT TRUE.
WE HAVE A CHANCE TO MAKE A DIFFERENCE. SO MANY SACRIFICES HAVE BEEN MADE ALREADY, AND YOU WANT TO STOP NOW?
YOU'RE TIRED, I KNOW. YOU'RE HURTING. YOU'RE SCARED. YOU THINK YOU'RE DONE.
YOU'RE NOT. NOTHING'S BEEN DECIDED. YOU'VE GONE UP AGAINST GODS, MONSTERS-- AND SURVIVED.
AND NOW YOU CAN DO BETTER THAN THAT.
YOU CAN WIN.
THE STRONG DETERMINE THEIR OWN DESTINIES.
CONTROL YOUR FATE. OR SOMEONE ELSE WILL.
GO TO HELL.

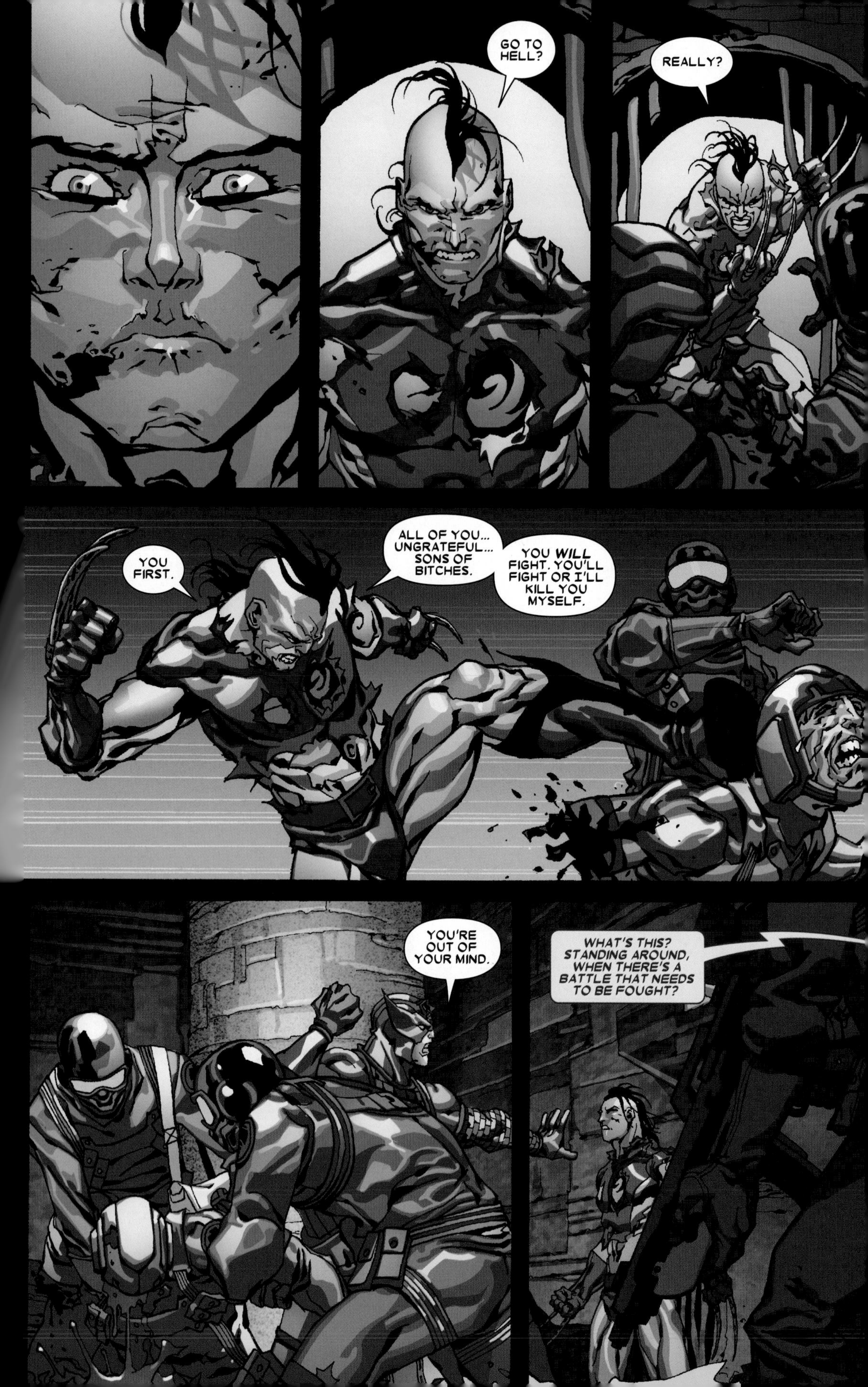
GO TO HELL?
REALLY?
YOU FIRST.
ALL OF YOU... UNGRATEFUL... SONS OF BITCHES.
YOU **WILL** FIGHT. YOU'LL FIGHT OR I'LL KILL YOU MYSELF.
YOU'RE OUT OF YOUR MIND.
WHAT'S THIS? STANDING AROUND, WHEN THERE'S A BATTLE THAT NEEDS TO BE FOUGHT?

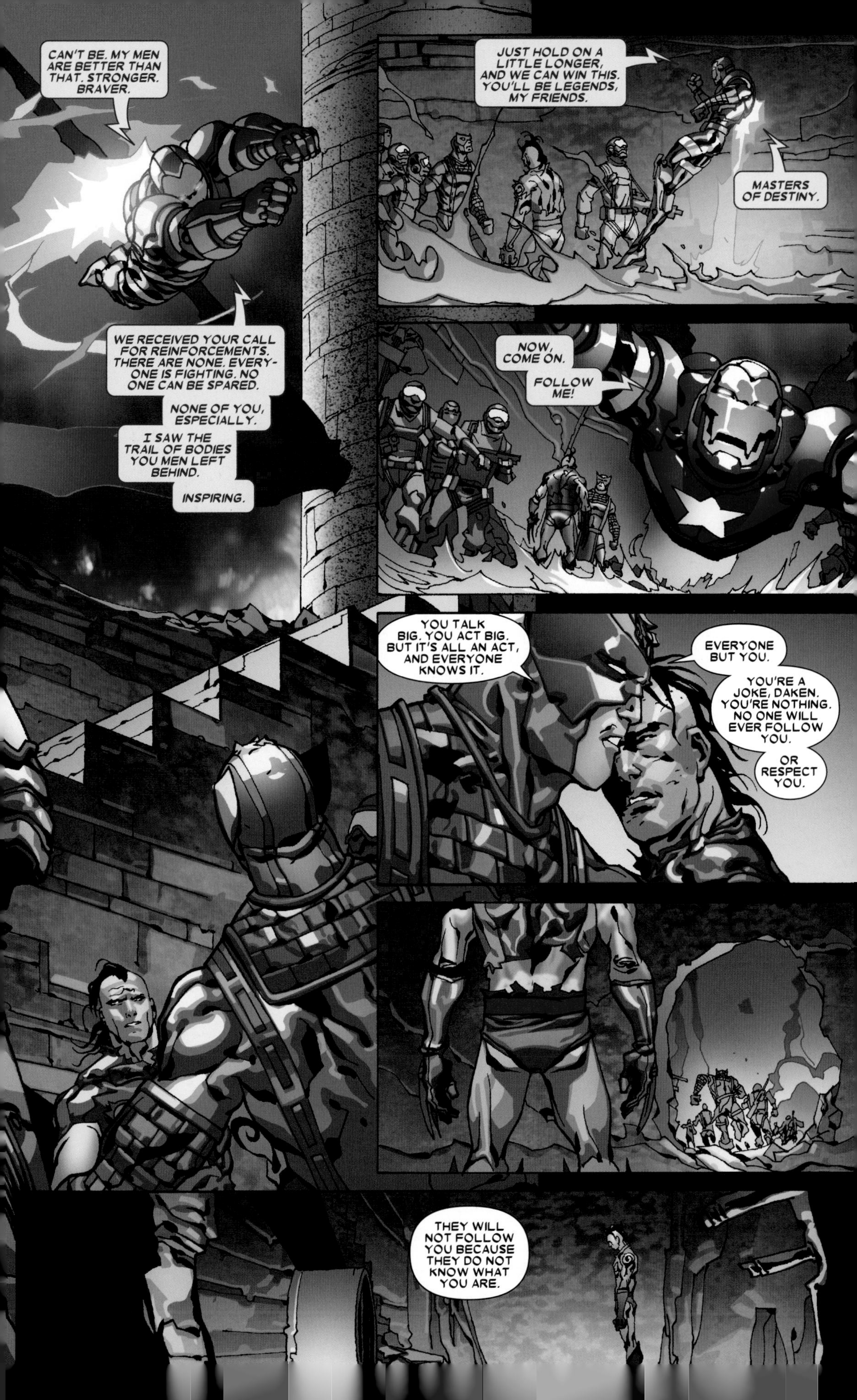
CAN'T BE. MY MEN ARE BETTER THAN THAT. STRONGER. BRAVER.
JUST HOLD ON A LITTLE LONGER, AND WE CAN WIN THIS. YOU'LL BE LEGENDS, MY FRIENDS.
MASTERS OF DESTINY.
WE RECEIVED YOUR CALL FOR REINFORCEMENTS. THERE ARE NONE. EVERY-ONE IS FIGHTING. NO ONE CAN BE SPARED.
NONE OF YOU, ESPECIALLY.
I SAW THE TRAIL OF BODIES YOU MEN LEFT BEHIND.
INSPIRING.
NOW, COME ON.
FOLLOW ME!
YOU TALK BIG. YOU ACT BIG. BUT IT'S ALL AN ACT, AND EVERYONE KNOWS IT.
EVERYONE BUT YOU.
YOU'RE A JOKE, DAKEN. YOU'RE NOTHING. NO ONE WILL EVER FOLLOW YOU.
OR RESPECT YOU.
THEY WILL NOT FOLLOW YOU BECAUSE THEY DO NOT KNOW WHAT YOU ARE.

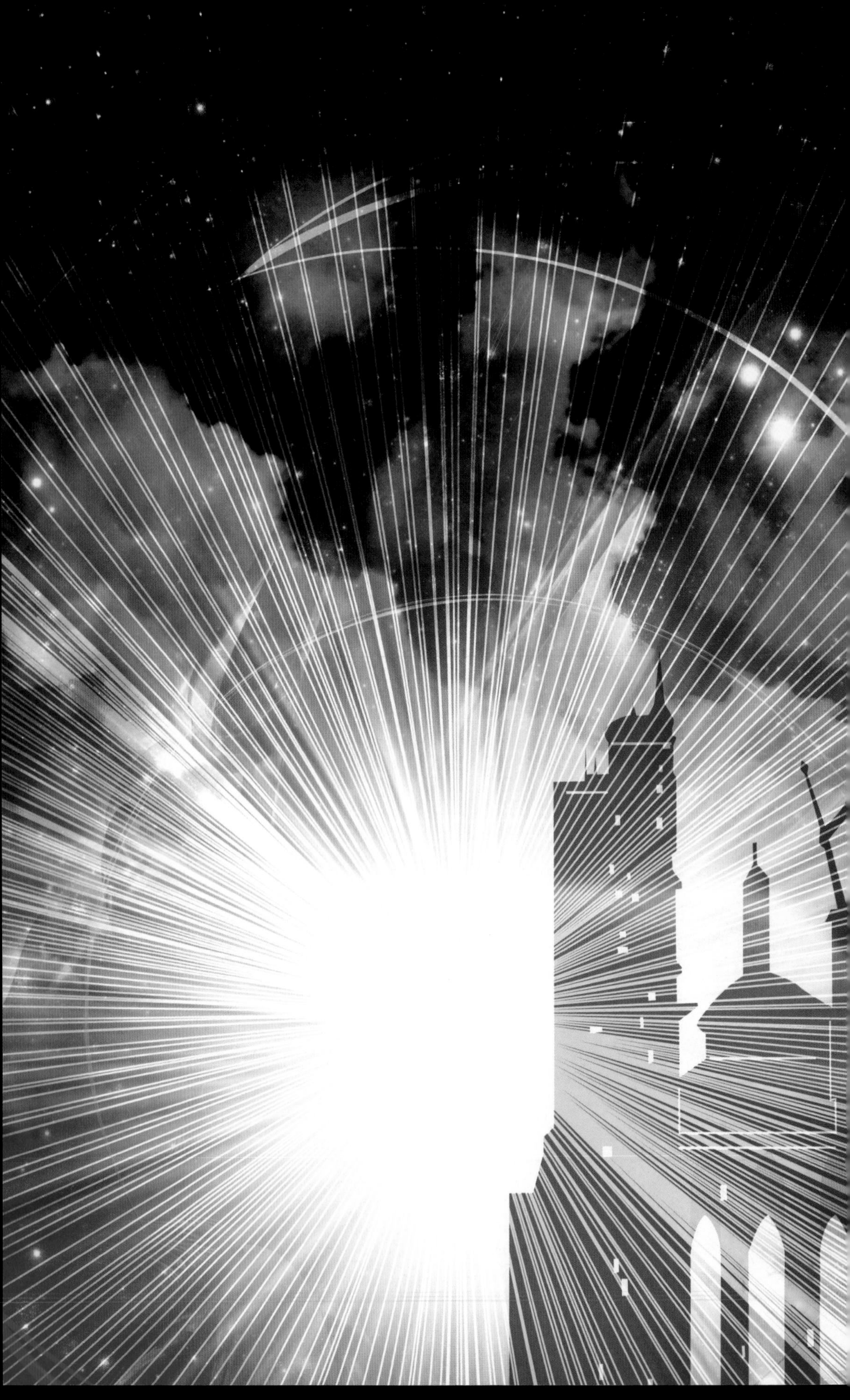

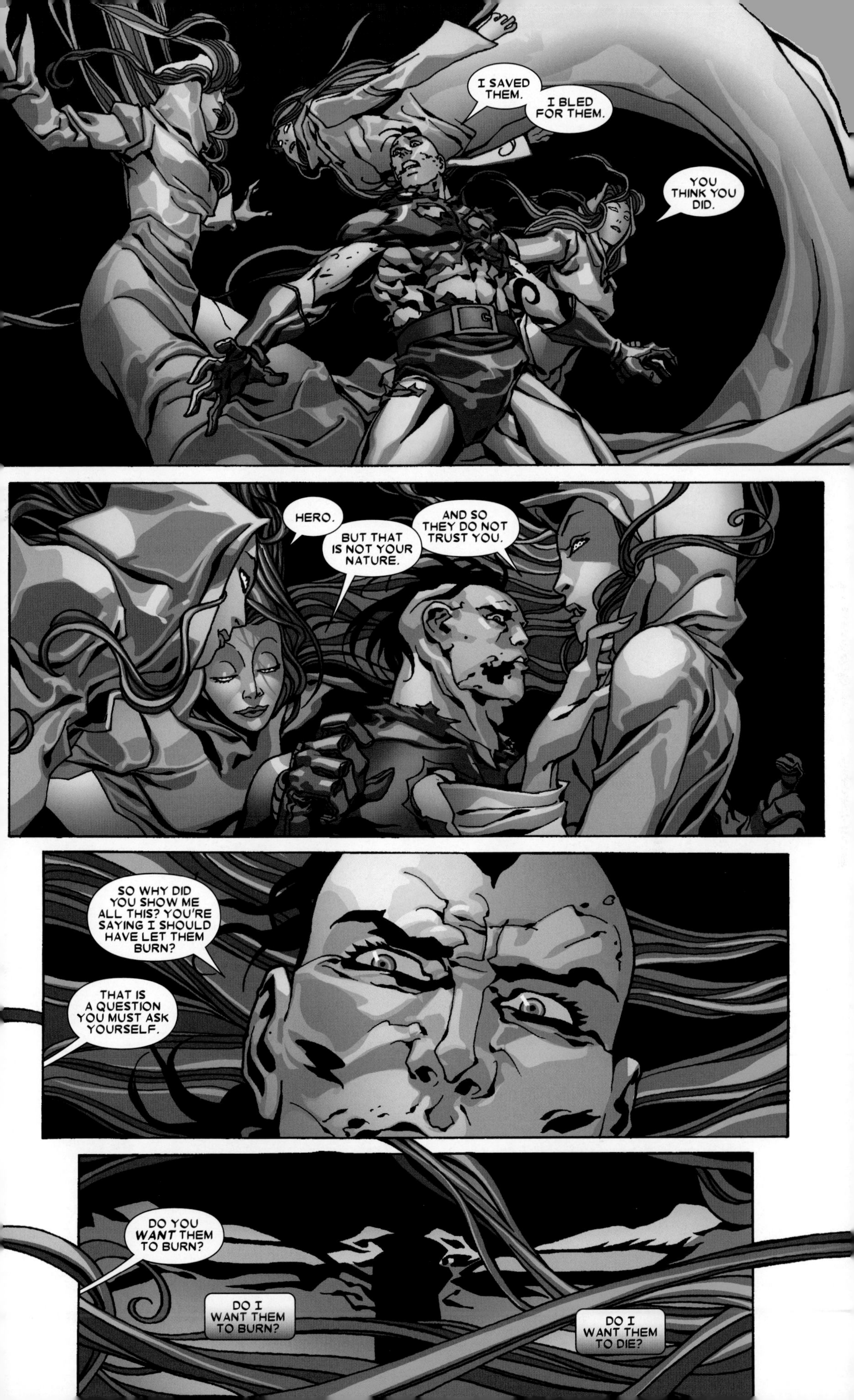
I SAVED THEM.
I BLED FOR THEM.
YOU THINK YOU DID.
HERO.
BUT THAT IS NOT YOUR NATURE.
AND SO THEY DO NOT TRUST YOU.
SO WHY DID YOU SHOW ME ALL THIS? YOU'RE SAYING I SHOULD HAVE LET THEM BURN?
THAT IS A QUESTION YOU MUST ASK YOURSELF.
DO YOU WANT THEM TO BURN?
DO I WANT THEM TO BURN?
DO I WANT THEM TO DIE?

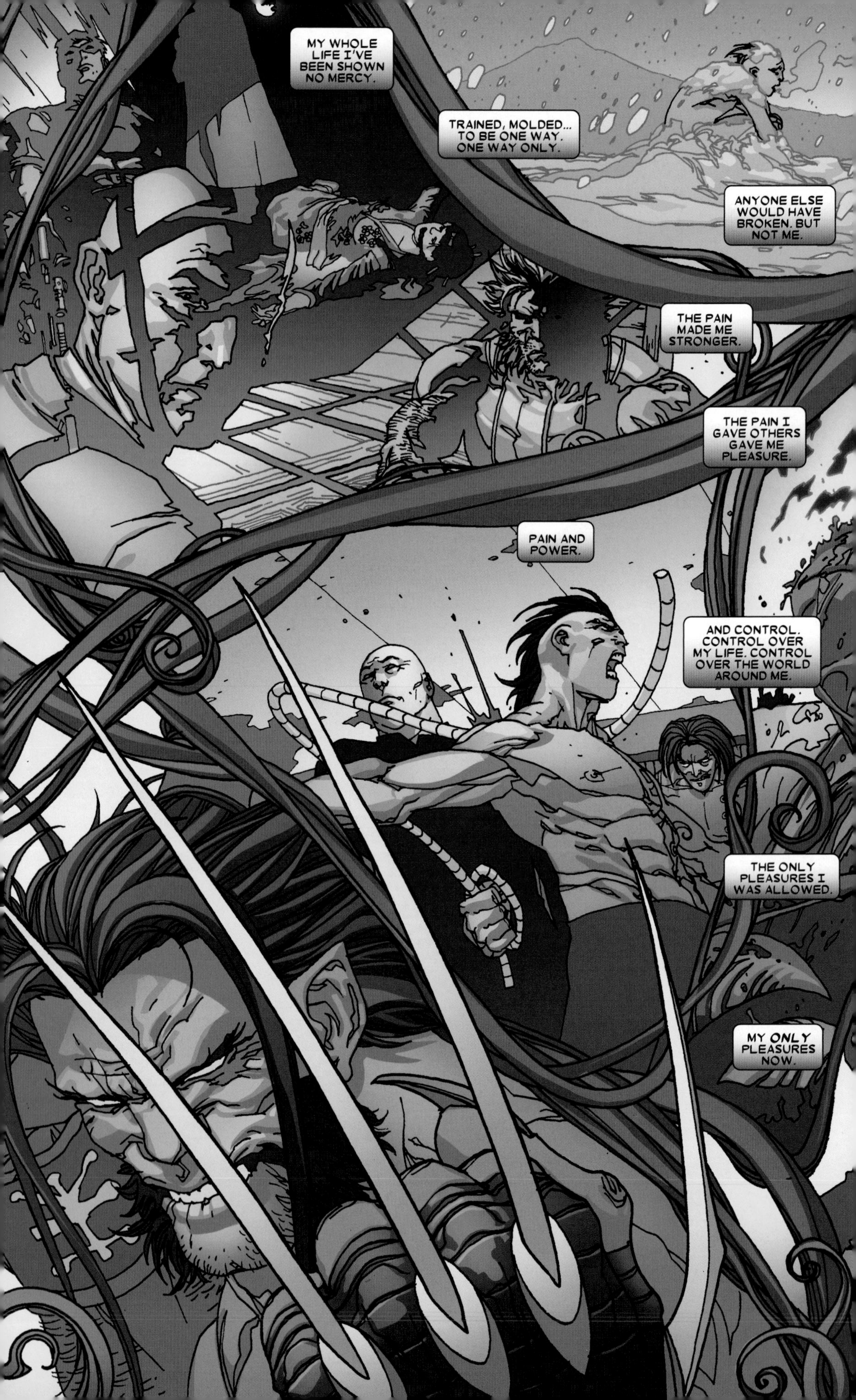

MY WHOLE LIFE I'VE BEEN SHOWN NO MERCY.
TRAINED, MOLDED... TO BE ONE WAY. ONE WAY ONLY.
ANYONE ELSE WOULD HAVE BROKEN. BUT NOT ME.
THE PAIN MADE ME STRONGER.
THE PAIN I GAVE OTHERS GAVE ME PLEASURE.
PAIN AND POWER.
AND CONTROL. CONTROL OVER MY LIFE. CONTROL OVER THE WORLD AROUND ME.
THE ONLY PLEASURES I WAS ALLOWED.
MY ONLY PLEASURES NOW.

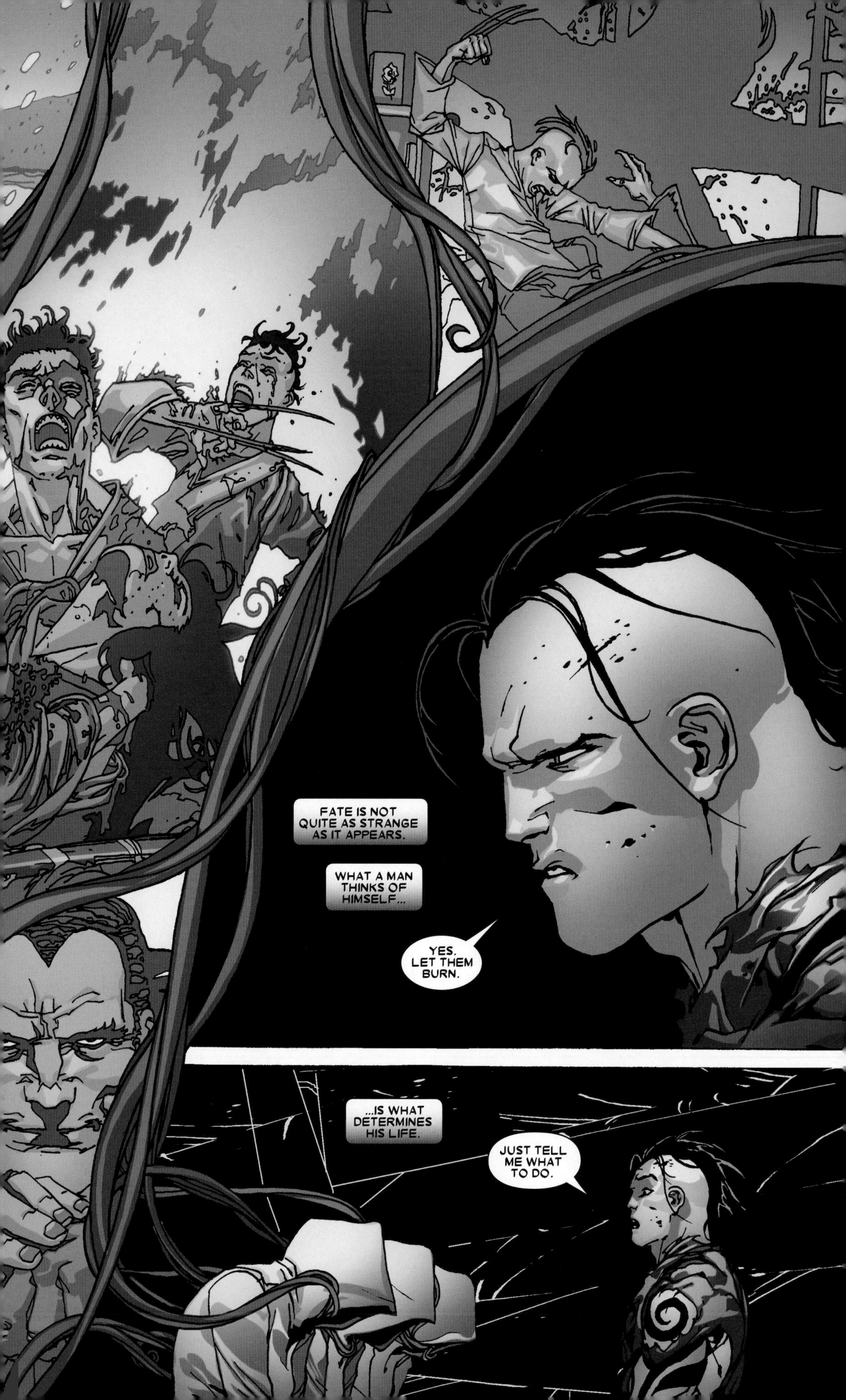
FATE IS NOT QUITE AS STRANGE AS IT APPEARS.
WHAT A MAN THINKS OF HIMSELF...
YES. LET THEM BURN.
...IS WHAT DETERMINES HIS LIFE.
JUST TELL ME WHAT TO DO.

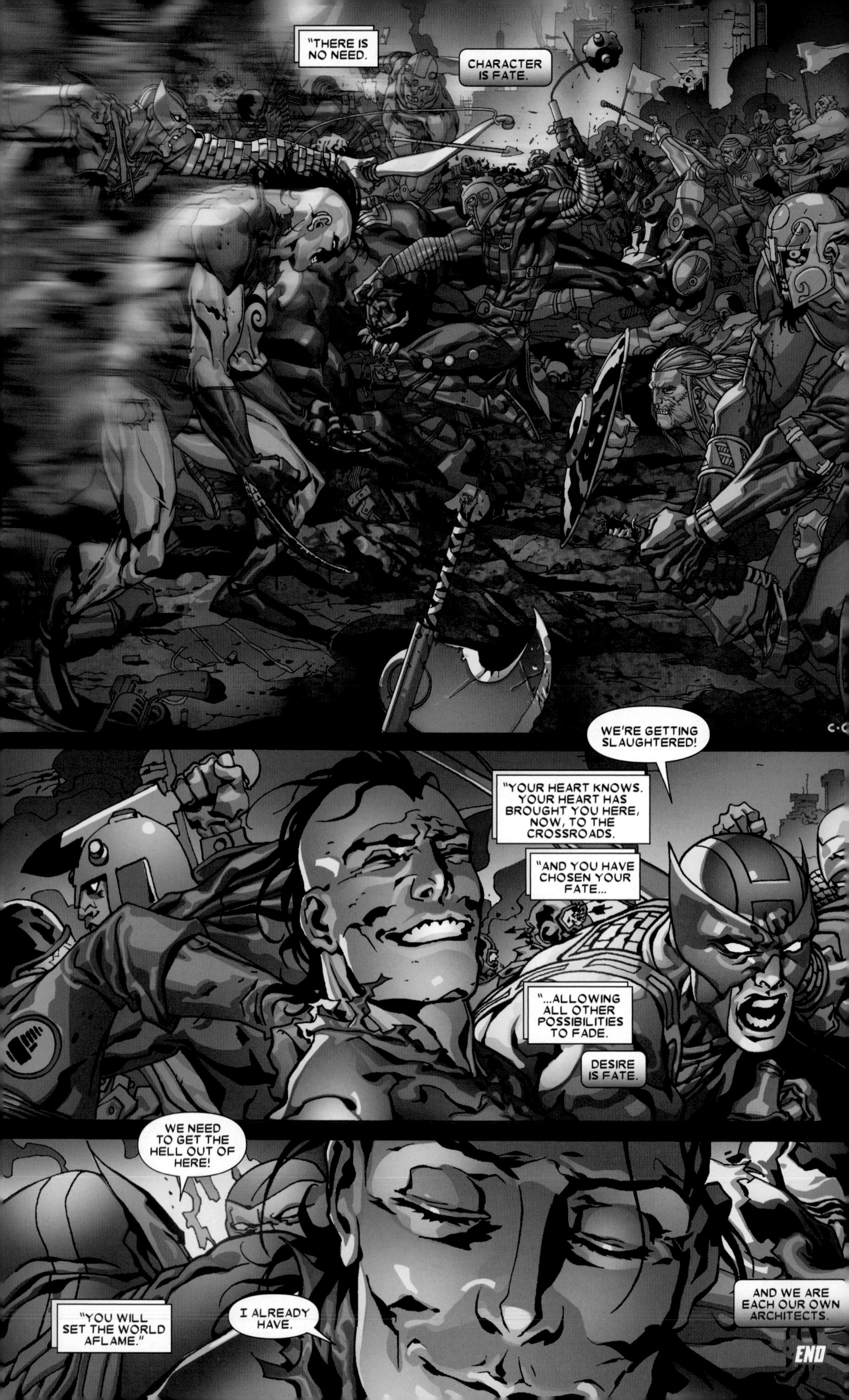
"THERE IS NO NEED.
CHARACTER IS FATE.
WE'RE GETTING SLAUGHTERED!
"YOUR HEART KNOWS. YOUR HEART HAS BROUGHT YOU HERE, NOW, TO THE CROSSROADS.
"AND YOU HAVE CHOSEN YOUR FATE...
"...ALLOWING ALL OTHER POSSIBILITIES TO FADE.
DESIRE IS FATE.
WE NEED TO GET THE HELL OUT OF HERE!
"YOU WILL SET THE WORLD AFLAME."
I ALREADY HAVE.
AND WE ARE EACH OUR OWN ARCHITECTS.
END

DARK WOLVERINE #84 DEADPOOL VARIANT

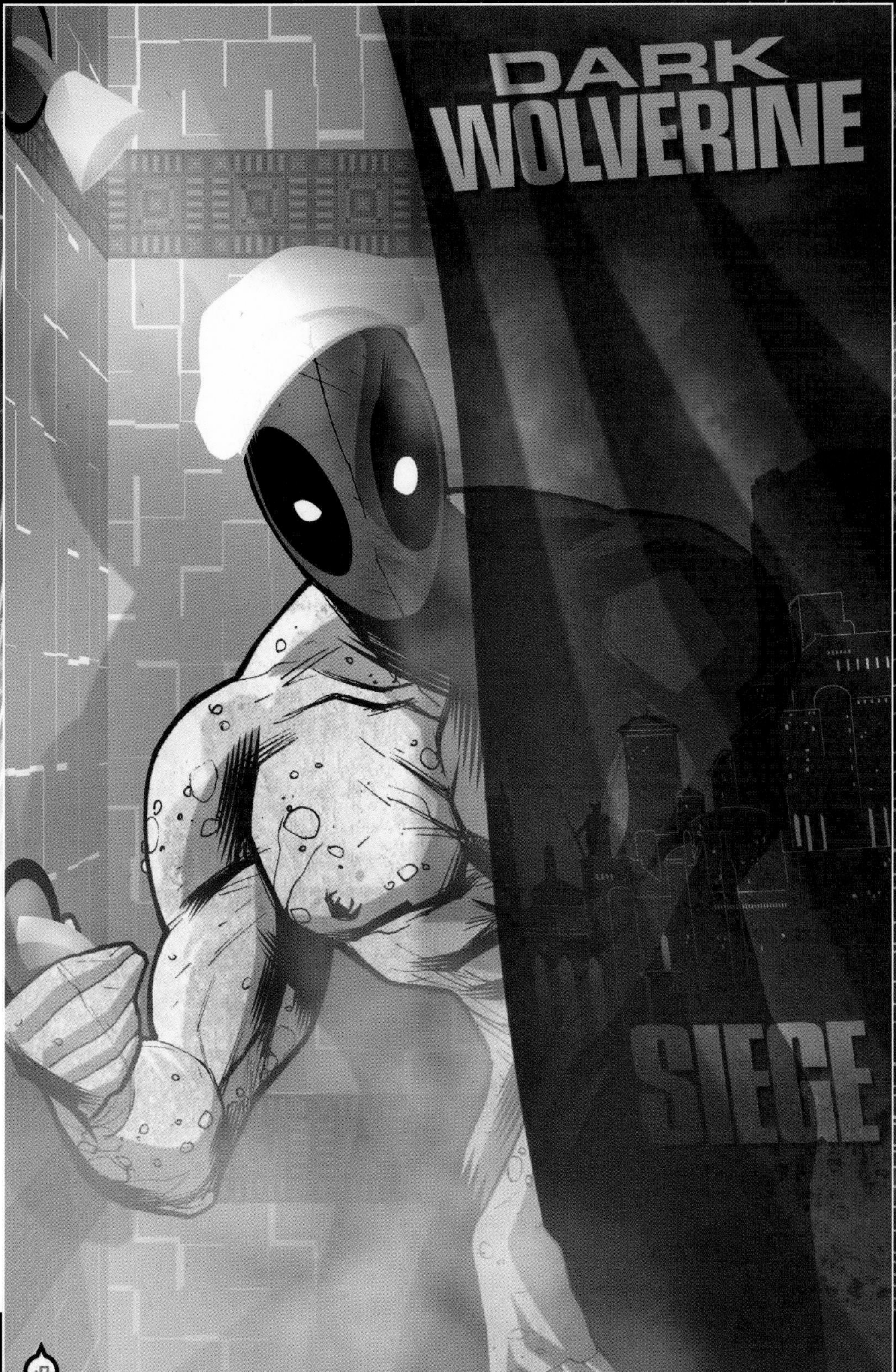
DARK
WOLVERINE
SIEGE

BY JUAN DOE

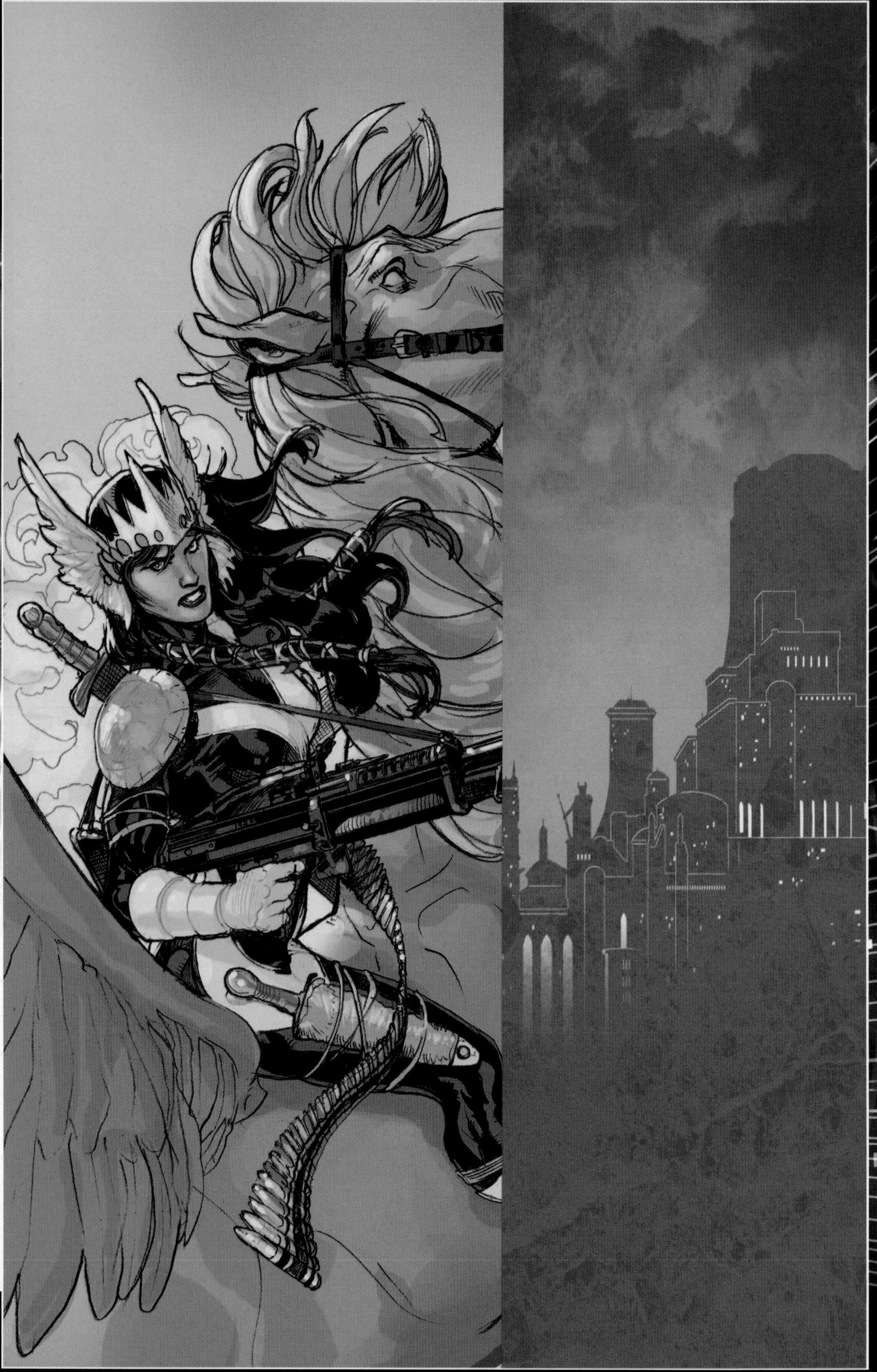

NEW MUTANTS

When Norman Obsorn, leader of the Dark Avengers, waged war on the X-Men, team leader Cyclops created a plan for fighting back. A key component of his strategy involved Dani Moonstar—depowered mutant and former Asgardian Valkyrie. Moonstar went to Hela, Asgardian goddess of death, and made a bargain with her: Hela would imbue Moonstar with the power of a Valkyrie once more so that she could repel the Dark Avengers' attack on the X-Men, but in turn, Moonstar would be indebted to the goddess.

"HEL'S VALKYRIE"

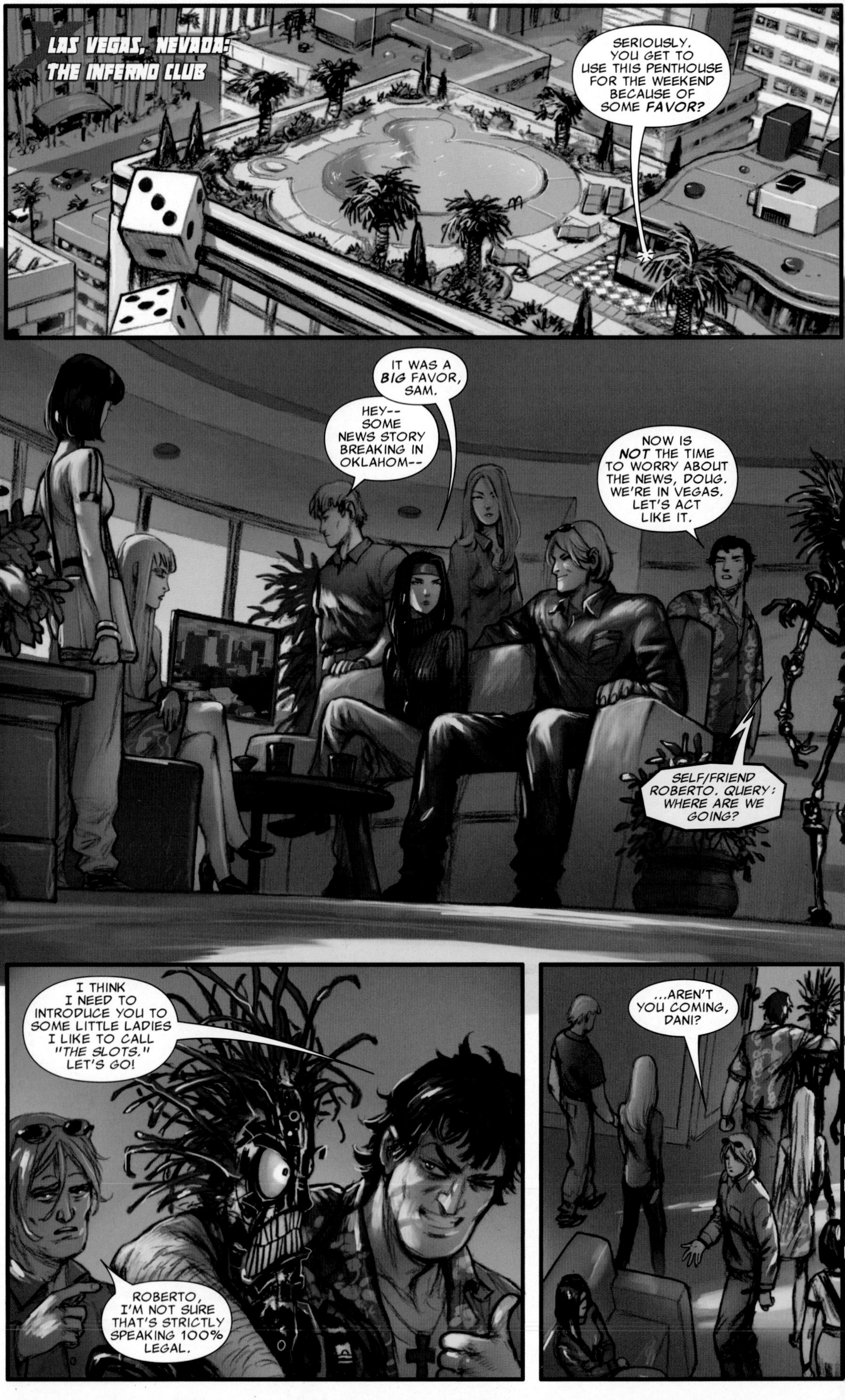
LAS VEGAS, NEVADA: THE INFERNO CLUB
SERIOUSLY. YOU GET TO USE THIS PENTHOUSE FOR THE WEEKEND BECAUSE OF SOME FAVOR?
IT WAS A BIG FAVOR, SAM.
HEY-- SOME NEWS STORY BREAKING IN OKLAHOM--
NOW IS NOT THE TIME TO WORRY ABOUT THE NEWS, DOUG. WE'RE IN VEGAS. LET'S ACT LIKE IT.
SELF/FRIEND ROBERTO. QUERY: WHERE ARE WE GOING?
I THINK I NEED TO INTRODUCE YOU TO SOME LITTLE LADIES I LIKE TO CALL "THE SLOTS." LET'S GO!
ROBERTO, I'M NOT SURE THAT'S STRICTLY SPEAKING 100% LEGAL.
...AREN'T YOU COMING, DANI?

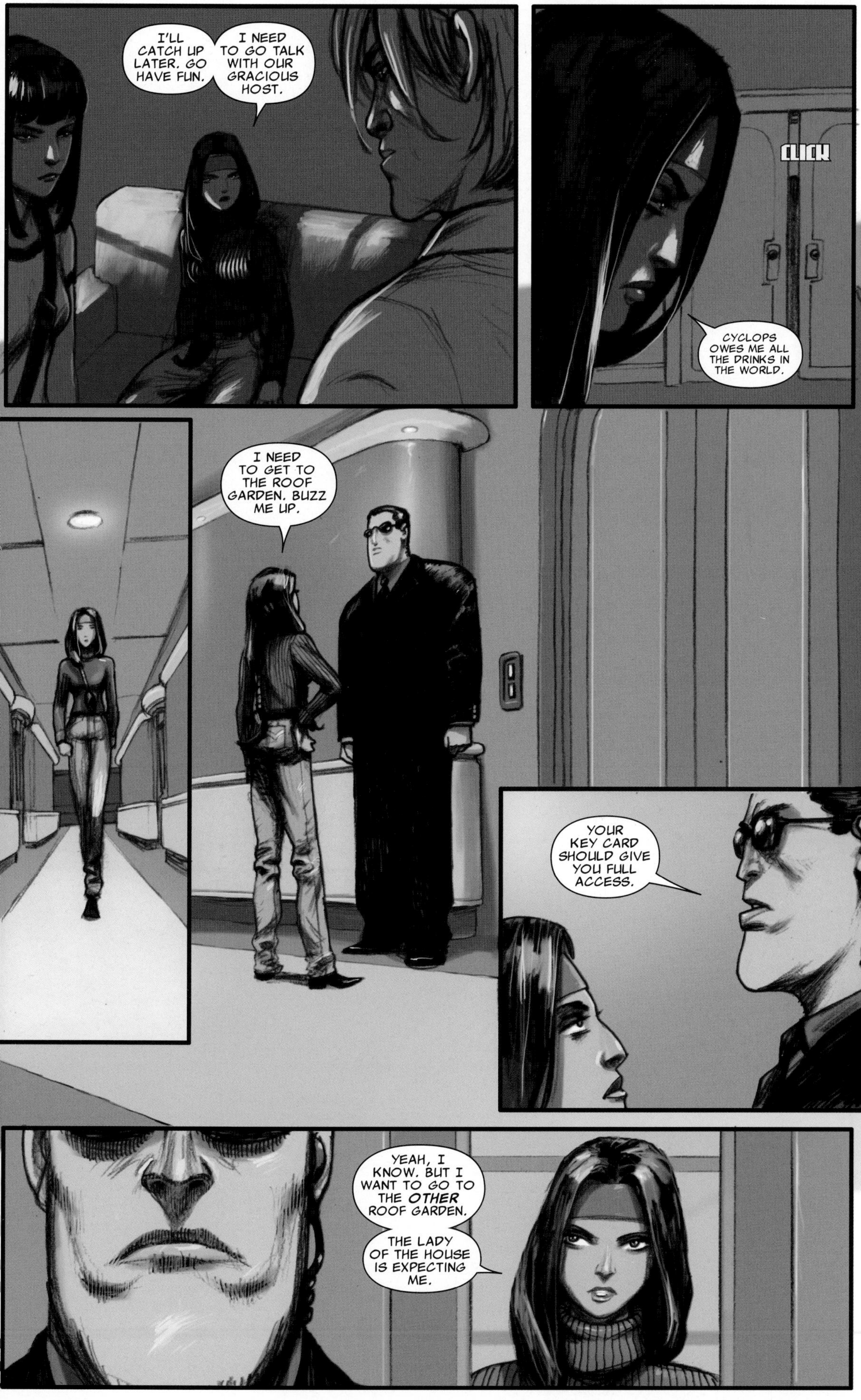
I'LL CATCH UP LATER. GO HAVE FUN.
I NEED TO GO TALK WITH OUR GRACIOUS HOST.
CLICK
CYCLOPS OWES ME ALL THE DRINKS IN THE WORLD.
I NEED TO GET TO THE ROOF GARDEN. BUZZ ME UP.
YOUR KEY CARD SHOULD GIVE YOU FULL ACCESS.
YEAH, I KNOW. BUT I WANT TO GO TO THE *OTHER* ROOF GARDEN.
THE LADY OF THE HOUSE IS EXPECTING ME.

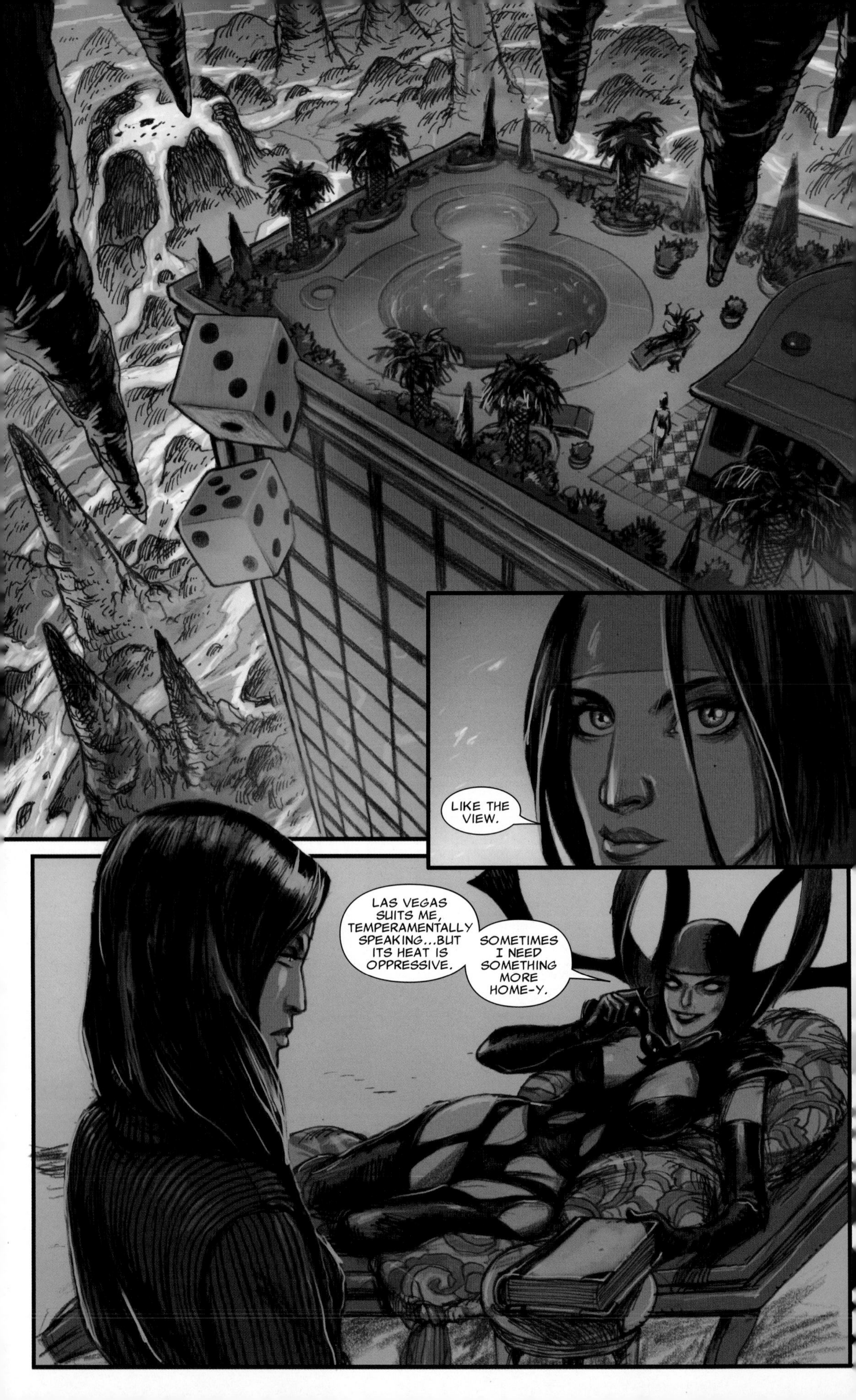
LIKE THE VIEW.
LAS VEGAS SUITS ME, TEMPERAMENTALLY SPEAKING...BUT ITS HEAT IS OPPRESSIVE.
SOMETIMES I NEED SOMETHING MORE HOME-Y.

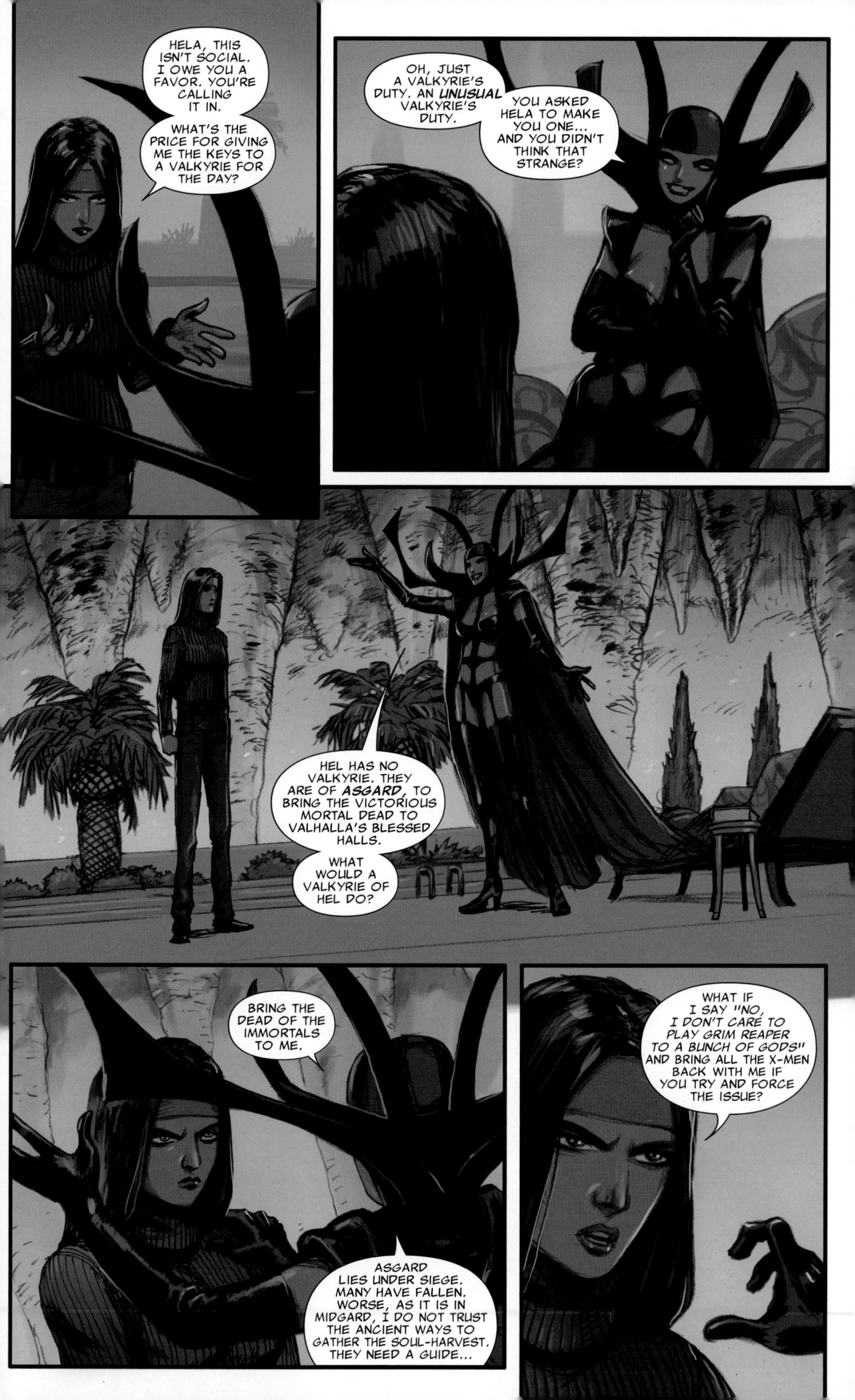
HELA, THIS ISN'T SOCIAL. I OWE YOU A FAVOR. YOU'RE CALLING IT IN.
WHAT'S THE PRICE FOR GIVING ME THE KEYS TO A VALKYRIE FOR THE DAY?
OH, JUST A VALKYRIE'S DUTY. AN UNUSUAL VALKYRIE'S DUTY.
YOU ASKED HELA TO MAKE YOU ONE... AND YOU DIDN'T THINK THAT STRANGE?
HEL HAS NO VALKYRIE. THEY ARE OF ASGARD, TO BRING THE VICTORIOUS MORTAL DEAD TO VALHALLA'S BLESSED HALLS.
WHAT WOULD A VALKYRIE OF HEL DO?
BRING THE DEAD OF THE IMMORTALS TO ME.
ASGARD LIES UNDER SIEGE. MANY HAVE FALLEN. WORSE, AS IT IS IN MIDGARD, I DO NOT TRUST THE ANCIENT WAYS TO GATHER THE SOUL-HARVEST. THEY NEED A GUIDE...
WHAT IF I SAY "NO, I DON'T CARE TO PLAY GRIM REAPER TO A BUNCH OF GODS" AND BRING ALL THE X-MEN BACK WITH ME IF YOU TRY AND FORCE THE ISSUE?

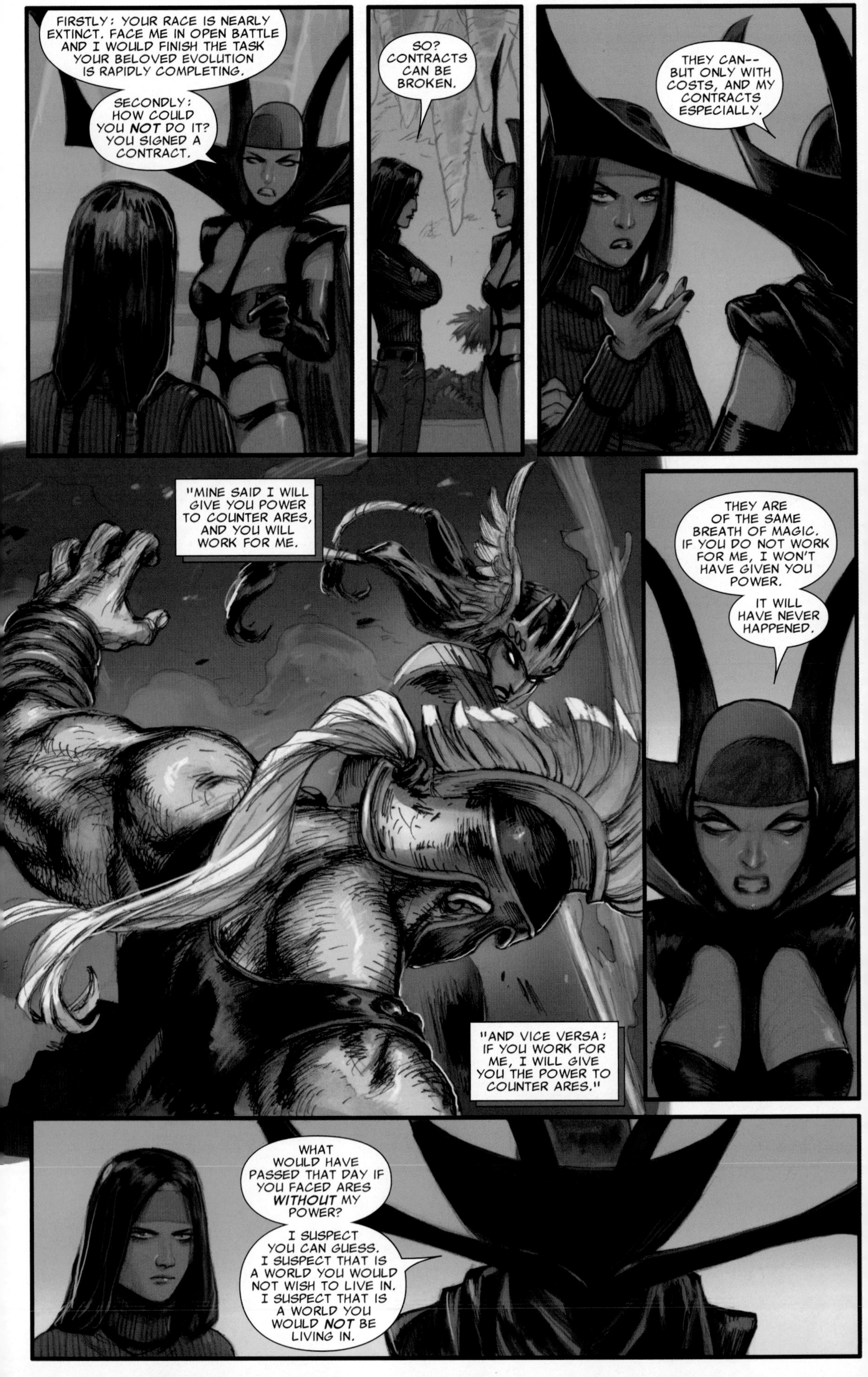
FIRSTLY: YOUR RACE IS NEARLY EXTINCT. FACE ME IN OPEN BATTLE AND I WOULD FINISH THE TASK YOUR BELOVED EVOLUTION IS RAPIDLY COMPLETING.
SECONDLY: HOW COULD YOU NOT DO IT? YOU SIGNED A CONTRACT.
SO? CONTRACTS CAN BE BROKEN.
THEY CAN-- BUT ONLY WITH COSTS, AND MY CONTRACTS ESPECIALLY.
"MINE SAID I WILL GIVE YOU POWER TO COUNTER ARES, AND YOU WILL WORK FOR ME.
"AND VICE VERSA: IF YOU WORK FOR ME, I WILL GIVE YOU THE POWER TO COUNTER ARES."
THEY ARE OF THE SAME BREATH OF MAGIC. IF YOU DO NOT WORK FOR ME, I WON'T HAVE GIVEN YOU POWER.
IT WILL HAVE NEVER HAPPENED.
WHAT WOULD HAVE PASSED THAT DAY IF YOU FACED ARES WITHOUT MY POWER?
I SUSPECT YOU CAN GUESS. I SUSPECT THAT IS A WORLD YOU WOULD NOT WISH TO LIVE IN. I SUSPECT THAT IS A WORLD YOU WOULD NOT BE LIVING IN.

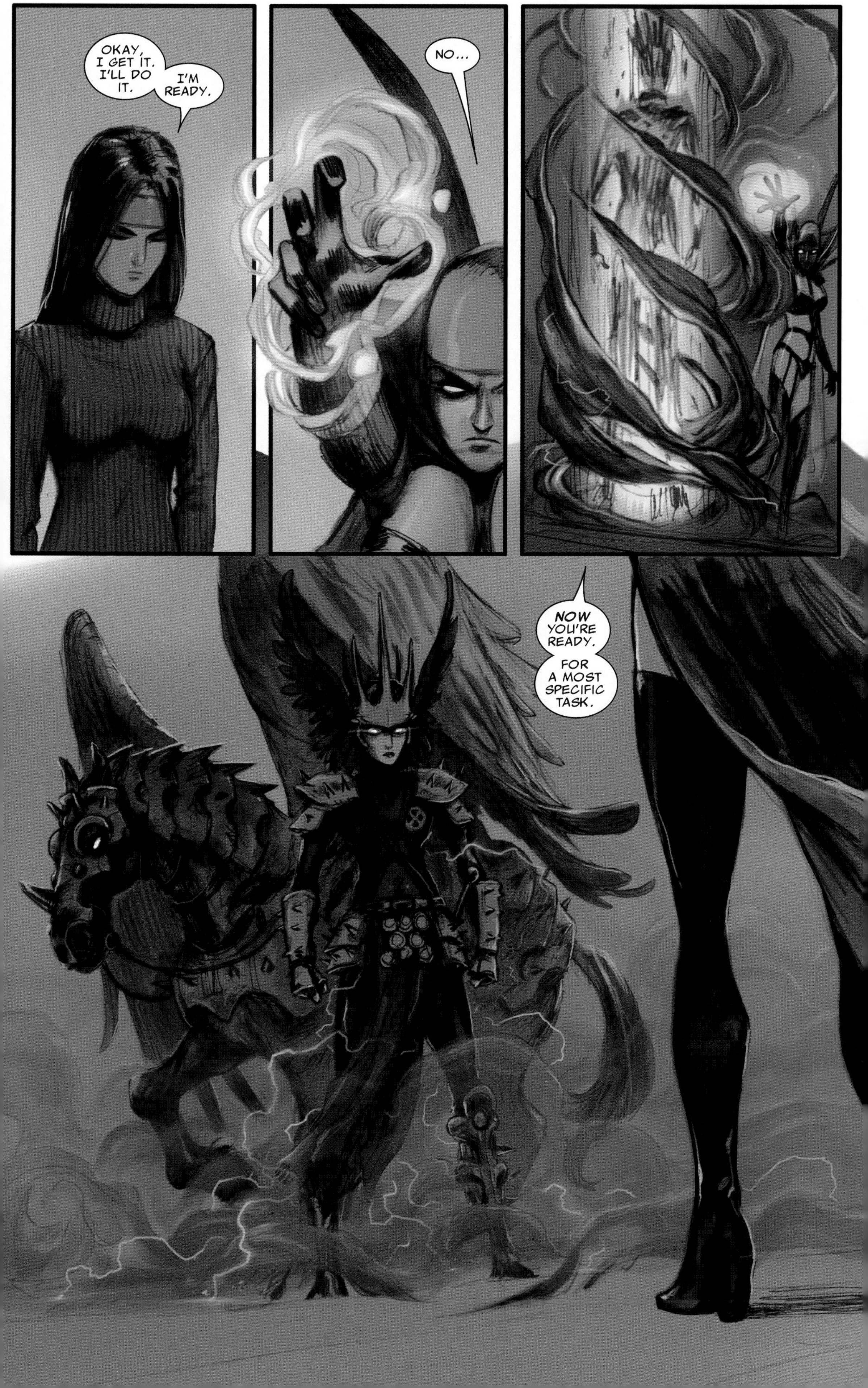
OKAY, I GET IT. I'LL DO IT.
I'M READY.
NO...
NOW YOU'RE READY.
FOR A MOST SPECIFIC TASK.

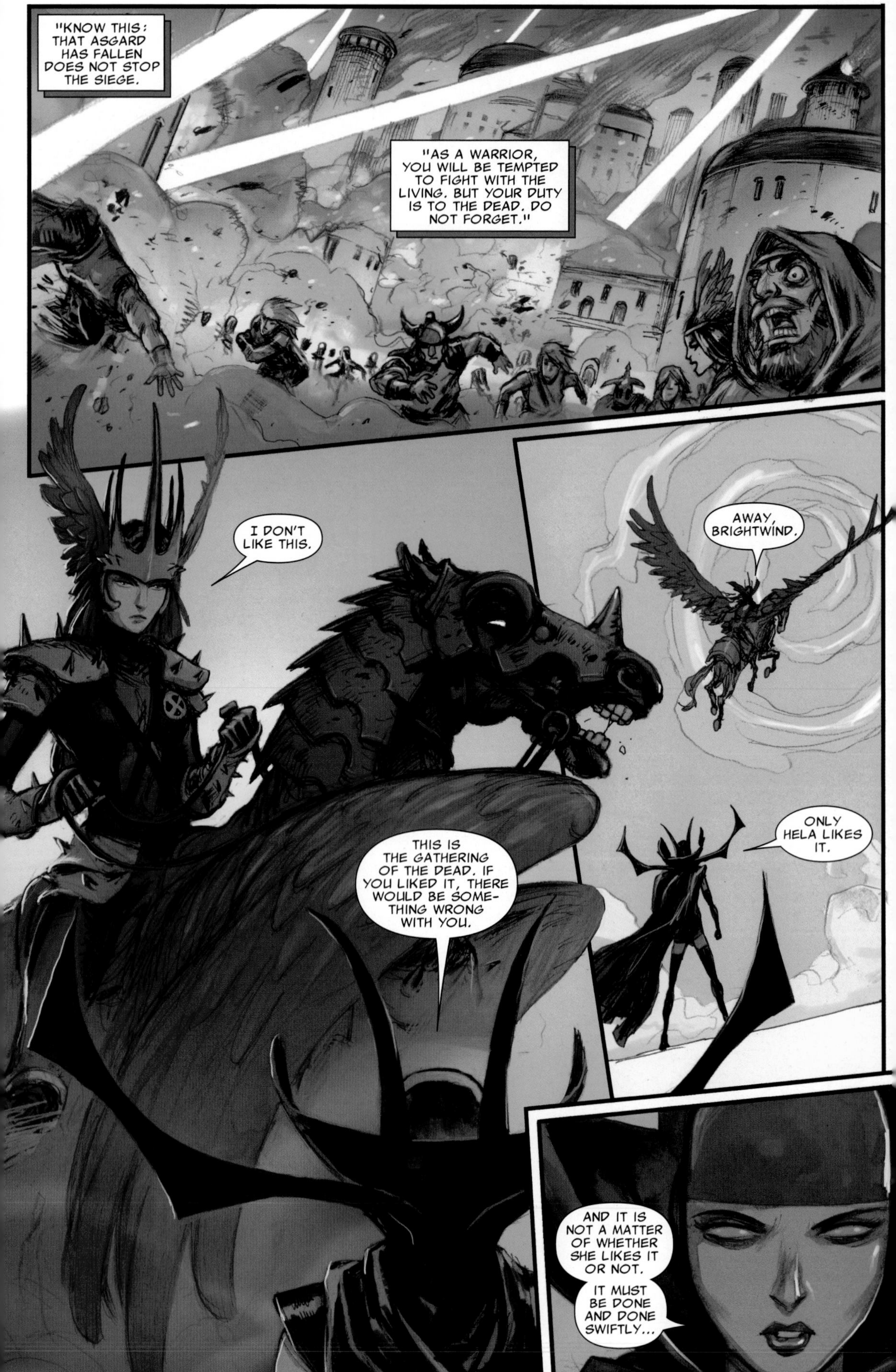
"KNOW THIS: THAT ASGARD HAS FALLEN DOES NOT STOP THE SIEGE.
"AS A WARRIOR, YOU WILL BE TEMPTED TO FIGHT WITH THE LIVING. BUT YOUR DUTY IS TO THE DEAD. DO NOT FORGET."
I DON'T LIKE THIS.
AWAY, BRIGHTWIND.
THIS IS THE GATHERING OF THE DEAD. IF YOU LIKED IT, THERE WOULD BE SOME-THING WRONG WITH YOU.
ONLY HELA LIKES IT.
AND IT IS NOT A MATTER OF WHETHER SHE LIKES IT OR NOT.
IT MUST BE DONE AND DONE SWIFTLY...

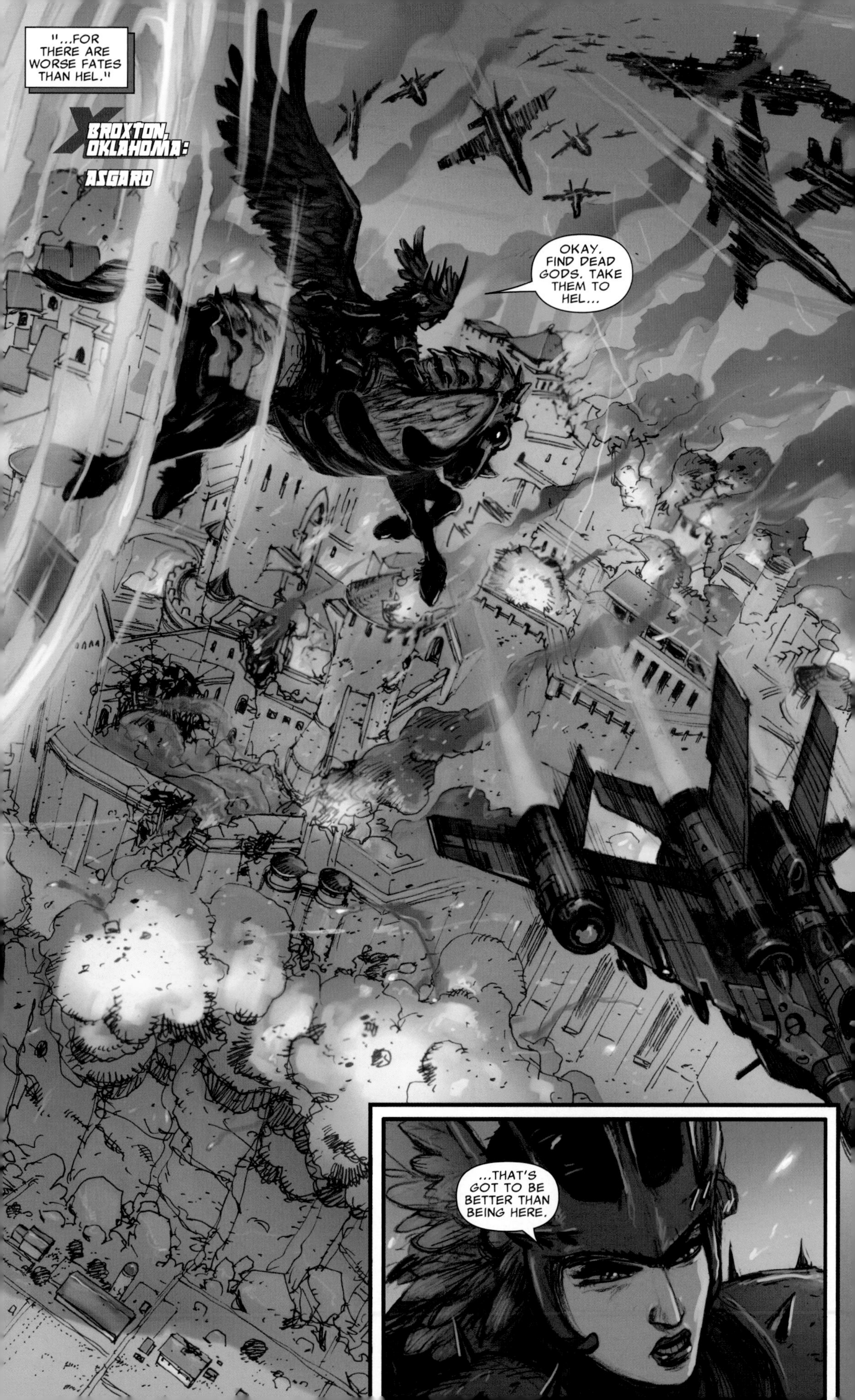
"...FOR THERE ARE WORSE FATES THAN HEL."
BROXTON, OKLAHOMA:
ASGARD
OKAY. FIND DEAD GODS. TAKE THEM TO HEL...
...THAT'S GOT TO BE BETTER THAN BEING HERE.

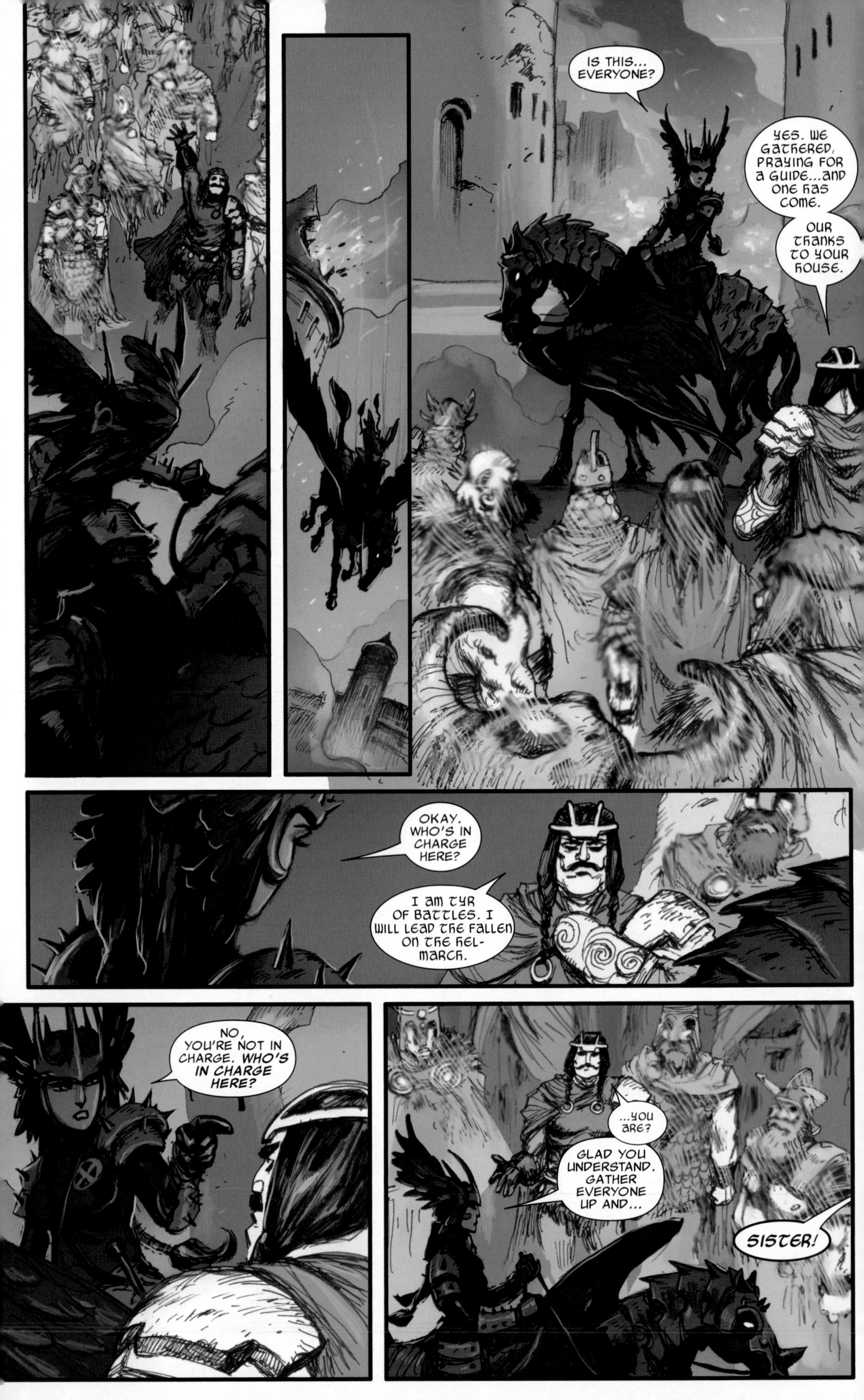
IS THIS... EVERYONE?
YES. WE GATHERED, PRAYING FOR A GUIDE...AND ONE HAS COME.
OUR THANKS TO YOUR HOUSE.
OKAY. WHO'S IN CHARGE HERE?
I AM TYR OF BATTLES. I WILL LEAD THE FALLEN ON THE HEL-MARCH.
NO, YOU'RE NOT IN CHARGE. *WHO'S IN CHARGE HERE?*
...YOU ARE?
GLAD YOU UNDERSTAND. GATHER EVERYONE UP AND...
SISTER!

WHAT ARE YOU DOING? IT IS NO TIME TO CONVERSE WITH ONESELF. ASGARD CALLS.

YOU WILL ANSWER?

WAIT! THERE ARE HUNDREDS OF WARRIORS HERE, ALL FIGHTING FOR THE LIVING.

WHO WILL FIGHT FOR THE DEAD?

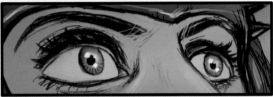

YOU'RE DEAD, TYR. THE WORST HAS ALREADY HAPPENED.

THERE'S STILL TIME TO STOP ANYONE ELSE ENDING UP LIKE YOU. DON'T WORRY...

...YOU GUYS HAVE NOTHING TO BE SCARED OF ANYMORE.

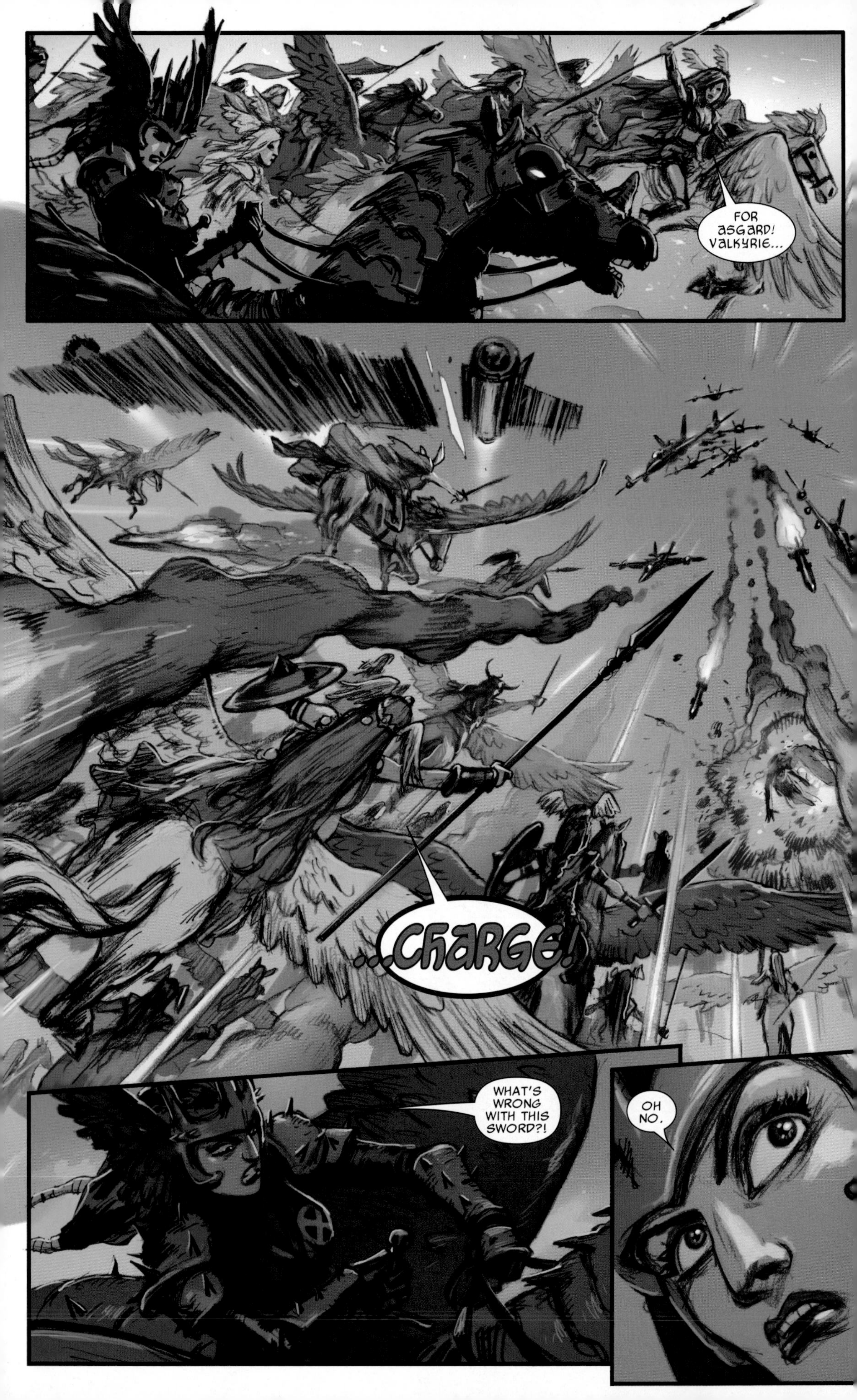
FOR ASGARD! VALKYRIE...
...CHARGE!
WHAT'S WRONG WITH THIS SWORD?!
OH NO.

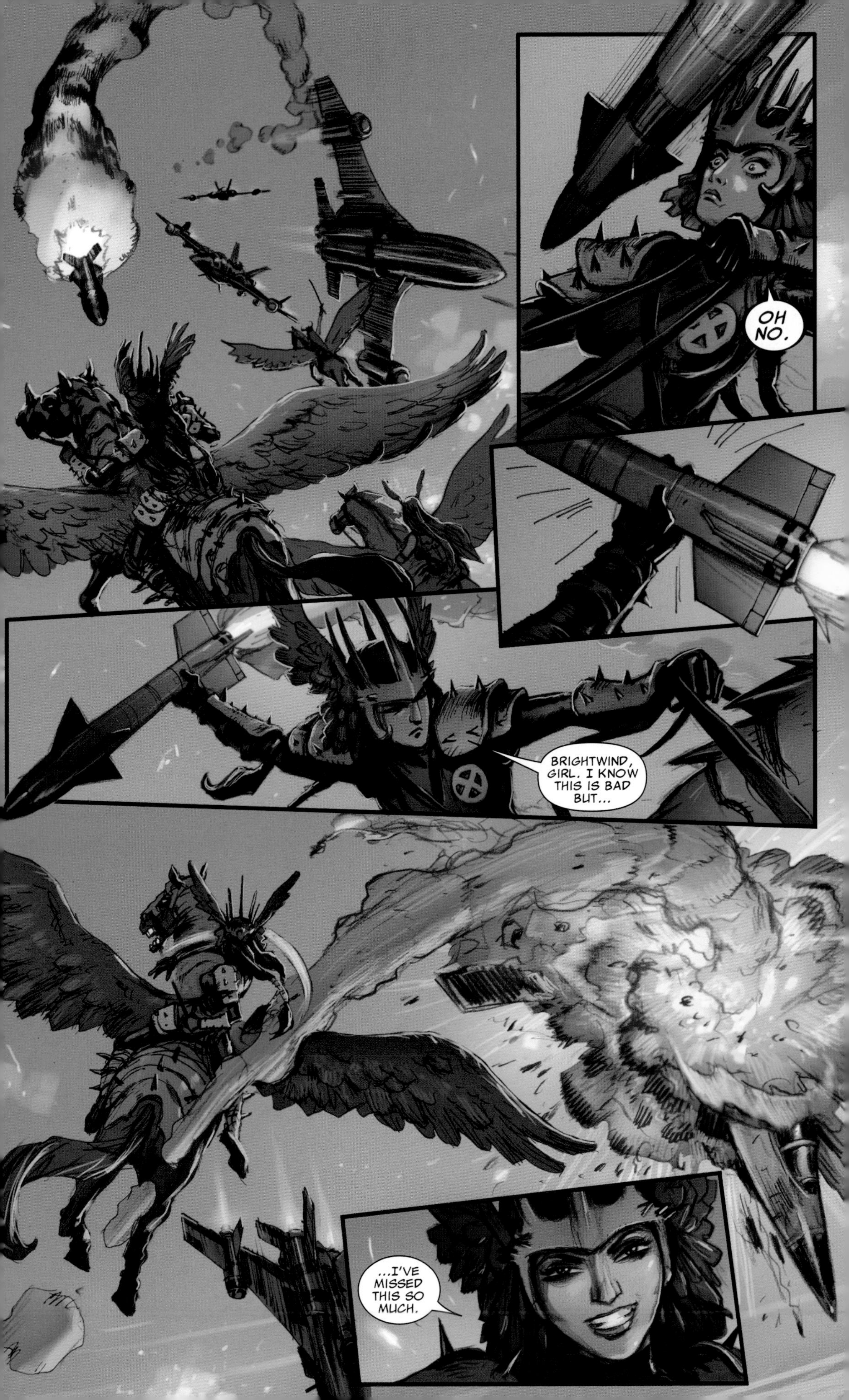
OH NO.
BRIGHTWIND, GIRL. I KNOW THIS IS BAD BUT...
...I'VE MISSED THIS SO MUCH.

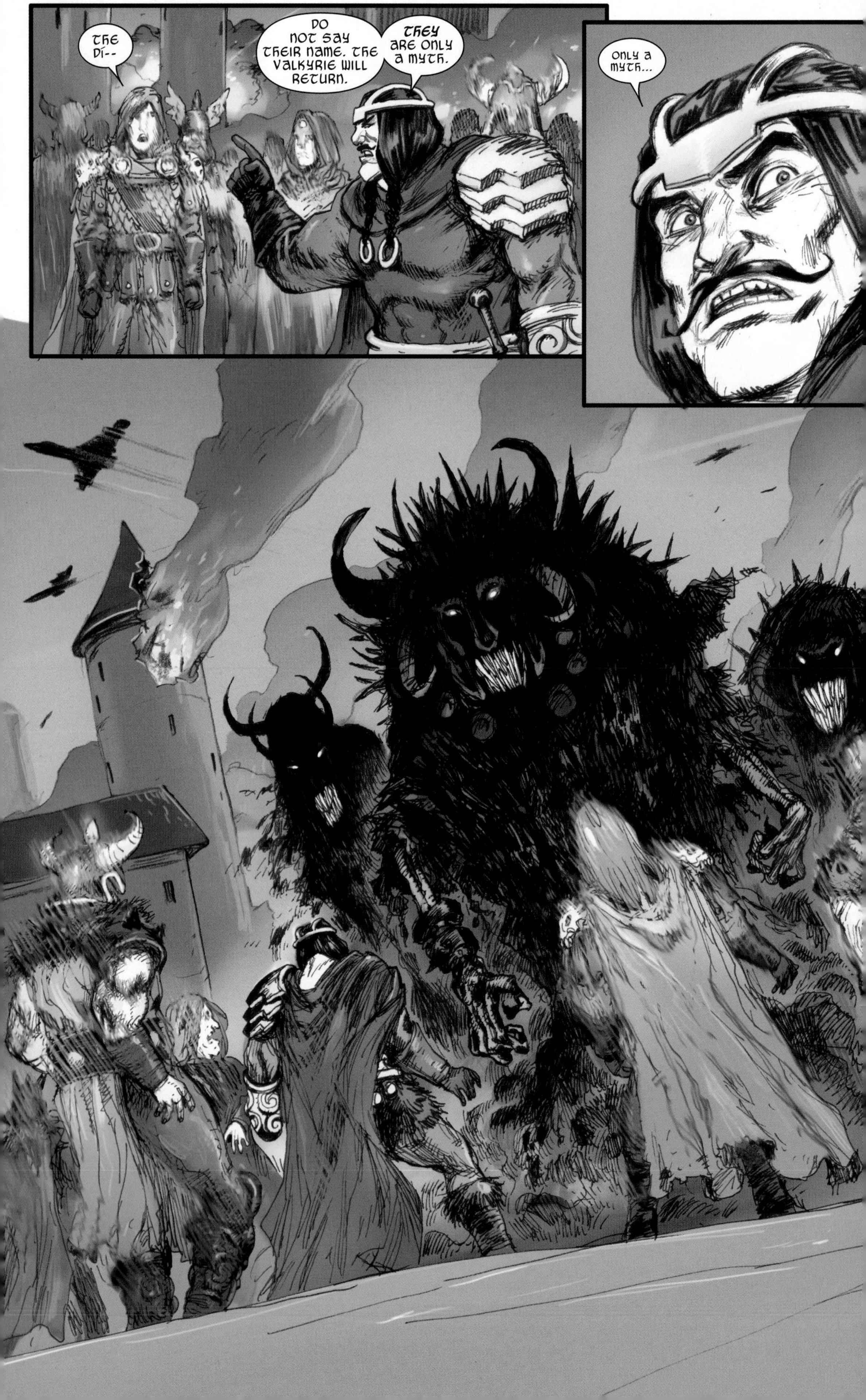
THE DÍ--
DO NOT SAY THEIR NAME. THE VALKYRIE WILL RETURN.
THEY ARE ONLY A MYTH.
ONLY A MYTH...

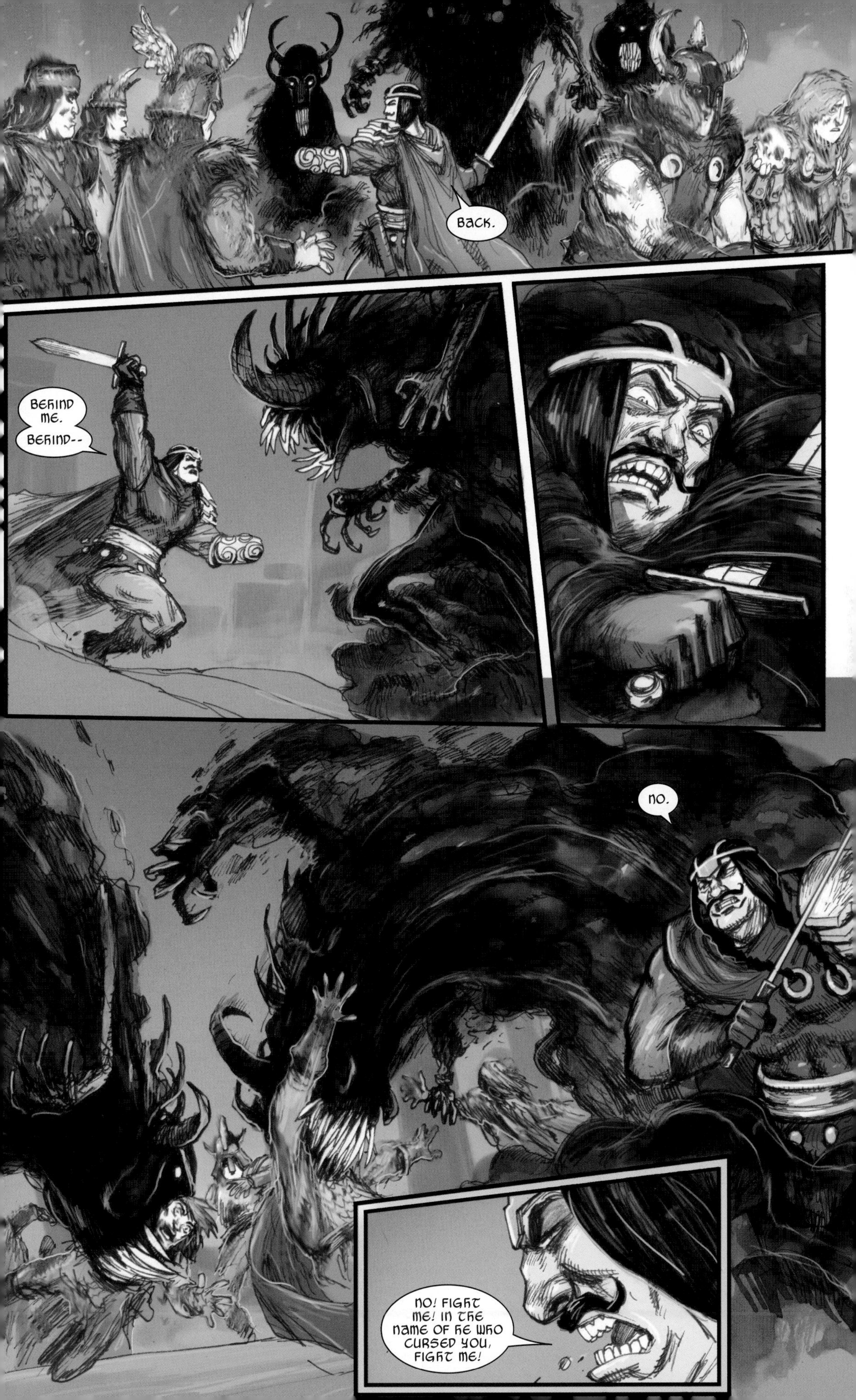
BACK.
BEHIND ME. BEHIND--
NO.
NO! FIGHT ME! IN THE NAME OF HE WHO CURSED YOU, FIGHT ME!

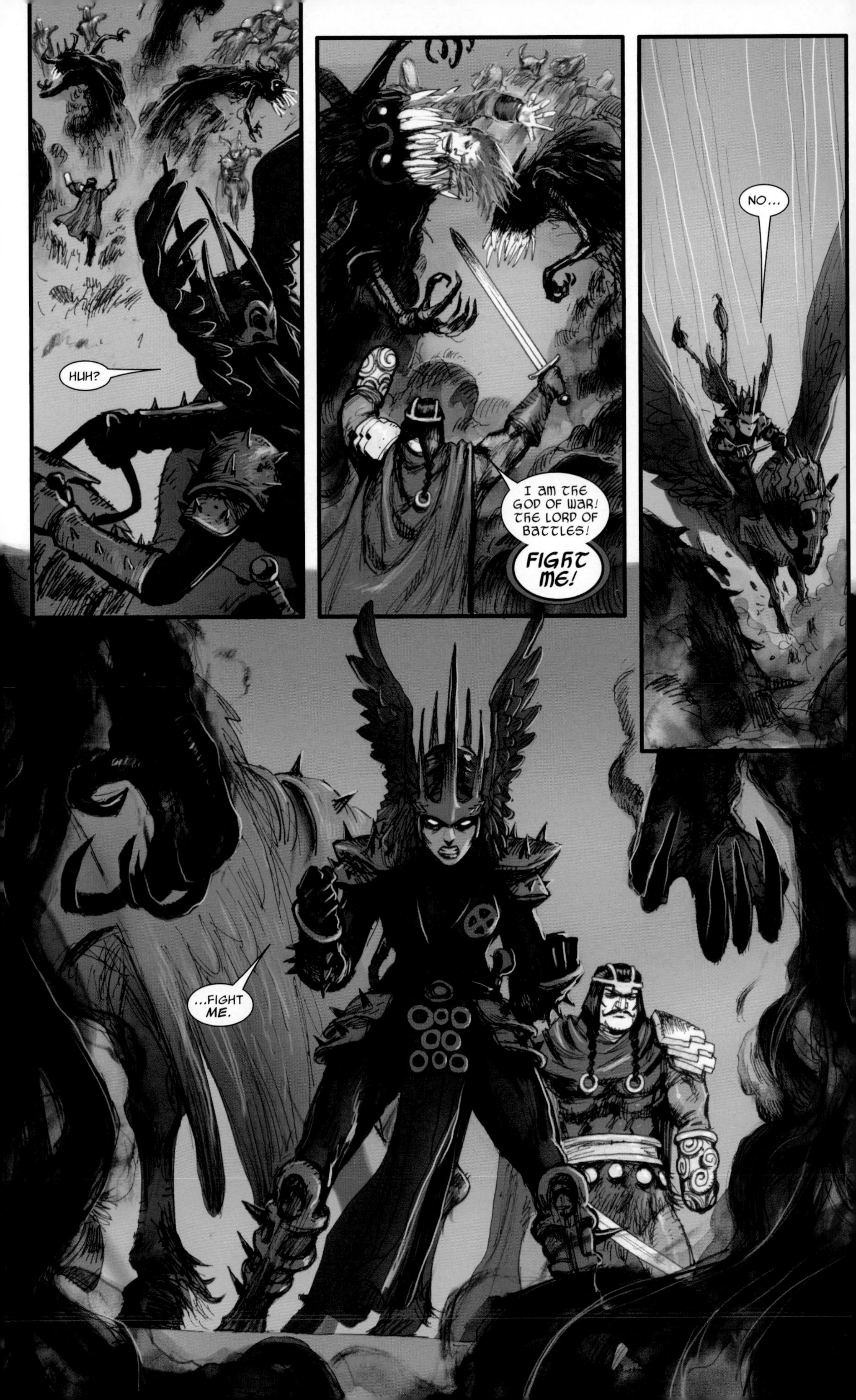
HUH?
I AM THE GOD OF WAR! THE LORD OF BATTLES!
FIGHT ME!
NO...
...FIGHT ME.

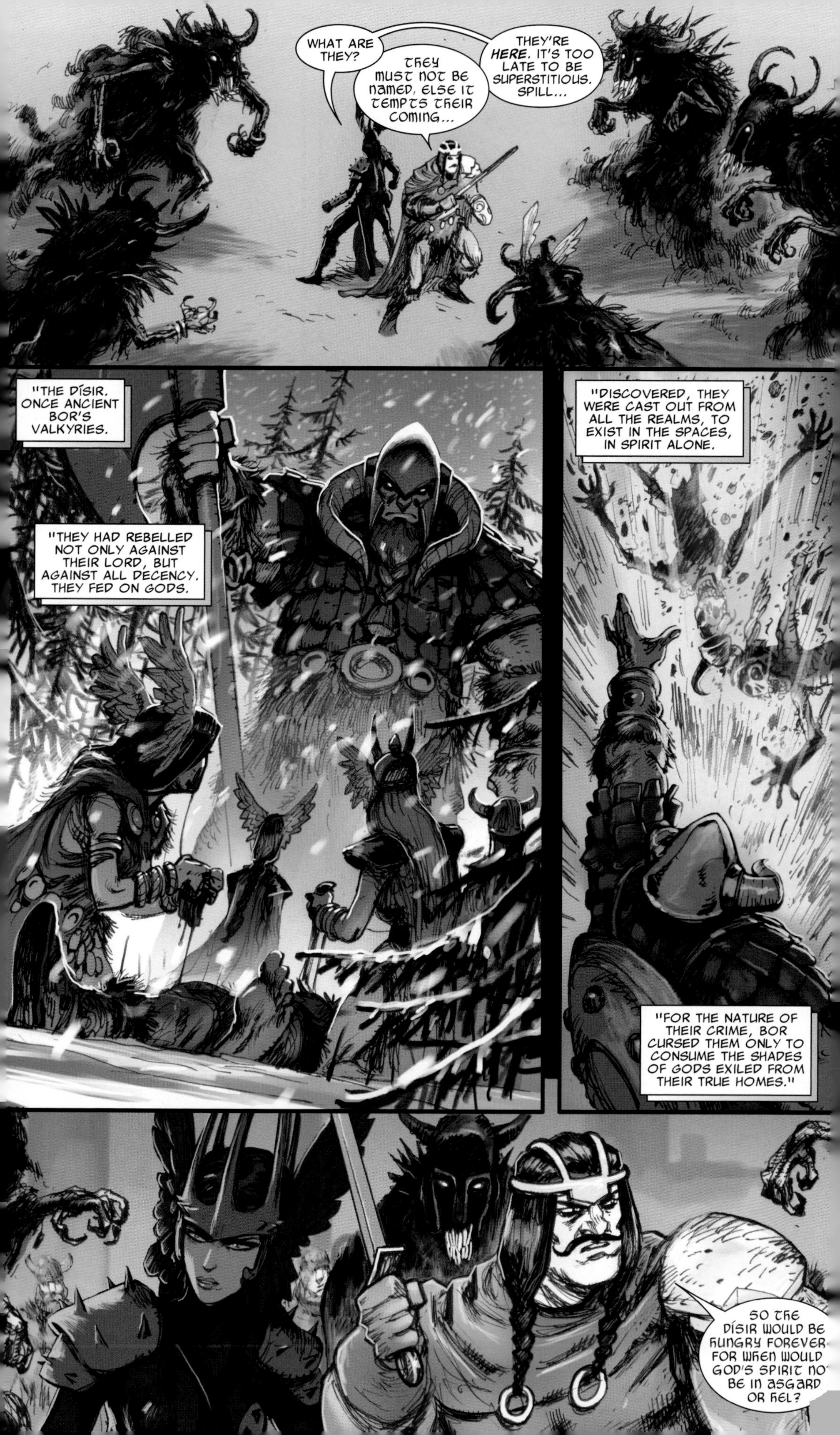
WHAT ARE THEY?
THEY MUST NOT BE NAMED, ELSE IT TEMPTS THEIR COMING...
THEY'RE HERE. IT'S TOO LATE TO BE SUPERSTITIOUS. SPILL...
"THE DÍSIR. ONCE ANCIENT BOR'S VALKYRIES.
"THEY HAD REBELLED NOT ONLY AGAINST THEIR LORD, BUT AGAINST ALL DECENCY. THEY FED ON GODS.
"DISCOVERED, THEY WERE CAST OUT FROM ALL THE REALMS, TO EXIST IN THE SPACES, IN SPIRIT ALONE.
"FOR THE NATURE OF THEIR CRIME, BOR CURSED THEM ONLY TO CONSUME THE SHADES OF GODS EXILED FROM THEIR TRUE HOMES."
SO THE DÍSIR WOULD BE HUNGRY FOREVER FOR WHEN WOULD GOD'S SPIRIT NOT BE IN ASGARD OR HEL?

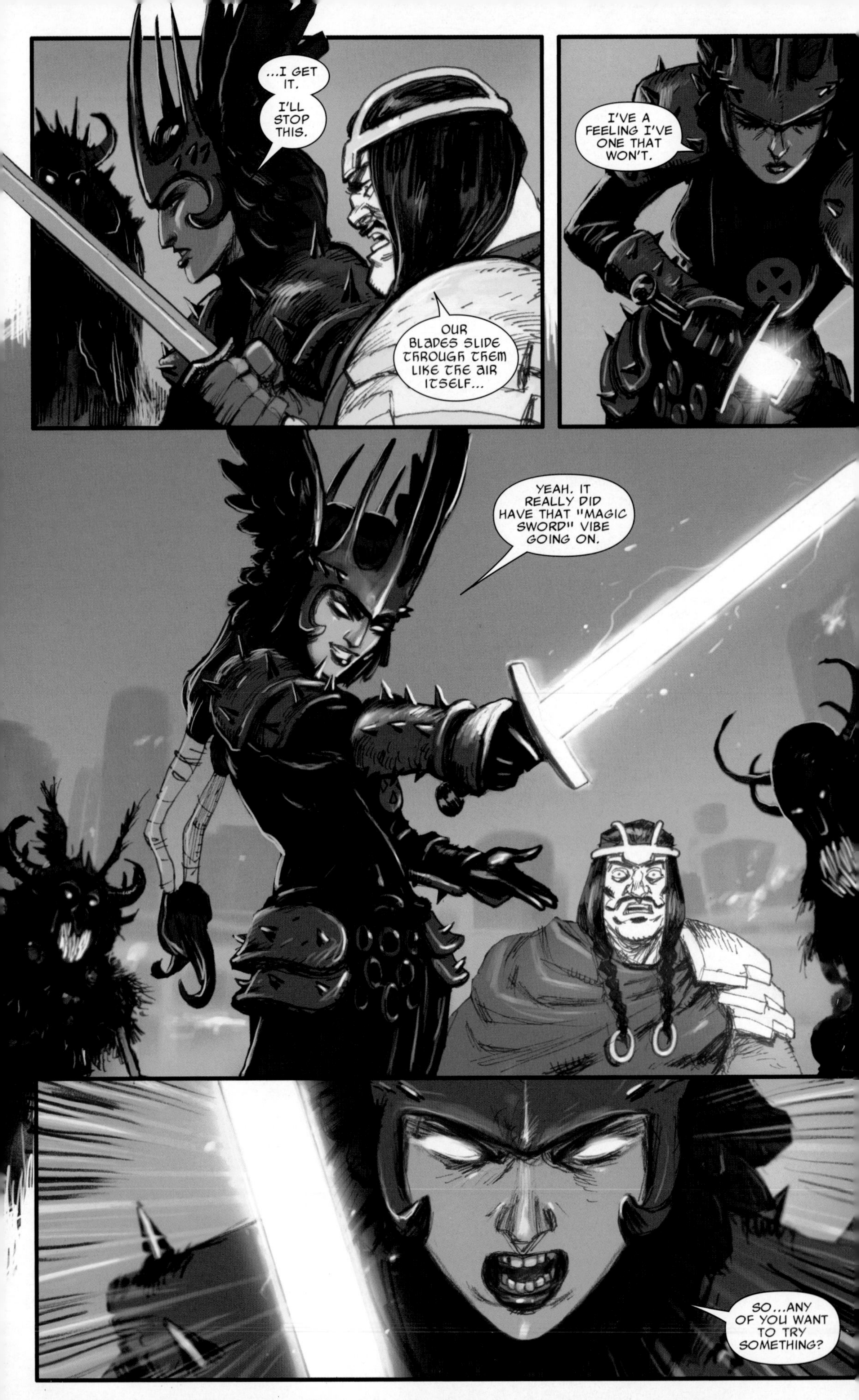
...I GET IT.
I'LL STOP THIS.
OUR BLADES SLIDE THROUGH THEM LIKE THE AIR ITSELF...
I'VE A FEELING I'VE ONE THAT WON'T.
YEAH. IT REALLY DID HAVE THAT "MAGIC SWORD" VIBE GOING ON.
SO...ANY OF YOU WANT TO TRY SOMETHING?

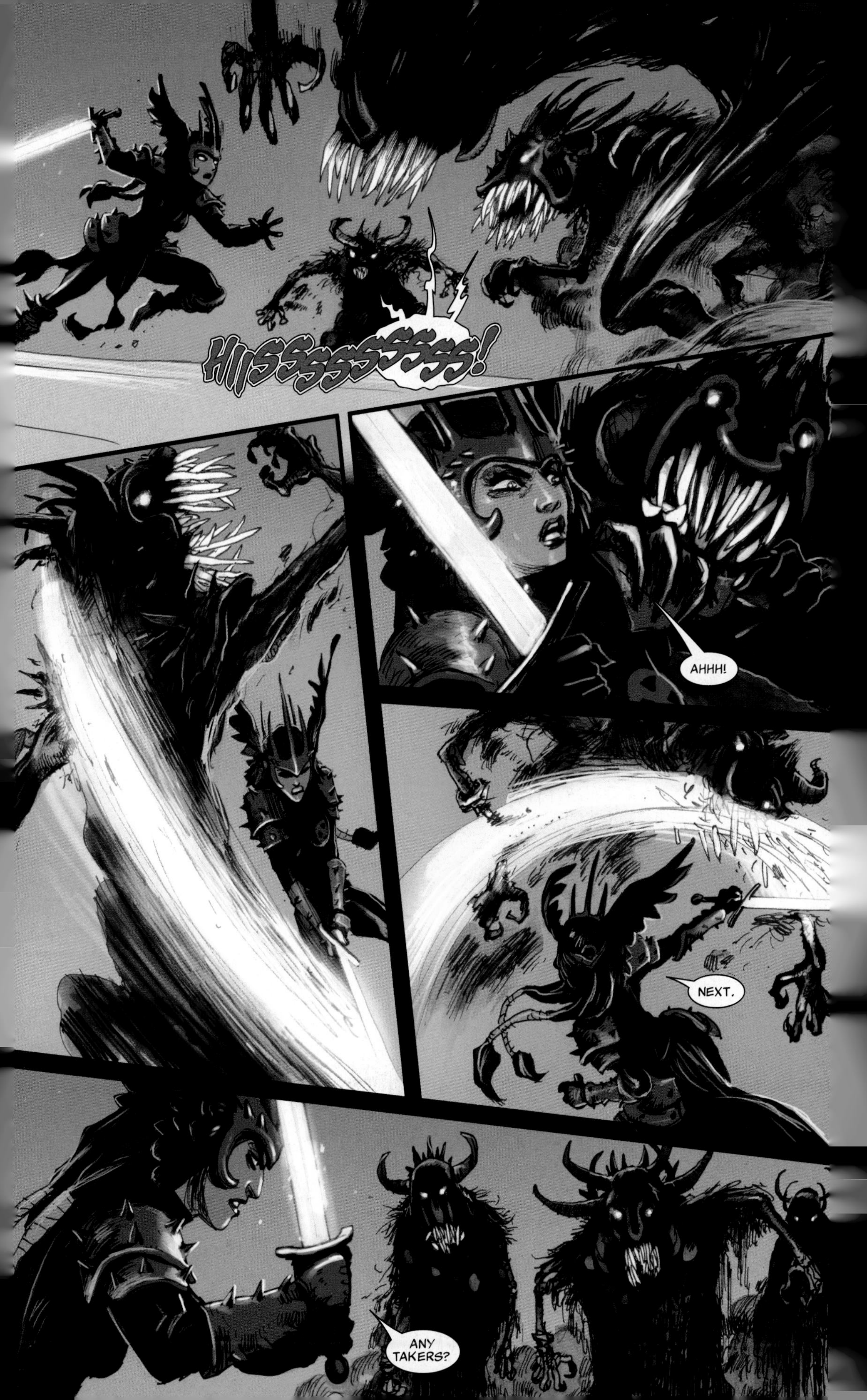
HIISSSSSSSSS!
AHHH!
NEXT.
ANY TAKERS?

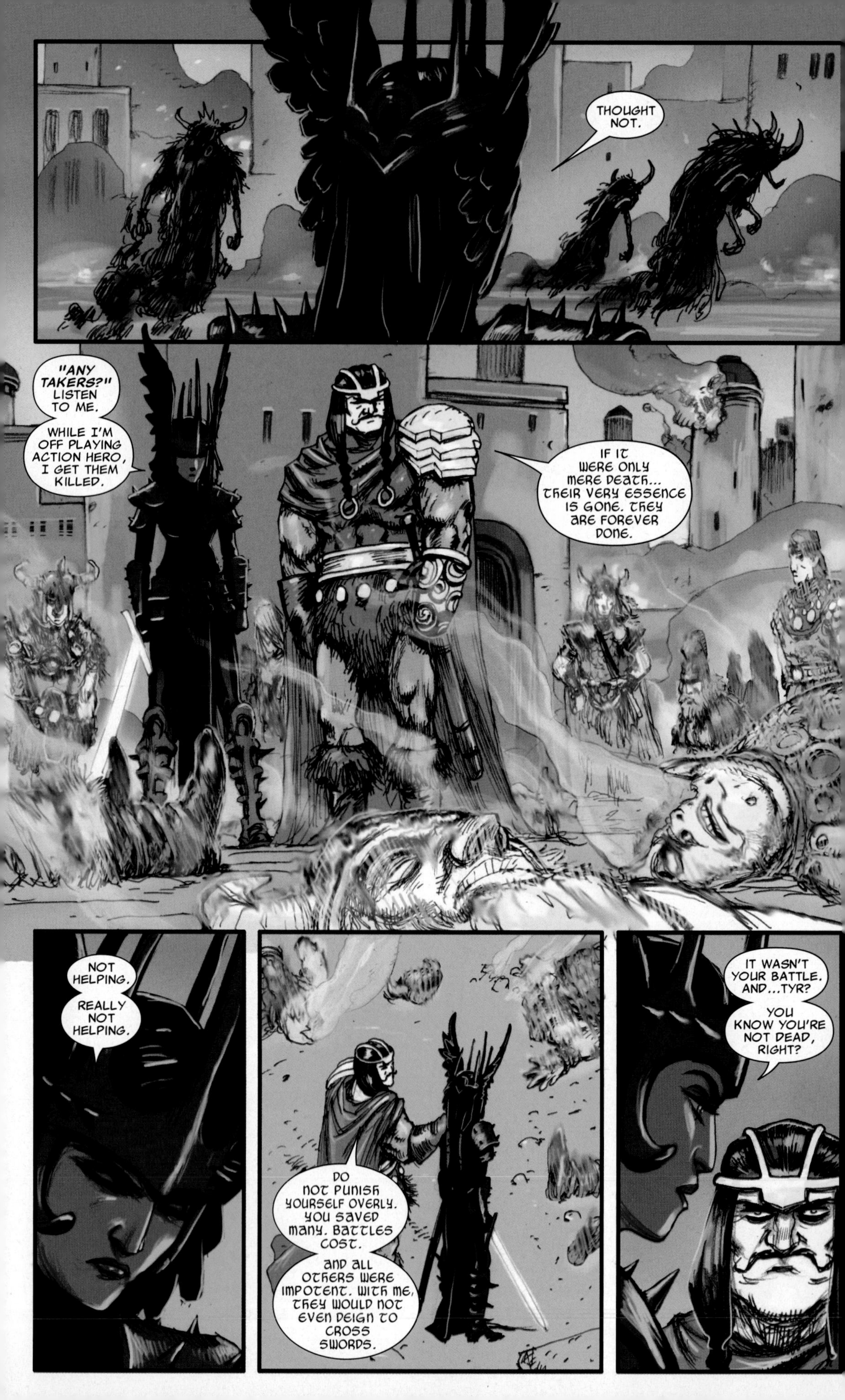
THOUGHT NOT.
"ANY TAKERS?" LISTEN TO ME.
WHILE I'M OFF PLAYING ACTION HERO, I GET THEM KILLED.
IF IT WERE ONLY MERE DEATH... THEIR VERY ESSENCE IS GONE. THEY ARE FOREVER DONE.
NOT HELPING.
REALLY NOT HELPING.
DO NOT PUNISH YOURSELF OVERLY. YOU SAVED MANY. BATTLES COST.
AND ALL OTHERS WERE IMPOTENT. WITH ME, THEY WOULD NOT EVEN DEIGN TO CROSS SWORDS.
IT WASN'T YOUR BATTLE. AND...TYR?
YOU KNOW YOU'RE NOT DEAD, RIGHT?

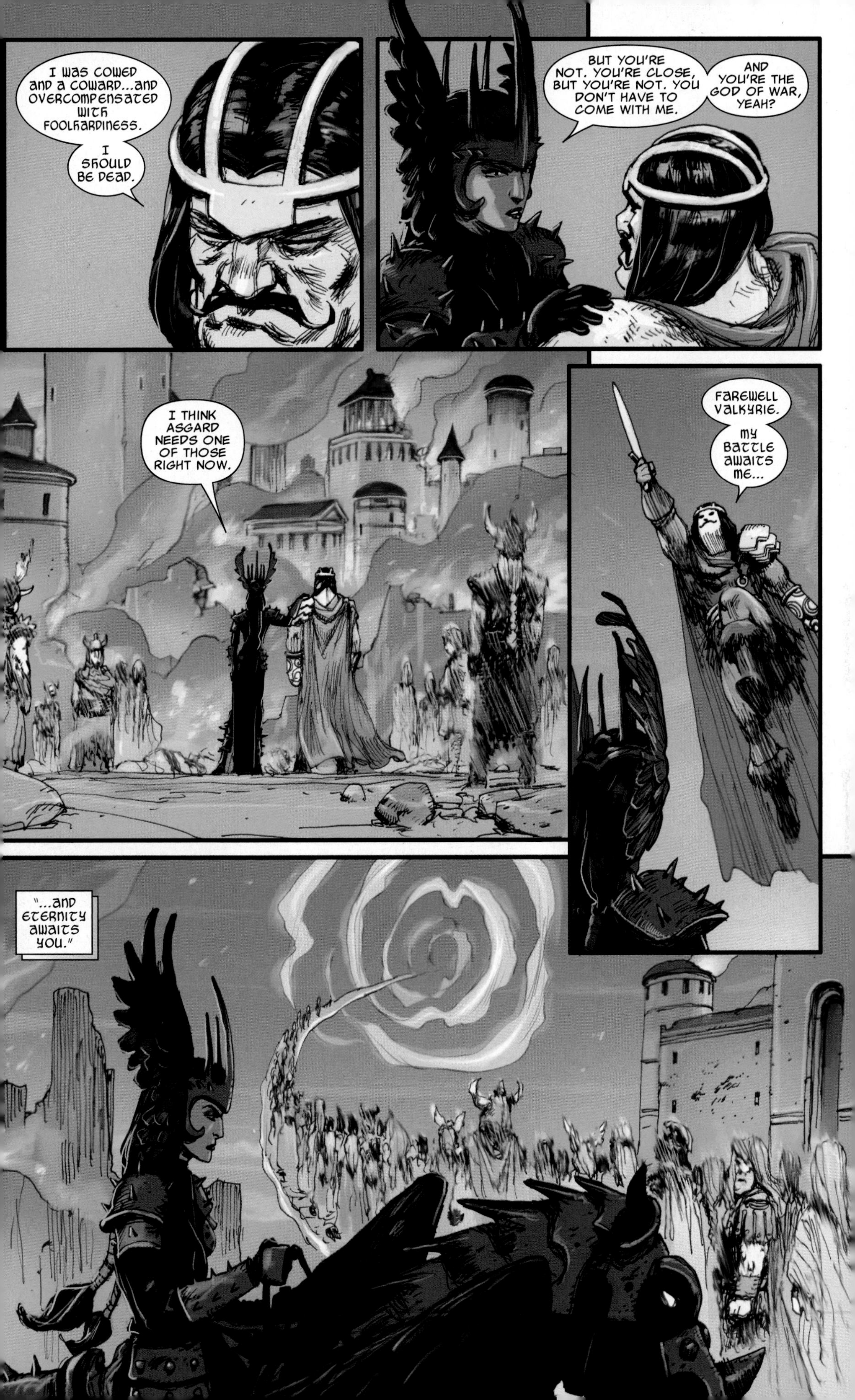
I WAS COWED AND A COWARD...AND OVERCOMPENSATED WITH FOOLHARDINESS.
I SHOULD BE DEAD.
BUT YOU'RE NOT. YOU'RE CLOSE, BUT YOU'RE NOT. YOU DON'T HAVE TO COME WITH ME.
AND YOU'RE THE GOD OF WAR, YEAH?
I THINK ASGARD NEEDS ONE OF THOSE RIGHT NOW.
FAREWELL VALKYRIE.
MY BATTLE AWAITS ME...
"...AND ETERNITY AWAITS YOU."

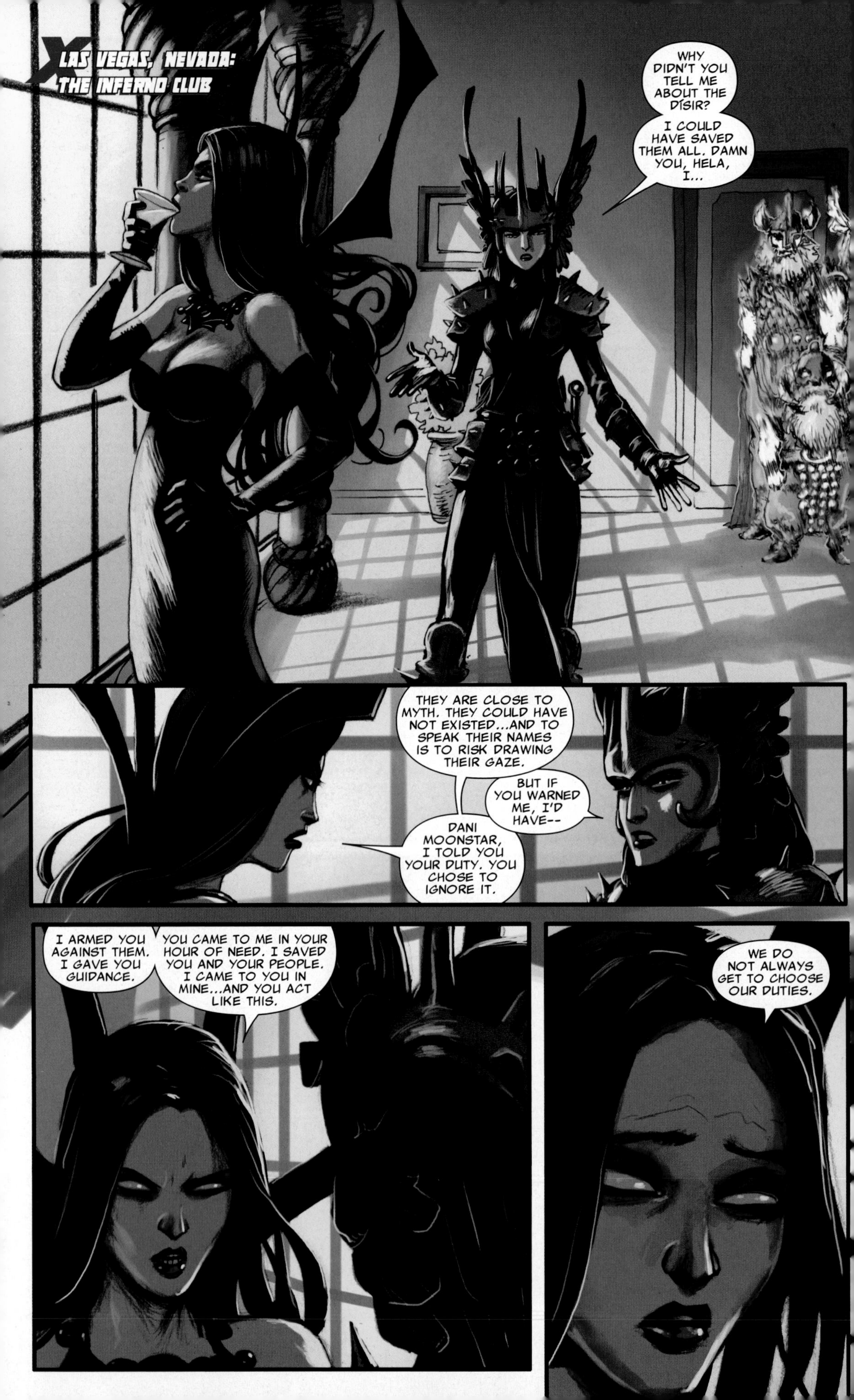
LAS VEGAS, NEVADA: THE INFERNO CLUB
WHY DIDN'T YOU TELL ME ABOUT THE DÍSIR?
I COULD HAVE SAVED THEM ALL. DAMN YOU, HELA, I...
THEY ARE CLOSE TO MYTH. THEY COULD HAVE NOT EXISTED...AND TO SPEAK THEIR NAMES IS TO RISK DRAWING THEIR GAZE.
BUT IF YOU WARNED ME, I'D HAVE--
DANI MOONSTAR, I TOLD YOU YOUR DUTY. YOU CHOSE TO IGNORE IT.
I ARMED YOU AGAINST THEM. I GAVE YOU GUIDANCE.
YOU CAME TO ME IN YOUR HOUR OF NEED. I SAVED YOU AND YOUR PEOPLE. I CAME TO YOU IN MINE...AND YOU ACT LIKE THIS.
WE DO NOT ALWAYS GET TO CHOOSE OUR DUTIES.

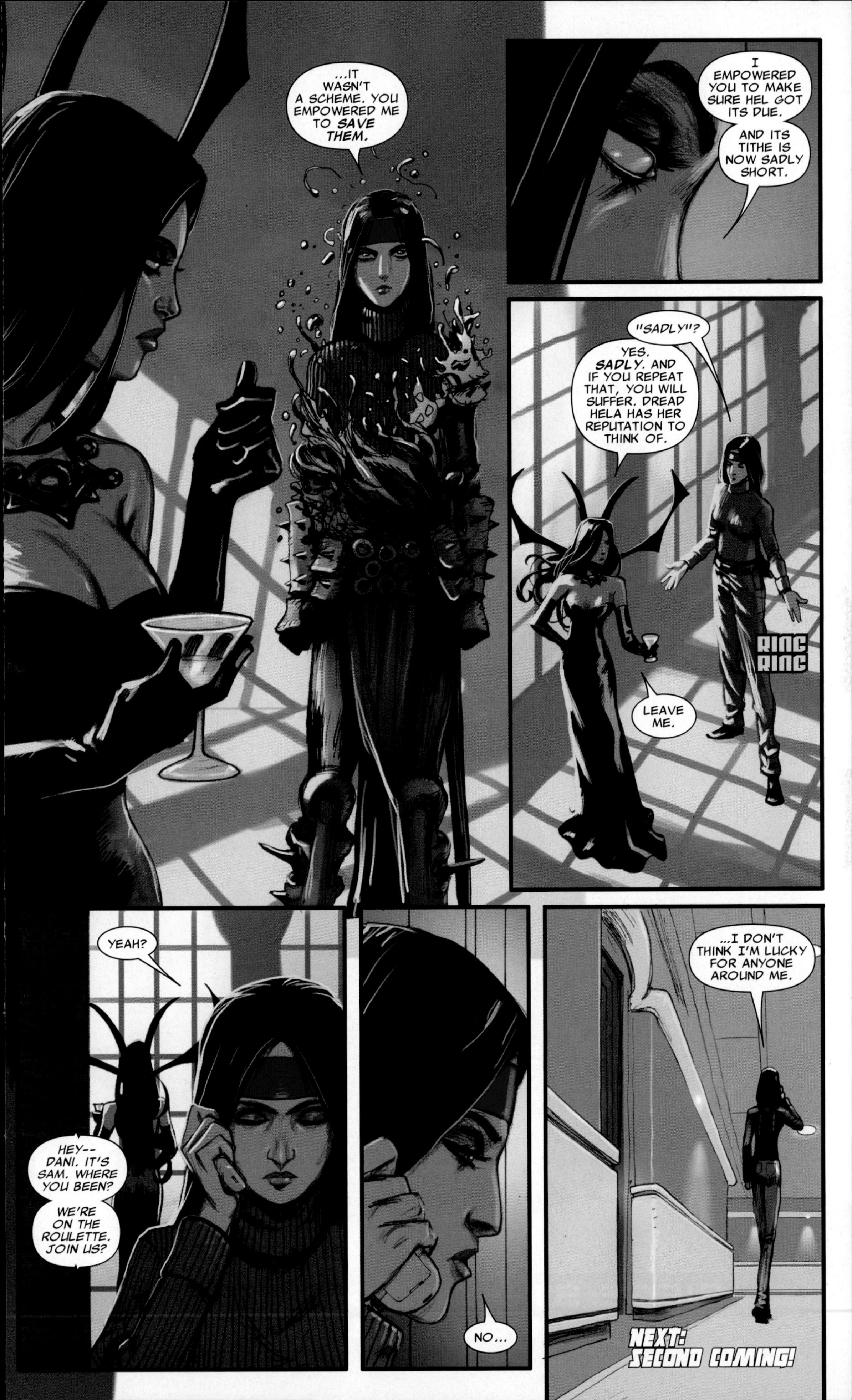
...IT WASN'T A SCHEME. YOU EMPOWERED ME TO **SAVE THEM.**
I EMPOWERED YOU TO MAKE SURE HEL GOT ITS DUE.
AND ITS TITHE IS NOW SADLY SHORT.
"SADLY"?
YES. **SADLY.** AND IF YOU REPEAT THAT, YOU WILL SUFFER. DREAD HELA HAS HER REPUTATION TO THINK OF.
RING RING
LEAVE ME.
YEAH?
HEY-- DANI. IT'S SAM. WHERE YOU BEEN?
WE'RE ON THE ROULETTE. JOIN US?
NO...
...I DON'T THINK I'M LUCKY FOR ANYONE AROUND ME.
NEXT: SECOND COMING!

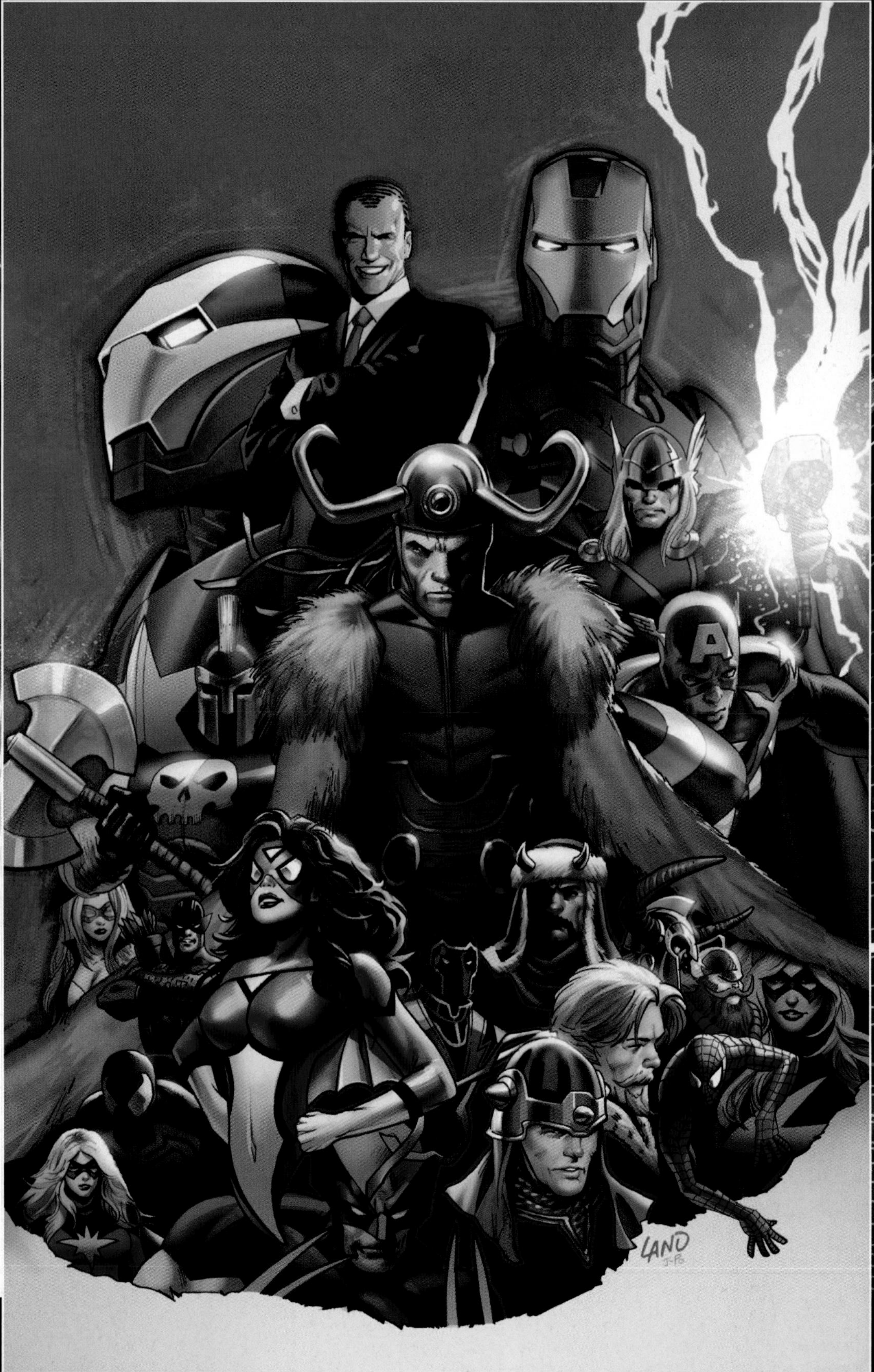
LAND
J-PB

SIEGE: STORMING ASGARD — HEROES & VILLAINS

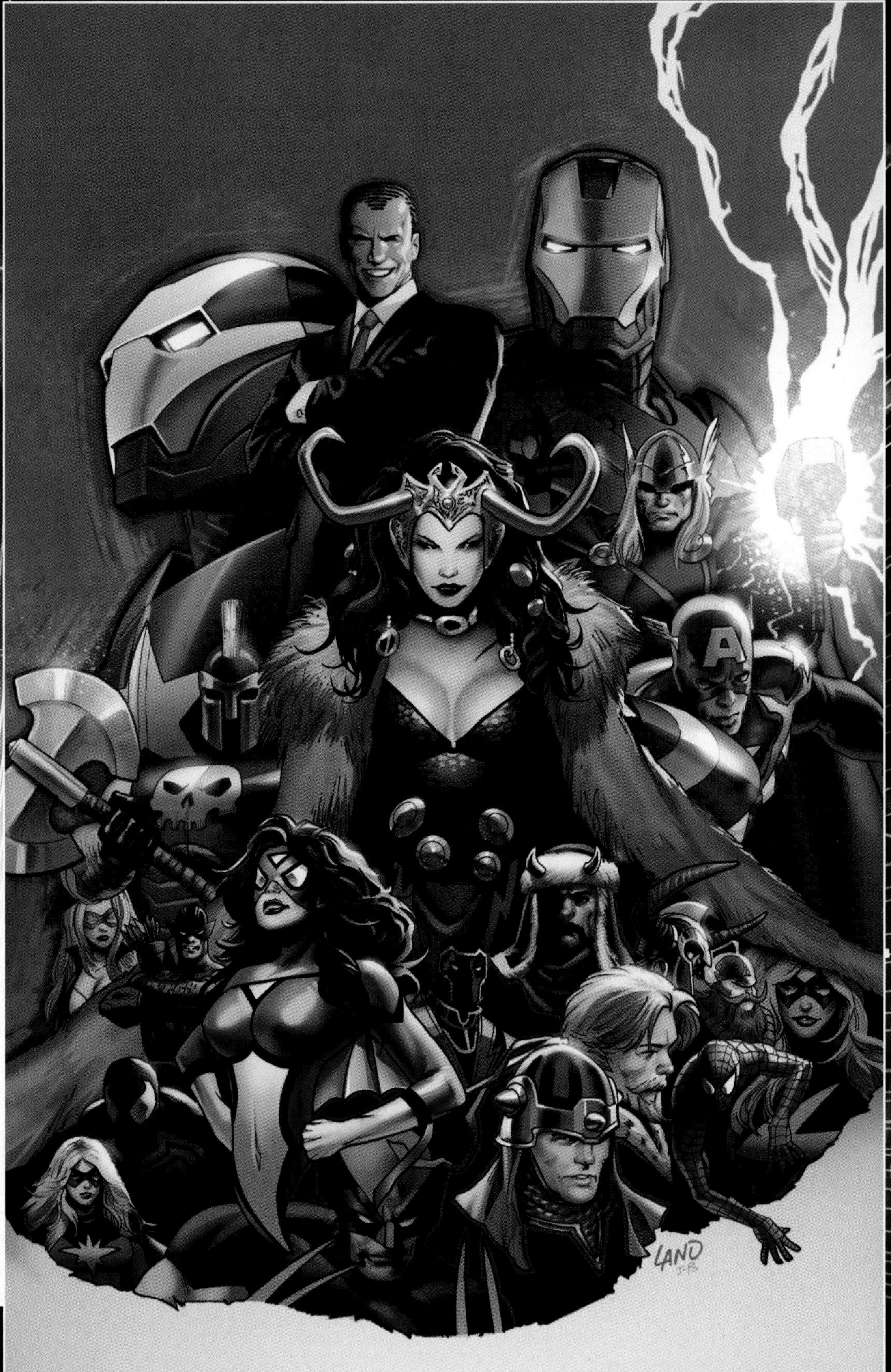

SIEGE: STORMING ASGARD — HEROES & VILLAINS VARIANT

USER: •••••••••
PASSWORD: •••••••••

WATCHING OVER YOU

Norman,

This dossier represents one of our last preparations for the Siege. Storming Asgard is the final stage of a plan long in developement, and H.A.M.M.E.R. has done a thorough review of the threat we face from Asgard's protectors as well as our own assets we are bringing to bear. H.A.M.M.E.R. agents Jess Harrold and Dugan Trodglen have culled data from interviews done in the field with Loki, the Hood, and other Cabal associates, as well as fellow H.A.M.M.E.R. field agent Kieron Gillen, a psych evaluator assessing Ares.

DEFINING TERMS

For easy reference, we developed a shorthand when making mention of any of the myriad teams of Avengers now dotting the landscape. These are:

DARK AVENGERS: The officially sanctioned Avengers under the Iron Patriot's leadership; a roster of "under the radar" personalities.

NEW AVENGERS: The team of Avengers formed in the wake of the disassembly of the originals, currently underground and led by Ronin, Luke Cage, Spider-Man and others.

MIGHTY AVENGERS: The newest collection of classic Avengers, led by Hank Pym in his new guise as the Wasp.

AVENGERS RESISTANCE: A loose affiliation of classic Avengers, Initiative alumni and New Warriors, led by Tigra, Justice and Gauntlet.

THE INITIATIVE: Future Avengers from H.A.M.M.E.R. training. Led by Taskmaster.

And the epochal events that have altered superhuman history:

CIVIL WAR: The clash between superhumans on either side of the Registration issue.

SECRET INVASION: The stealth insurgency by Skrulls.

These encrypted files are for your eyes only. They deal directly with the Siege and its many contingencies, but their relevance may well extend beyond our successful Siege campaign and battle against Thor.

It's our H.A.M.M.E.R. against his. Let's go get him.

Victoria Hand
Siege Operations Manager

CREDITS

Head Writer/Editor: John Rhett Thomas
Spotlight Bullpen Writers: Jess Harrold & Dugan Trodglen

Senior Editor, Special Projects: Jeff Youngquist
Editors, Special Projects: Mark D. Beazley
    & Jennifer Grünwald
Assistant Editors: John Denning & Alex Starbuck
Vice President of Sales, Publishing: David Gabriel
Book Design: BLAMMO! Content & Design,
    Rommel Alama, Mike Kronenberg
Editor in Chief: Joe Quesada
Publisher: Dan Buckley
Executive Producer: Alan Fine

Cover Artists: Greg Land &
Justin Ponsor

Special Thanks to Kieron Gillen,
Paul Cornell and Christos N. Gage

The views and opinions expressed in this issue are solely those of the writers, commentators or creative talent and do not express or imply the views or opinions of Marvel Entertainment, Inc.

USER: ••••••••••

PASSWORD: ••••••••••

NAME:

LOKI

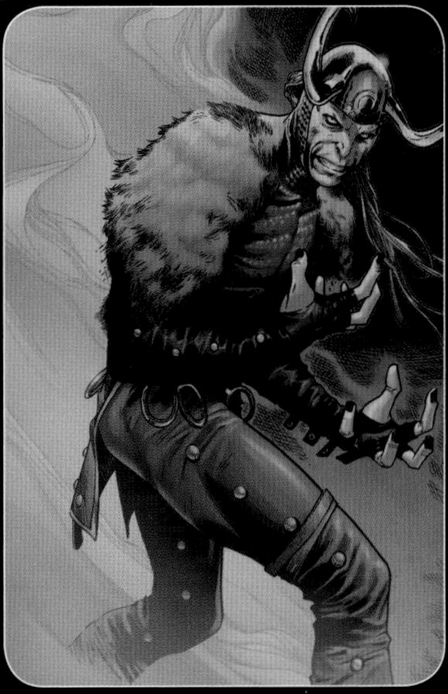

ART BY AGENT MARKO DJURDJEVIC

BACKGROUND:

From what we've been able to gather, Loki is Thor's half-brother and has been Thor's rival forever. Every plan Loki ever concocted has eventually been thwarted by Thor; in fact, according to old S.H.I.E.L.D. files it was a failed scheme of Loki's that brought the original Avengers together. This time may be different, however. He has thus far succeeded in running Thor out of Asgard, leaving a power vacuum filled by Balder, exactly as Loki had planned. .

Interestingly, when Loki first returned from the dead he was in the form of a female. We have no idea how this happened, but this female form seemed to serve Loki well. He/she was able to, if not exactly gain Thor's trust, at least not get beaten to a pulp or banished from the city. It was shortly after this that Loki once again became male, presumably because he had accomplished all he wanted in his female guise. Whether he can go back and forth is not known, nor does it seem relevant at this point.

ANALYSIS: AGENT TRODGLEN

It's pretty obvious that Loki is central to our plans to invade Asgard. Without his involvement, the Siege simply would not be happening. Let me start by saying I don't know if Loki, Thor, etc. are actually gods or that "Asgard" is the Asgard of Norse mythology. Ascertaining that as fact in no way changes either our goals or our methods. Whether or not these people are gods, they are immensely powerful and cannot be underestimated if this campaign is to work. I will be referring to these beings in my report as though they are the gods of myth rather than get bogged down in this detail. They look like gods, they have power like gods, and the Siege by its very conception treats them like gods; labels at this stage are beside the point. Now, as to Loki...

Loki can't be trusted. He simply cannot be trusted. He is the God of Mischief. He lies, therefore he is. Director Osborn has factored this into his strategic thinking from the beginning. Thus, our plan of attack must be Loki-proof. It must position Director Osborn in a way that will protect him from a sudden but inevitable betrayal on the part of Loki. But for now we must proceed as though he is our ally. This entire operation is doomed without Loki as an ally. With neither Thor nor Odin in power – and we have Loki to thank for this – Asgard has never been this vulnerable. He is the source of all of our intelligence, which amounts to quite a lot. We certainly have a common enemy, and H.A.M.M.E.R. and the Dark Avengers undoubtedly provide the resources to accomplish a siege of Asgard far beyond anything Loki can conjure on his own. So it's a good bet he wants us to succeed, and that he needs us.

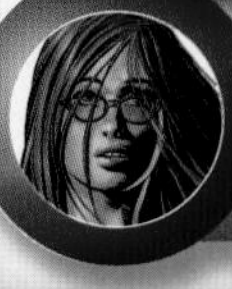

EXECUTIVE ASSESSMENT:
Forge ahead. But never turn your back on him.

USER: ••••••••••

PASSWORD: ••••••••••

NAME:

THE HOOD

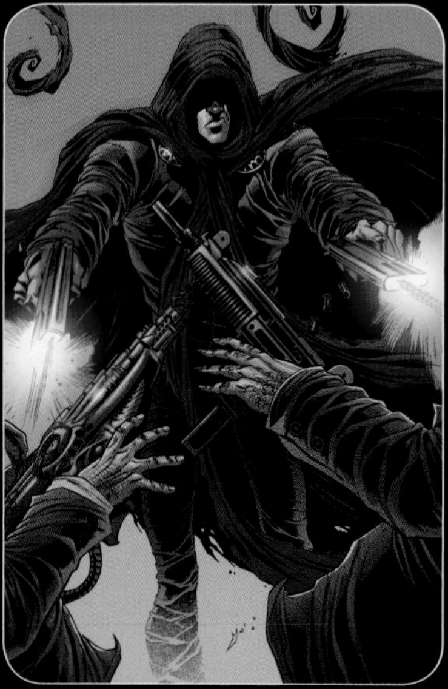

ART BY AGENT KYLE HOTZ

BACKGROUND:

Parker Robbins started out as a reliable ally for Director Osborn but recently has become anything but. His history has been hard to come by, but from what we can gather, he started out as a small-time hood. He was just another worthless street criminal until he came into possession a few years ago of an apparently **magical red cloak**, which granted him great power. If our sources are to be believed, these powers came from an other-dimensional demon, though that seems to no longer be a part of Robbins' makeup. Thanks to Loki he is now apparently in possession of something called **Norn Stones** and these are the source of his power now.

For a while he seemed content to go after his slice of the criminal pie, merely to support his girlfriend, small child, invalid mother, and personal indulgences, but sometime shortly before the Secret Invasion he was struck with inspiration. He assembled a virtual army of superpowered criminals and created his own super-crime syndicate. At first, while there were a few problems, things went much better than they usually do for groups like this, and Robbins, now calling himself The Hood, can claim much of the credit for his fresh approach. He didn't rely on the group's numbers, or even their power; instead, everything was carefully organized and everything they did had a specific, logical goal.

After the invasion, when Director Osborn came to power, he recognized The Hood as a valuable ally. They have worked together ever since. Among their agreements, the Hood was placed in charge of the **Initiative** program, and Director Osborn has agreed to overlook the activities of the Hood's group, with the understanding that the Director would occasionally call in favors. He was confronted by, if not a coup, at least a betrayal by most of his syndicate, who attempted to broker a deal with Director Osborn separate from the Hood's, who would have none of it. The Hood returned, and while their relationship was seemingly damaged, they remain allies.

ANALYSIS: AGENT TRODGLEN

If power corrupts, what happens when the already corrupt gain power? Parker Robbins seems to be a case study in this question. While he has shown excellent business acumen and a knack for self-preservation, over time he has grown increasingly unstable. The good news is that there is reason to believe even his new source of power is actually less dangerous to his mental faculties, but it is too early to know for sure.

But this potential stability comes at another cost. If indeed Loki is responsible for the Hood gaining new, even greater powers, where do you think the Hood's loyalty will ultimately lie? Yes, Loki is our ally, but he will remain an ally for only as long as it suits him. If and when the time comes when we find ourselves at odds with Loki, we need to be prepared for the fact that we will have lost the Hood as well, or take steps to ensure his loyalty to us before that happens.

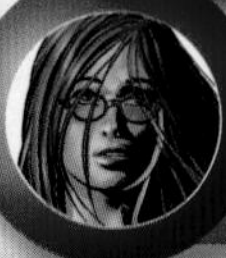

EXECUTIVE ASSESSMENT: A loose cannon, now in Loki's pocket? How does that sound to you?

USER: •••••••••••

PASSWORD: •••••••••••

NAME:

TASKMASTER

BACKGROUND:

Taskmaster has "photographic reflexes," which is the ability to mimic any physical movement or activity he witnesses, and he has used this not so much to carve out a career in crime as a career in training criminals. With his ability, he has studied and learned the fighting and weapon-wielding techniques of just about everyone you can think of, but just as his only abilities come from taking cues from others, he similarly seems to have no ambition of his own, at least in the traditional sense. Hence, ever since Director Osborn has been in power, Taskmaster has eagerly followed orders and risen through the ranks. He took over the Initiative program to great success, including leading the mission that took back the Negative Zone prison. He apparently recently met with Director Osborn to discuss an increase in his responsibility and influence before becoming injured during an undisclosed skirmish, protecting Director Osborn.

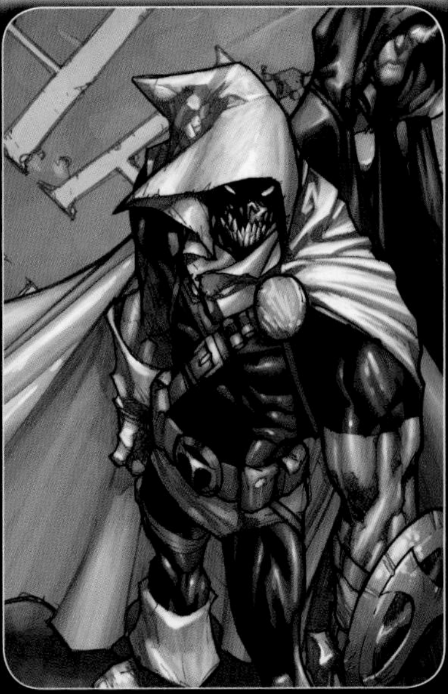

ART BY AGENT HUMBERTO RAMOS

ANALYSIS: AGENT TRODGLEN

Taskmaster is quite content to follow the money and power without ever really seeming to seek that power for himself. Director Osborn loves this about him. I have, however, spoken with some fellow agents who have trained under Taskmaster and while they applaud his skill and his ability to train others, they are dubious about his ability to actually assume any sort of executive or administrative responsibility, and has been known to extract himself from any given situation when the heat starts to come down. He really doesn't like to get his own hands dirty.

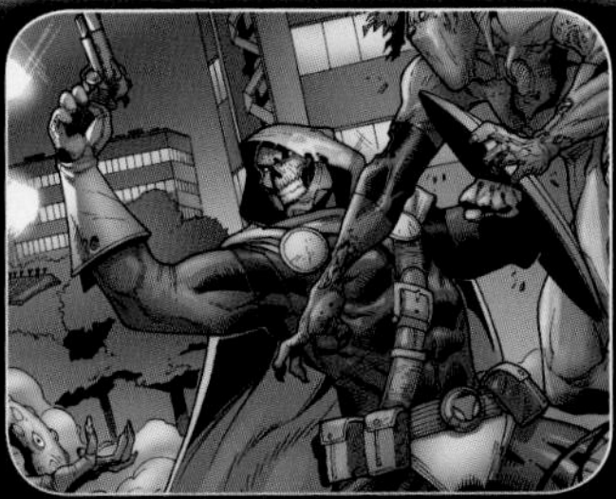

ART BY AGENT JORGE MOLINA

Director Osborn obviously sees something in him, and a lot of what I am reporting comes from hearsay, but my impression is that he wants to get by while doing as little work as possible. Some agents have also reported that under his watch, the maintenance of Camp H.A.M.M.E.R. was a bit more freewheeling than he'd have Director Osborn believe. In short, I have formed a profile of Taskmaster as someone who is mentally lazy and am surprised to see him even want to move as far up the ladder as Director Osborn is leading him. Don't be too shocked to turn around one day to find him gone.

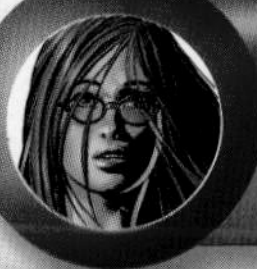

EXECUTIVE ASSESSMENT: A good ally in the minor leagues. But are you sure he's fit for your Cabal?

USER: ••••••••••

PASSWORD: ••••••••••

NAME:

DOCTOR DOOM

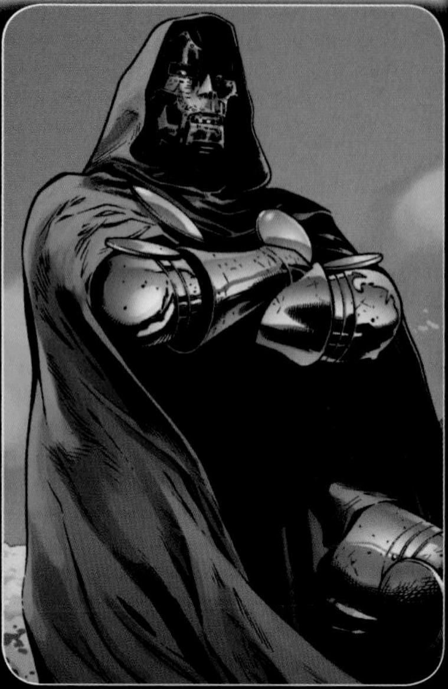

ART BY AGENT OLIVIER COIPEL

BACKGROUND:

As one of his first acts as head of H.A.M.M.E.R., Director Osborn arranged for the release of Victor Von Doom from S.H.I.E.L.D. custody and his extradition back to Latveria, in return for Doom's allegiance. Shortly thereafter, the Dark Avengers stepped in to save Doom from the sorceress Morgan Le Fay amidst the wreckage of the tyrant's homeland. Doom's castle and nation were somehow rebuilt from scratch in time for him to offer Latveria as a new home for Asgard, in a pact with Loki. However, Doom's relationship with Asgard, and its ruler Balder, is now at an end following the revelation that he had been carrying out vivisection experiments on Asgardians. As yet, it is unknown to what extent Doom's personal relationship with Loki has been affected. Doom resigned somewhat dramatically from Director Osborn's Cabal in a devastating confrontation at Avengers Tower.

ANALYSIS: AGENT HARROLD

More so than any member of Director Osborn's inner circle, Doom was always going to be difficult to control. We gave him everything he wanted – freedom, his kingdom back, and saved him from Morgan Le Fay. But while he purports to be a man of honor, Doom was never likely to keep his side of the bargain for long. It is to be assumed that Doom was plotting against Director Osborn from the start, most likely together with his long-time associate Namor. Indeed, it was a dispute over Namor that led to the confrontation that ended Director Osborn's involvement with Doom. Only Director Osborn knows for sure what started the physical confrontation in his private office at Avengers Tower, but the retaliation of a Doombot, sent in Doom's place, almost killed the Taskmaster. The robotic insectoid attack that followed would have crippled the facility were it not for the Sentry, and Doom even had the audacity to threaten Director Osborn's son in the event of any retaliation. He is to be considered a top-level threat, one not to be engaged without very careful planning. As well as technological know-how that puts him among the most intelligent men on Earth, Doom has harnessed the power of time travel to research arcane and long-forgotten dark magicks. His powerful sorcery can be the only explanation for the rapid rise of Latveria from the ashes of destruction. It remains to be seen what new threats his experimentation on the Asgardians has added to his already considerable arsenal. However, this is a problem for another day. It is felt unlikely that he will involve himself in the Asgardian conflict in the light of his own dispute with Balder. In this respect, as his enemy's enemy, it may be that we are inadvertently Doom's friend. Once Asgard is conquered, however, Doom will find himself high on our list of subsequent issues to address.

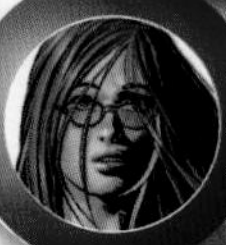

EXECUTIVE ASSESSMENT:
Today Asgard. Tomorrow Latveria.

NAME:

SUB-MARINER/ NAMOR

BACKGROUND:

At first an apparently obedient and willing member of Director Osborn's Cabal, Namor attempted to apprehend Iron Man on our behalf. However, when asked to denounce and exterminate Atlantean terrorists responsible for loss of lives in Los Angeles, Namor showed where his true allegiances lie and refused. Against his better judgment, Director Osborn was persuaded by Emma Frost to allow Namor onto the team of **Dark X-Men** sent in to resolve the mutant riots in San Francisco. With the Bay Area secured, and Director Osborn apparently victorious, the extent of Frost and Namor's treachery stood revealed: They had been working with Cyclops all along. Fending off the Dark Avengers, Namor, Frost, Cyclops and the X-Men evacuated the mutants and established a stronghold on the island of Utopia, the rocky surface of Magneto's Asteroid M newly raised by the mutants. In retaliation, Director Osborn obtained Namor's former wife Marrina in her mutated Plodex form. Genetically enhancing her to induce a voracious appetite for Atlantean flesh, he unleashed her into the oceans where she began the slaughter of thousands of the scattered seadwellers. Namor captured the monster, slew it, and hurled it through the windows of Oscorp's Atlantean offices before issuing a grave threat to Director Osborn: if he'd do something like that to his wife, imagine what he would do to an enemy.

ART BY AGENT ALAN DAVIS

ANALYSIS: AGENT HARROLD

Such is Namor's tremendous arrogance, self-importance and disdain for "surface-dwellers," his alliance with Director Osborn was always likely to be fragile. They can now be considered bitter enemies. The Atlantean monarch has found his way onto the growing list of targets for whom Director Osborn's well-earned enmity outstrips any strategic imperative. Having seemingly found a permanent home with the X-Men on Utopia, Namor should be considered highly unlikely to involve himself in the Siege on Asgard. He will be of greater significance in any future engagement with his frequent ally, Doctor Doom. Doom vehemently objected to Director Osborn's treatment of Namor, leading to the confrontation that saw him removed from the Cabal. Meanwhile, Atlantean troops are believed to have been given refuge in Latveria. Any attack on either man is likely to be considered a declaration of war upon the other. Namor is one of the few men alive to have held his own against the Sentry, and can command forces of unknown numbers currently scattered throughout the oceans. Further engagement with him or Doom is not recommended until detailed projections of acceptable losses can be prepared.

EXECUTIVE ASSESSMENT: Interference with Siege unlikely, but keep your nose open for that smell...

USER: ••••••••••

PASSWORD: ••••••••••

NAME:

WHITE QUEEN/ EMMA FROST

BACKGROUND:

When Emma Frost was recruited to Director Osborn's Cabal, the lure was an invitation to save her species. With the mutant population in seemingly terminal decline, Director Osborn offered her a way to stave off the prospect of those remaining mutants being rounded up and forced into concentration camps. He offered her the opportunity to become the face of mutantkind, with her own team of X-Men, albeit a line-up he himself would choose. She agreed, on the condition that **Namor** could take a place on the team. Her **Dark X-Men** helped quell mutant riots in San Francisco, and took the protestors into custody in H.A.M.M.E.R.'s remodeled Alcatraz facility. However, Frost discovered that the alternate reality Dark Beast was experimenting on the captured mutants and painfully siphoning their powers to augment Weapon Omega. She betrayed Director Osborn, aided the mutants in their escape, and returned to the side of her lover, **Cyclops,** on the newly raised island of **Utopia,** a haven for mutantkind outside of H.A.M.M.E.R.'s jurisdiction. During the ensuing battle with the Dark Avengers, Frost – who has served as an occasional therapist for the troubled Sentry – managed to unsettle him enough to make him flee. Sources confirm that whatever she did left her with a sliver of some sort of negative energy inside her head that requires her to remain in diamond form.

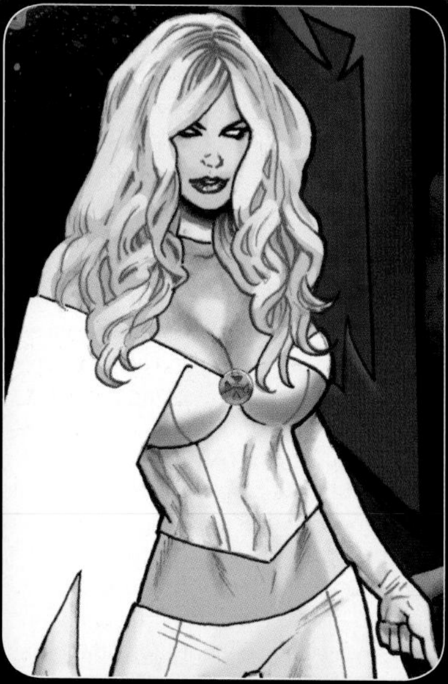

ART BY AGENT GREG LAND

ANALYSIS: AGENT HARROLD

Frost was a useful member of the Cabal, one whose psychic powers served to encourage honesty among its members. Had she remained in charge of the Dark X-Men, the resolution of the mutant problem in San Francisco would have been an excellent public relations boost. Nevertheless, Director Osborn was still able to claim victory when looking at the big picture. Frost and Cyclops' X-Men are confined to an island prison of their own making, and the mutant menace is under control. However, Frost's treachery could lead to further provocation if left unpunished. H.A.M.M.E.R. must be vigilant for probable cause that would justify a strike upon Utopia. In the meantime, Frost and the beleaguered X-Men are unlikely to be drawn into an involvement in the conflict in Asgard that could further reduce their dwindling numbers. Vigilance is nonetheless recommended, due to Frost's personal and professional history with the Sentry. She is one of the few people on Earth capable of taking Reynolds down. Reports of her current condition make interesting reading in the light of psych reports that evaluate "the Void," the dark half the Sentry claims to harbor deep inside. Further investigation is highly recommended. To that end, it should be noted that, while Frost's current permanent diamond form considerably increases her physical threat, it prevents her from using her far more deadly psychic powers.

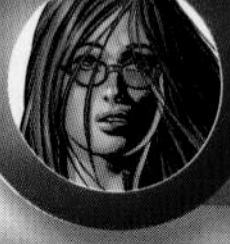

EXECUTIVE ASSESSMENT: Keep both eyes open and your mind closed around this witch.

USER: ••••••••••

PASSWORD: ••••••••••

SIEGE ASGARD

NAME:

THOR

BACKGROUND:

Some time ago, Asgard suffered through Ragnarok, which saw the seeming death of Thor, Odin, and every other citizen. As is often the case with the superhuman community, this death was not permanent, and a few months ago Thor returned. He eventually brought back all of the citizens of Asgard save Odin, and even returned Asgard itself to existence, although now the majestic city found itself not in the heavens but floating above rural Broxton, Oklahoma. With Odin not among the returned, Thor was the new ruler of Asgard.

Soon after, Loki returned to the living Bor, Odin's father and Thor's grandfather, and placed him in the middle of New York City in a berserker rage. Thor could only halt Bor's rampage by killing him. This led to Thor's exile (Loki's ultimate goal), Thor having essentially slain the King of Asgard. Balder became the new ruler of Asgard and Thor was forced to go down and live on earth. Curiously, Thor seems not to be around that often, as though he leaves the planet, or perhaps our dimension itself, for significant periods of time. It is also not known if his major weapon asset, his hammer Mjolnir, is in working condition.

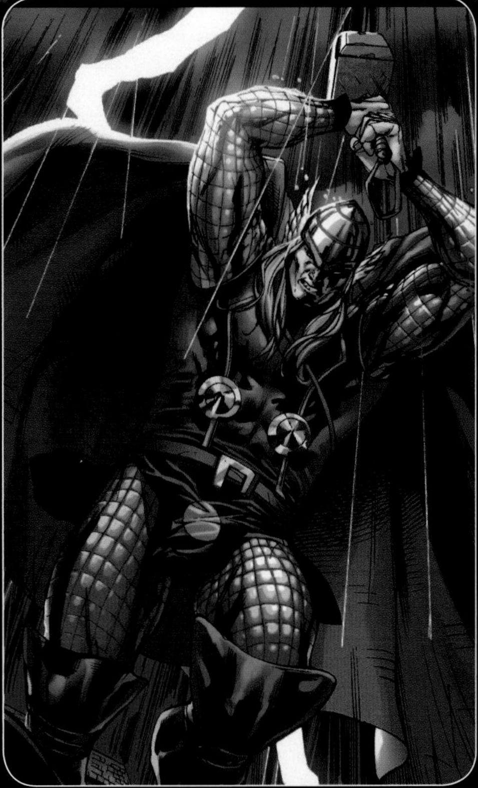

ART BY AGENT BILLY TAN

ANALYSIS: AGENT TRODGLEN

There is no question Thor represents the greatest threat to victory in Asgard. Even exiled, he will stop at nothing to defend his homeland, nor will the Asgardians hesitate to call on him to return home to do so. One wonders if even the Sentry is enough to deal with Thor. While comparable in terms of power, Thor would have the distinct advantage of fighting for the homeland that means everything to him. In short, it will take more than the Sentry to bring Thor down. It will take the combined efforts of all of our most powerful resources to take Thor down. The other possibility is that a proper threat to all of Asgard might be enough to persuade Thor to consider surrender.

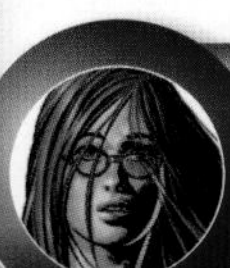

EXECUTIVE ASSESSMENT: Thor should keep us up at night. Dealing with him is beyond my pay grade.

USER: ••••••••••

PASSWORD: ••••••••••

BROXTON, OKLAHOMA

BACKGROUND: When Thor restored Asgard and positioned it on Earth, for some reason he chose Broxton, OK, 150 miles west of Oklahoma City, as its new locale. Broxton is fly-over country at its most insufferable. Everyone there is, by all accounts, the "salt of the earth." They have welcomed the Asgardians into their lives as only Mayberry-types could, and seem to have mostly gotten over the incredible nature of what they are dealing with. The bottom line is that a conflict with Asgard could turn into a conflict with Broxton, and from a PR standpoint, that could be trouble. Another threat the citizens of Broxton represent is the possibility of actually mixing with the Asgardians. The relationship between "Bill" (last name unknown) and the Asgardian Kelda proved to be dynamite that blew up in Loki's face.

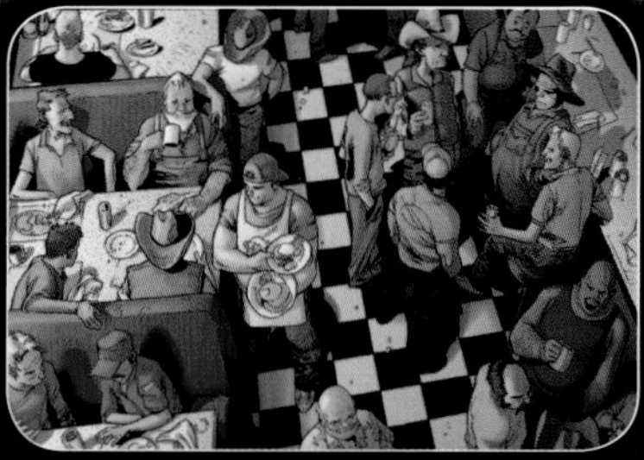

ART BY AGENT OLIVIER COIPEL

ANALYSIS: AGENT TRODGLEN
Bill's discovery of Doom's vivisection lab illustrates how easily a simple hick can fly under the radar when dealing with larger-than-life adversaries. Real damage to our cause can come of this. We have got to avoid getting Broxton involved. In addition, we have to keep the media away from the citizens of Broxton. We cannot let Ma Kettle look into the camera and tell America that we're the bad guys here.

EXECUTIVE ASSESSMENT: Fifty square mile cordon, total population evac and standard issue media blackout.

FRONT LINE

BACKGROUND: Front Line is the left-wing rag run by **Ben Urich**, along with fellow executive **Robbie Robertson**, staff reporters **Sally Floyd** and **Norah Winters**, and longtime Spider-Man ally, photographer **Peter Parker**. Even before he started Front Line, Urich had been a thorn in Director Osborn's side for years as a reporter for the Daily Bugle. He and his paper are the only significant members of the media to have never backed Director Osborn in his position of power. It is not expected that he will in any way support the Siege with either fair and balanced reporting or objective editorializing.

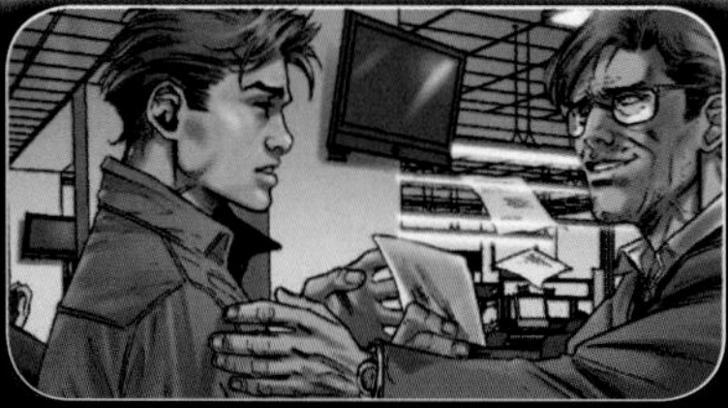

ART BY AGENT MARCO CHECCHETTO

ANALYSIS: Ben Urich will undertake every effort to be at the scene in Broxton somehow. His tenacity is legendary. Count on it: His narrative will make villains out of us, and the way information travels these days, he will likely prove our greatest enemy in the war of public opinion. We need eyes on him. There ought to be multiple opportunities to lock him up, as he and his minions are sure to break the law in their attempts to gain access to our operation. As well, we need to be mindful of the Freedom of Information Act requests that are sure to come from Urich and other media outlets. Safeguard all paper trails and information exchanges so we can hide the design of Siege.

EXECUTIVE ASSESSMENT: I would drive to Broxton for the chance to put a bullet in him myself.

USER: ••••••••••

PASSWORD: ••••••••••

NAME: BALDER

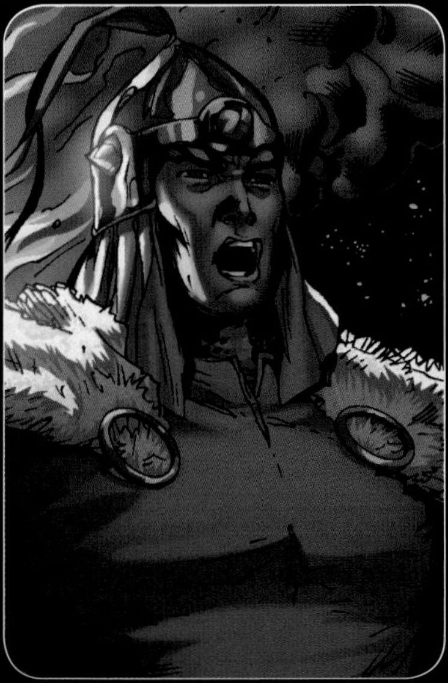

ART BY AGENT OLIVIER COIPEL

BACKGROUND: Balder is currently the ruler of Asgard, son of **Odin** and half-brother of both **Loki** and **Thor,** taking the throne after Loki's machinations exiled Thor. Loki considered the idealistic Balder an easily manipulated figure whose presence on the throne was a key component in his/her plans. Balder agreed to move his people to Latveria where it wasn't long until the Asgardians found themselves at odds with Doom. Loki appeared caught in the middle and Balder's trust of Loki diminished.

ANALYSIS: AGENT TRODGLEN

While we can certainly expect Thor to take the lead at some point, as it stands, Balder rules Asgard. In battles like this, it's always desirable to break a people's will, but that would appear to be a near-impossible task when it comes to Asgard. Even before he was their leader, he was among their most inspiring warriors, second only to Thor. It is highly doubtful that we can look for surrender on the part of Balder, so a sound strategy must involve his swift removal. This won't be easy. It will take someone in the highest weight class to take out a warrior of Balder's strength and resolve.

EXECUTIVE ASSESSMENT: Eliminate quickly: Ares and/or Sentry.

NAME: SIF

BACKGROUND: Lady Sif has long been **Thor's** ally and lover. She was the final Asgardian returned to life by Thor after Ragnarok, and Loki recognizing her stature as both a warrior and stabilizer of Thor's emotional well-being — nearly succeeded in preventing her return. But he didn't, she's here, and we have to deal with that.

ANALYSIS: A significant adversary on her own, her greatest role and one we'd like to exploit is that of Thor's lover. Her presence helps bring focus and resolve to Thor. If we can eliminate her, it could damage Thor's morale, but it would also threaten to enrage him beyond our ability to contain. Somehow capturing her and using her as a bargaining tool is a high risk/high reward approach we may wish to consider.

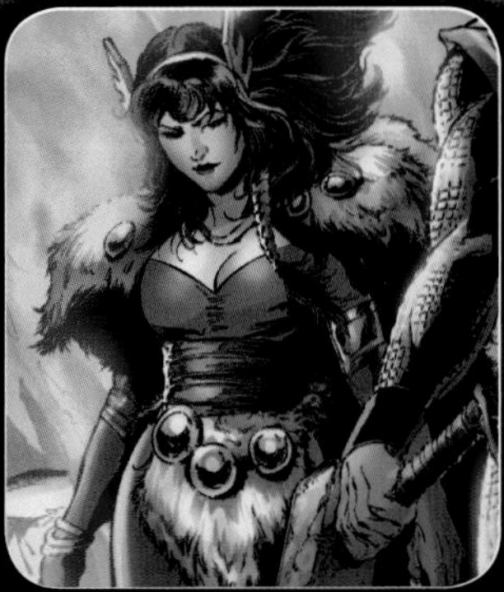

ART BY AGENT MARKO DJURDJEVIC

EXECUTIVE ASSESSMENT: Disappear the $%#@& and we distract and potentially have leverage against Thor.

SIEGE ASGARD

USER: ••••••••••

PASSWORD: ••••••••••

THE WARRIORS THREE

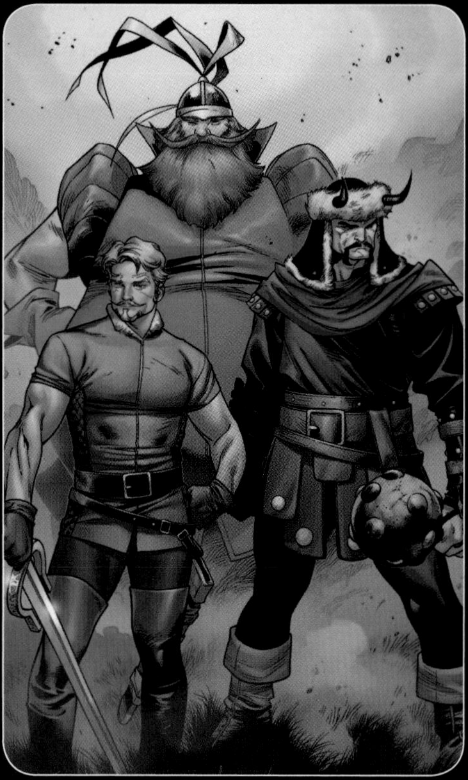

ART BY AGENT OLIVIER COIPEL

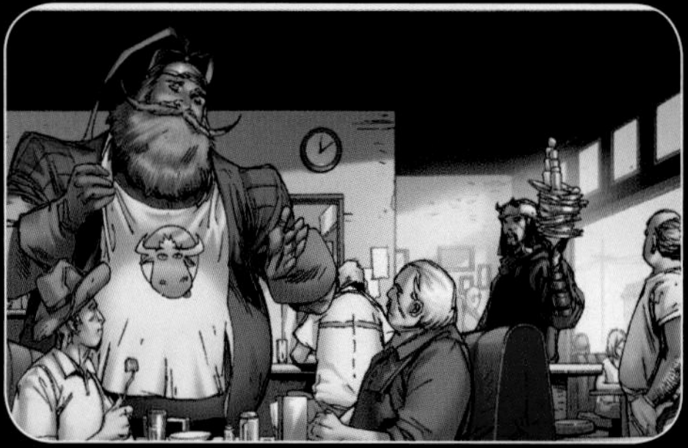

ART BY AGENT BILLY TAN

BACKGROUND:

Along with Balder, the so-called Warriors Three – **Fandral, Hogun** and **Volstagg** (the fat one) – are the foremost defenders of Asgard this side of Thor. They are as powerful as they are fiercely loyal, to Thor in particular. It is this loyalty – and a distrust of Loki – that led the trio to stay behind when Balder took the Asgardians from Broxton, Oklahoma to Latveria. They seem content, for now, to get to know their human neighbors and seemingly bide the time until what they assume will be Thor's eventual return to power. They currently run a diner in Broxton. That's not a typo. We saw it for ourselves. (Our stealth agents recommend the country fried steak.)

ANALYSIS:

AGENT TRODGLEN

Like Balder, there is no sound strategy that involves either capturing the Warriors Three or counting on their surrender. They must be eliminated. Again, it will take the most powerful beings at our disposal to accomplish this. Somehow separating them would probably be best.

One thing about their presence in the "outside world" is intriguing. With Asgard isolated, it's not easy to contrive any sort of aggression on their part. In discussing ways by which Asgard can be viewed publicly as aggressors, Loki mentioned the loyalty of these three as ripe for exploitation. He also thinks they are pretty dumb, particularly Volstagg ("oaf" was the term he used), and plans on discussing ways to take advantage of this with Director Osborn. If by this point the Director's strategy in this regard has gone beyond the talking stage, our analysis is perhaps moot.

EXECUTIVE ASSESSMENT: Sounds like Loki has this one.

NAME: **HEIMDALL**

ART BY AGENT OLIVIER COIPEL

BACKGROUND:
The brother of Sif, Heimdall is **Asgard's all-seeing sentry**. And as sentries go, our understanding is that he is pretty extraordinary. Through Asgardian magic he can see everything on earth.

ANALYSIS: With Heimdall around, we cannot count on ever having the element of surprise. So we may as well forget about that. We want this guy out of the picture fast. What we'll need to do is remove Heimdall as a resource as soon as we can for the sake of any future strategy. We're working on ways to confound his magical senses, but so far we're stumped. Loki may ultimately be the best source for that.

EXECUTIVE ASSESSMENT: Suggest gouging this guy's eyeballs out be a priority for Loki. (And fast, please.)

NAME: **TYR**

ART BY AGENT BILLY TAN

BACKGROUND:
Tyr is the **Norse God of War**. He is their Ares. He had not made his presence known in Asgard until their battle with Doom, insisting that he is there only when needed.

ANALYSIS: (Well, they'll be needing him now.) He represents a more headfirst battle mentality (the kind Ares encompasses) than the other Asgardians. This aggression could be trouble but it could also lead to injudicious movements on the battlefield that ultimately help the enemy – in this case, us. The right sort of emotional manipulation can lead him to make mistakes, Loki assures us.

EXECUTIVE ASSESSMENT: Wind Ares up and turn him loose. (How are we on our stocks of popcorn?)

NAME:

THE HOOD'S ARMY

ART BY AGENT STUART IMMONEN

BACKGROUND: The Hood has gathered a very impressive group — the "Masters of Evil," if you will (he would never refer to them as that). Their goal is to pool resources, make each other aware of goals, and when necessary, go in together on certain activities and split the profits. Members of this group have included:

Madame Masque	Dr. Demonicus	Deathwatch	Living Laser
Dr. Jonas Harrow	Scarecrow	Blackout	Jigsaw
Wrecker	Bulldozer	Answer	Armadillo
Bulldozer	Mentallo	Centurius	Mr. Hyde
Piledriver	Mandrill	Controller	Mr. Fear
Thunderball	Razor Fist	Corruptor	The U-Foes
Griffin	Chemistro	Cutthroat	Graviton
Bushwacker	Piledriver	Purple Man	Grey Gargoyle
Crossfire	Brothers Grimm	Vermin	Shocker

ANALYSIS: AGENT TRODGLEN

The Hood's army screwed themselves and ended up in a position that is very beneficial to us. By assigning this powerful group to take down Cage's New Avengers, they will at the very least keep themselves occupied for the duration of the Siege of Asgard. At best, they'll permanently remove some serious thorns in Director Osborn's side.

EXECUTIVE ASSESSMENT:
Cannon fodder. They have their mission.

USER: ••••••••••
PASSWORD: ••••••••••

NAME:

MADAME MASQUE

BACKGROUND: When the Hood gathered his army of costumed criminals, **Whitney Frost** quickly became part of his inner circle and soon their relationship grew beyond the professional. She was not among the group when it attempted its coup. Instead, she escorted Robbins as he journeyed with Loki to gain the Norn Stones.

Director Osborn did attempt to use her in his plan to assassinate Tony Stark, but instead she found herself trapped by Pepper Potts inside the Rescue armor and had to be cut out. This embarrassing incident was part of a successful strategy by Potts to spring Maria Hill and Black Widow from detention at Avengers Tower, which did not endear her to Director Osborn.

ART BY AGENT SALVADOR LARROCA

ANALYSIS: AGENT TRODGLEN
There are a number of ways to use Miss Frost going forward, but her greatest value has to come from Robbins' feelings for her, the pair having engaged in a persistent romantic affair. His army is a key component of this operation and if we need to use her to keep him focused on the matter at hand then let's do it. In other words, we need an agent ready at any moment to take her down so we can use her as a bargaining chip with Robbins.

EXECUTIVE ASSESSMENT: After the Iron Man fiasco, I want no part of her.

**ART BY AGENT
KYLE HOTZ**

NAME: JOHN KING

BACKGROUND: John King is Parker Robbins' longtime right hand man. Robbins trusts him, probably more than anyone. Robbins and King are cousins and their business relationship goes back to their days as petty criminals. Whatever caper got the Hood his powers, King was there, and has been his confidant ever since his successful play for power.

ANALYSIS: AGENT TRODGLEN
Now that Director Osborn has pretty much seized control of the Hood's Army, there is less need to keep up with the comings and goings of someone like King. If Robbins goes off the reservation again, it's doubtful King would last very long in that group and Director Osborn would probably look to someone else as a liaison. Although looking at The List of names, he may prefer to assign someone from outside.

EXECUTIVE ASSESSMENT: Has chump written all over him.

NAME: U-FOES

BACKGROUND:

Director Osborn requested we specifically include the U-Foes in this dossier. The U-Foes – Iron Clad, Vapor, Vector, and X-Ray – have been loyal members of both the Hood's army and the Initiative (they currently serve as North Carolina's team in the Fifty State Initiative). They were recently used to go after the Heavy Hitters, after the Nevada team seceded from the Initiative, successfully capturing Prodigy.

ART BY AGENT OLIVIER COIPEL

ANALYSIS: AGENT TRODGLEN

Having apparently lost all ambition of their own, but still retaining quite a lot of firepower, the U-Foes have proven to be valuable assets and should continue to be so. They aren't able to lead normal lives and seem to genuinely appreciate being more or less taken care of in exchange for doing whatever is asked of them. If Director Osborn requested info on these guys because he's looking for someone for a specific mission, I can't think of a better group. They are much less trouble than the Wrecking Crew.

EXECUTIVE ASSESSMENT: Creepy, but effective group.

NAME: ZODIAC

BACKGROUND:

Zodiac is an anarchist. He is the thorn in the side of whoever is in power, so he is currently an enemy to Director Osborn. He is the antithesis of the Hood, as he favors dissension, disorganization and chaos. He apparently liked the name Zodiac so he killed the twelve leaders of the crime cartel known as Zodiac to clear up use of the name. He was also able to hack into H.A.M.M.E.R.'s planetary defense network, triggering false positives of the arrival of Galactus. He did this as a distraction while he unleashed the giant Japanese robot Red Ronin on New York City. He is currently at large.

ART BY AGENT NATHAN FOX

ANALYSIS: Zodiac is as psycho as anyone in our files. A perfect example of the kind of individual not even Norman Osborn or Parker Robbins has any hope of reasoning with, Zodiac is notable only as someone we should be wary of. He could unleash terror at any time and threatens to derail anything we attempt at any moment. He would do so not for any greater good, but for the love of sticking it to anyone in power. He tortured and killed 100 H.A.M.M.E.R. agents and would gladly do so again.

EXECUTIVE ASSESSMENT: Should have been on The List, Norman.

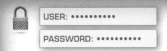

USER: •••••••••

PASSWORD: •••••••••

NAME:
ARES

BACKGROUND:

Ares claims to be the bona fide Greek god of war, who has turned his back on Olympus and chosen to raise his son, **Alexander**, on Earth in an effort to be a better father than he feels Zeus ever was to him. Ares has long been a thorn in the side of his half-brother, Hercules, and has been drawn into repeated conflict with the demigod's allies Thor and the Avengers. However, following the superhuman Civil War, Tony Stark hand-picked Ares for his Mighty Avengers, presumably seeking to combine the raw power of Thor and Hercules with the ruthlessness Wolverine brought to the team. Ares gladly remained with the Avengers after Director Osborn took charge. Of interest are numerous reports, including chaotic footage from the recent battle with the Skrulls, of a young boy matching Alexander's description currently serving with Nick Fury's band of Secret Warriors using the code name Phobos.

ART BY AGENT MIKE DEODATO

ANALYSIS: AGENT GILLEN

As an immortal Greek god, Ares brings great strength and resilience to the team, and a mastery of a wide array of weaponry from all eras. However, sheer power is not his most vital asset: it's how Ares thinks that sets him apart. He's a brilliant tactician and military strategist, the consummate soldier. It just happens that his idea of what that entails is at least a thousand years out of step with the rest of the world.

His experience is a great advantage: He led his exhaustively trained special forces team, the Shades, in a successful mission against overwhelming odds, instilling in them a camaraderie and desire for self-sacrifice. It can also, at times, be a disadvantage: The Shades all ended up dead. For the forthcoming siege of Asgard, Ares has promised a "Cannaean" victory, referring to the greatest of Hannibal's victories over the forces of Rome. Historians put Roman fatalities at about 50,000 in a single day – half of their men. Ares plans a similarly devastating, decapitating ambush that will ensure victory. But it must be remembered that one in eight of Hannibal's forces also lost their lives at Cannae, and Hannibal did not win the war. Ares may deliver the most striking victory imaginable, but there will be a price in blood. And Ares will savor every moment.

Fortunately, he has utmost respect for the chain of command. He shows fierce loyalty to Director Osborn, and disdain towards more reluctant teammates. His very nature means he is willing to lay down his life for his cause. But a word of caution: Ares has great nobility at his core. Woe betide anyone who manipulates him into fighting an unjust cause, especially one that pits him against a foe he respects. The rumors about Alexander and Fury raise a further concern: has he turned a blind eye to his son fraternizing with the enemy? Ares was notably absent during Fury's recent infiltration of Avengers Tower. What happens if Ares and Alexander find themselves on opposite sides? In Greek legend, when father is pitted against son, it almost always ends in tragedy.

EXECUTIVE ASSESSMENT: Ultimate Ballbuster.
We position him strategically, he takes it from there.

NAME:

SENTRY

ART BY AGENT MIKE DEODATO

BACKGROUND:

Everyone knows the **Sentry** has the power of a million exploding suns. What eludes our scientists, despite months of study, is exactly what that means. His power defies measure. Tests indicate that the man known as **Robert Reynolds** differs from regular humans on the molecular level, giving him limitless strength and speed, the power of flight and remarkably acute senses. He has survived more than one apparent "death," leading to a considerable body of opinion that he is effectively immortal. Files impounded during the S.H.I.E.L.D. handover suggest he may also have revived **his wife**, **Lindy**, after she was reportedly killed by Ultron. What little we know of his early history is derived from the medical records of psychiatrist Dr. Cornelius Lunt (accessed under H.A.M.M.E.R.'s Alpha Priority clearances).

Reynolds says he received his abilities from a formula far more potent than Captain America's super soldier serum. He claims to have removed the world's memories of him for years, after realizing that he and his arch-nemesis, the deadly **Void**, were one and the same. As will be seen, his belief that he harbors a murderous dark side has caused him troubling mental problems. Fuller documentation begins when Reynolds found himself in the middle of the jailbreak at the Raft, where he was being held as a prisoner. His heroic actions earned him a place on Captain America's New Avengers. However, he went on to side with Iron Man during the Civil War and served on Stark's Mighty Avengers, before remaining with the team after Director Osborn took control.

ANALYSIS: AGENT HARROLD

Reynolds' only ostensible weakness is his own mind. He has a proven vulnerability to mental attack, and his hyper-senses were once exploited by Iron Man: Stark overwhelmed him with details of simultaneous global disasters. On the battlefield, H.A.M.M.E.R. should be vigilant to keep Reynolds away from psychic or technological threats of this kind, and preventive measures should be thoroughly researched. Director Osborn has taken special interest in Reynolds, perhaps seeing in him a kindred spirit. Having overcome his own personal demons, Director Osborn has tried to convince Reynolds that there is no Void; that it is all in Reynolds' head. Though Reynolds has no need for food or sleep, Director Osborn has encouraged him to indulge in such everyday pleasures as a means of retaining his humanity. In return, the Sentry has shown unswerving loyalty, following orders without question. In strategic terms, he provides a vital role as the team's first – and often decisive – strike; he is "shock and awe" incarnate. As such, he has shown a surprisingly ruthless streak – annihilating an Atlantean terror cell, and ripping off sorceress Morgana Le Fay's head – though he has demonstrated almost childlike concern over whether such actions are good or bad. Clear concerns remain about Sentry's continuing fragile mental state after he abandoned the team during a confrontation with the X-Men. Our sources on the mutants' island nation Utopia report this had something to do with Emma Frost and the Void; the sliver of darkness now reported to be visible inside the diamond-form telepath's head suggest that perhaps there is more to this Void than Director Osborn believed. The Sentry's unpredictability and godlike power continue to cause considerable unease among his teammates and – according to S.H.I.E.L.D. files – even for his wife.

EXECUTIVE ASSESSMENT: Nutcase. Game-changing nutcase, but still... Proceed with caution.

USER: ••••••••••

PASSWORD: ••••••••••

SIEGE DARK AVENGERS

NAME: SPIDER-MAN

BACKGROUND: After years as the serial loser the **Scorpion**, former private detective **Mac Gargan** hit the big time when he bonded with the **Venom** symbiote. Drafted into Director Osborn's **Thunderbolts** to hunt unregistered superhumans, Venom became surprisingly popular with the public. But, unknown to the world at large, only electrical implants kept the murderous symbiote in check. Later, Gargan took a place in Director Osborn's Dark Avengers line-up as **Spider-Man**, thanks to potent medications that control the symbiote and also make it resemble the familiar black costume of the famous wallcrawler.

ART BY AGENT MIKE DEODATO

ANALYSIS: AGENT HARROLD
Gargan has been a problematic member of the team. Despite extensive tests, our labs have yet to hit on the ideal formula for his meds. Too weak and "Spider-Man" eats people. Too strong, and his effectiveness is severely compromised. He has recently shown much anxiety and/or inconsistency in battle; it remains a concern that his volatile teammates – particularly Hawkeye – may elect to take the Gargan problem into their own hands. As shown during the Secret Invasion, a fully effective Venom symbiote is devastating at close quarters on the battlefield. Gargan is one weapon of mass destruction we want to unleash on Asgard.

EXECUTIVE ASSESSMENT: For %&#$ sake will somebody get his meds right!

ART BY AGENT TOM RANEY

NAME: HAWKEYE

BACKGROUND: The former assassin-for-hire, aka **Bullseye**, is a phenomenal marksman, lethally accurate with any object he can lay his hands on. As he will never tire of telling you, he "never misses." As a **Thunderbolt**, he came under the leadership of Director Osborn, who rewarded him for his part in the downfall of the Secret Invasion by recruiting him for the Dark Avengers. Bullseye was given the name and costume of Hawkeye, his true identity fiercely guarded from the public.

ANALYSIS: AGENT HARROLD
More than any other member of the team, Hawkeye has delighted in being a Dark Avenger. Having been kept hidden from public view while with the Thunderbolts, he has relished his chance in the limelight. Psychologists believe that his status as an Avenger may give him a level of self-esteem he has never before enjoyed. While he may occasionally complain about the workload, he is a committed team member who has literally given blood for the cause many times over. Perhaps it is because he views himself as part of a team that is the ultimate instrument for killing, his favorite pastime.

An adamantium-laced spine and other grafts are the legacy of a lifetime of brutal injuries, increasing his resilience to the extent that he can take incredible punishment in battle. He is without equal when it comes to the instantly devastating surgical strike. However, none of this effectiveness in the field should detract from the fact that he remains a violent sociopath who has continued to take scores of lives even while serving as an Avenger.

EXECUTIVE ASSESSMENT: Smart-mouthed, sadistic, insane. But all he needs is one shot...

USER: ••••••••••

PASSWORD: ••••••••••

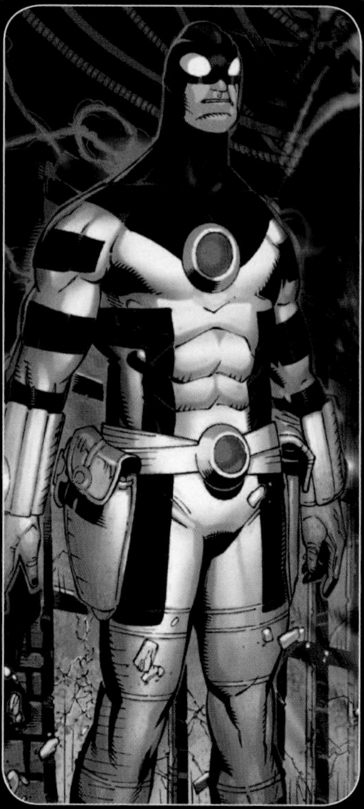

ART BY AGENT CHRIS BACHALO

NAME:

PROTECTOR

BACKGROUND:

The young **Kree** warrior known as **Noh-Varr** was the only survivor when his ship was shot down by the power-crazed Dr. Midas. Noh-Varr was captured by S.H.I.E.L.D., imprisoned in an escape-proof facility known as the Cube, and at one point used by his captors during the Civil War against the Young Avengers and fellow unregistered juvenile superhumans known as the Runaways. The chaos of the Secret Invasion gave him the opportunity to flee his prison. However, having privately declared war on the human race, he was then appointed its protector by a dying Skrull who had believed he was the legendary Kree warrior, Mar-Vell: Earth's Captain Marvel.

Suitably inspired, Noh-Varr donned the powerful **Nega Bands** and fought against the invading Skrulls. Director Osborn welcomed him onto his Avengers as a "war hero," dubbing him the new **Captain Marvel**. He soon fled the team (for reasons we have yet to discern) after spending the night with Karla Sofen. After weeks on the run, he recently resisted an attempt to reengage his services, managing to escape the Sentry and somehow elude both Reynolds' and Daken's heightened senses. Eyewitness reports refer to a man in a "black and white space suit" flying from the scene, which makes his escape unlikely to be a coincidence.

ANALYSIS: AGENT TRODGLEN

Noh-Varr showed initial promise as an Avenger, boasting tremendous speed, strength, resilience and agility that our geneticists attribute to his DNA being a remarkable hybrid of Kree and cockroach. (Sounds gross, but that's the Kree.) Not only is he a formidable combatant, but both his biology and his extensive knowledge of Kree science and weaponry could have proven invaluable for our research and development division. If any illustration was needed of how useful he and his toys could have been, take a look at the NYU surveillance tapes that captured the recent attempt to bring him back in the fold. Noh-Varr went head-to-head with our heaviest hitter until an as-yet-unidentified civilian managed to use one of his firearms to temporarily take the Sentry down.

Noh-Varr is very much an alien in our midst, unfamiliar with our ways and customs. It remains possible that confusion as to our own aims and purposes led him down the wrong path. Priority should be given to finding him, and helping him to see the error of his ways. It is vital that we reach him before Captain America, Clint Barton or Luke Cage fill his head with lies about us. Though we gave Noh-Varr the Captain Marvel name, the last thing we want is him embracing the legacy.

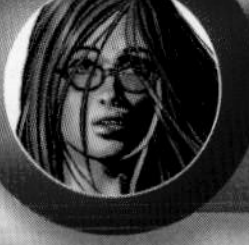

EXECUTIVE ASSESSMENT: Recapture, re-educate or, if necessary, retire. Permanently.

USER: •••••••••

PASSWORD: ••••••••••

NAME:
MS. MARVEL

BACKGROUND: Dr. Karla Sofen, an accomplished psychiatrist known for years as the villain **Moonstone**, was one of the few members of the **Thunderbolts** that remained with the team when Director Osborn came to power. She was given the name and original costume of Ms. Marvel when he took charge of the Avengers, though having been Thunderbolts team leader, she was disappointed when Director Osborn took command in the field as Iron Patriot. Her extensive powers, including enhanced strength and speed, the power of flight, intangibility, photon blasts and limited gravitational control, are derived from Kree Moonstones. Her powers of seduction have resulted in liaisons with at least two, though possibly up to four, members of the Dark Avengers.

ART BY AGENT MIKE DEODATO

ANALYSIS: AGENT TRODGLEN

Sofen has spent much of her life on the wrong side of the law. Even as part of the various incarnations of the Thunderbolts, she was a reluctant hero, most often pursuing her own agendas. Now she is in the public glare as the popular hero Ms. Marvel, freed of associations with her former guise – and she likes it. The extent to which she has embraced her role seems to have surprised even her, and she has shown great determination to be a more effective Ms. Marvel than her predecessor Carol Danvers.

As a Dark Avenger, however, she remains a potentially disruptive influence. She is a master manipulator with a thirst for power, and will push any button if it advances her own ends. When not in the field, she should be kept well away from Director Osborn during any times of stress. Sofen has wasted no time fraternizing with her male teammates, noticeably flirting with Ares and Daken. Noh-Varr left the team after a night in her bed, and even Hawkeye hasn't escaped her attentions. However, their liaison may have more to do with the costume than the man inside, giving rise to concerns that she may still harbor feelings for her former lover, Clint Barton. The footage of Barton's recent assault on Avengers Tower suggests her attack upon him may just have been for the cameras. When they meet again, we need to know where her loyalties will lie.

EXECUTIVE ASSESSMENT: Manipulative witch. Part of me recommends giving her the sack. (You know what I mean.)

SIEGE
DARK AVENGERS

USER: ●●●●●●●●●●

PASSWORD: ●●●●●●●●●●

NAME:
WOLVERINE

BACKGROUND:

The **son of Logan** boasts his father's ferocity, regenerative ability and trademark claws that extend from the underside of each wrist. But, unlike his father, Daken is a lifelong killer without remorse. He can also use his pheromones to influence others' emotions and actions. Daken's claws were recently laced with metal from the blade of the Muramasa sword, which S.H.I.E.L.D. files list as practically the only thing that can kill Wolverine. (Side note: How is this not in H.A.M.M.E.R. custody?) Director Osborn recruited Daken to the Dark Avengers primarily to annoy Logan. Daken, who grew up blaming the X-Man for the death of his mother, seemed happy to oblige, taking on his father's codename and iconic brown costume. As befits the identity, Daken was happy to pull double duty, for a time serving both on the Dark Avengers and Dark X-Men.

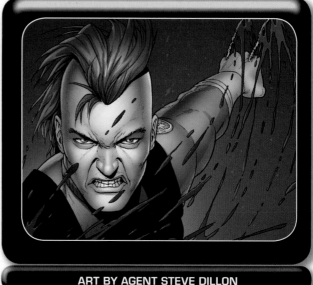

ART BY AGENT STEVE DILLON

ANALYSIS: AGENT TRODGLEN

Other than getting under his father's skin, Daken's motivations for joining and remaining with the Dark Avengers are completely unclear. He has proven almost impossible for our psych teams to evaluate, unsurprising for someone whose own pheromones can alter their perceptions. A recent encounter with Ms. Marvel left the usually unflappable Dr. Sofen clearly shaken. As a result, his loyalty should not be taken for granted.

Having a Wolverine on the team clearly serves its own purpose, and he may be the only one who can stop his father. So far, when Director Osborn points him at someone, he takes them down. But our intelligence suggests that Daken has denied truly working for the Director, and suspicions remain that he may be playing us all. The recent confrontation with the Fantastic Four had his fingerprints all over it, and may be evidence of some long-term plan of his own design. He did not seem upset that the Thing had thrown him out of the Baxter Building, while Ares was acting strangely out-of-character in the fracas that saw our vital footage of the incident destroyed. Is Daken powerful enough to control even a god? That could be useful – but only as long as he's on our side.

EXECUTIVE ASSESSMENT: Never, ever turn your back on him.

USER: ••••••••••
PASSWORD: ••••••••••

ART BY AGENT
MARKO DJURDJEVIC

NAME: RONIN

BACKGROUND: **Clint Barton**, the original **Hawkeye**, stepped up as leader of the renegade **New Avengers** following the Secret Invasion, and has made it a personal crusade to oppose Director Osborn and H.A.M.M.E.R. Barton declared Director Osborn and his Avengers killers on live TV, and after failing to turn the tide of public opinion, launched an unsuccessful assassination attempt and was placed under arrest. Following a successful rescue mission by the New Avengers, he is once again at large.

ANALYSIS: AGENT HARROLD

It's hard to imagine Director Osborn hating anyone as much as Spider-Man, but after the last few months, Barton is at least running a close second. Note that on his assassination attempt, he acted alone; it is likely that he acted without the approval of his teammates, which may cause dissension in their ranks. In infiltrating Avengers Tower and single-handedly taking down the three Dark Avengers, Barton showed himself to be resourceful and dangerous. Only Director Osborn's personal force field saved his life. Under arrest, Barton proved incredibly resilient, refusing to give up his colleagues under extreme duress. One button that might be pushed in a future confrontation is his resentment of our own Hawkeye, and his determination to take the costume back. Question marks remain over his reappearance after an apparent death at the hands of the Scarlet Witch. It is further recommended that tests should be carried out on Barton's DNA retrieved during his imprisonment, to investigate why Dr. Harrow's power drainer worked on him.

EXECUTIVE ASSESSMENT: Let's quit monkeying around with this B-lister: Kill on sight.

NAME: MOCKINGBIRD

BACKGROUND: **Bobbi Morse** was apparently one of the first superhumans to be captured and replaced by the Skrulls during their Secret Invasion of Earth. She was discovered, along with the other captives, on a Skrull vessel once the Invasion was thwarted. Though reports reach us that Mockingbird was captured during a period of separation from her husband, Clint Barton, the pair once again seem romantically involved while serving together with the New Avengers.

ART BY AGENT JO CHEN

ANALYSIS: AGENT HARROLD

Mockingbird lost years of her life to the Skrulls, and the exact psychological effects of that remain to be seen. She appears to have thrown herself into her work, thriving on the action during her team's encounters with the Hood's gang and our the Dark Avengers. She was the only one left standing after her team was downed by Harrow's power drainer. While confirming that Mockingbird has no superhuman abilities, the incident demonstrates that she should not be underestimated. She showed impressive combat ability and mastery of weapons, as one might expect from a former S.H.I.E.L.D. agent, and managed to pilot a quinjet to the rescue of her team. She also led Spider-Woman, Ms. Marvel and Jessica Jones on a rescue mission to spring Ronin from the H.A.M.M.E.R. brig. However, her thirst for action could leave her prone to recklessness.

EXECUTIVE ASSESSMENT: Mockingbird might produce valuable intelligence on Skrull methods of brainwashing. Capture and contain her.

USER: ••••••••••

PASSWORD: ••••••••••

NAME: SPIDER-MAN

ART BY AGENT BILLY TAN

BACKGROUND: Spider-Man has made it his apparent mission to discredit Director Osborn and undermine the H.A.M.M.E.R. regime. Once again an outlaw, Spider-Man has banded with his **New Avengers** allies to defy the Director at every turn. Acting individually, Spider-Man also played a key part in thwarting the Director's bid to recruit his son, Harry, as an inspirational addition to his Avengers team under the codename American Son. Spider-Man recently managed to infiltrate Avengers Tower and leak potentially damaging footage of Director Osborn's experimental procedures on live subjects to the media.

ANALYSIS: AGENT HARROLD

Director Osborn has decreed that Spider-Man must be brought to him alive. While there are many more potent threats to our regime, and certainly more troublesome obstacles to the assault on Asgard, Spider-Man will always be high on the Director's list of targets. The Director's hatred for Spider-Man knows no bounds. Their history is long and complex, and official records fail to tell the full story. It is clear, however, that Spider-Man holds a very personal grudge against the Director, and is a persistent thorn in H.A.M.M.E.R.'s side, acting both as part of the New Avengers and individually. Spider-Man's recent raid on Avengers Tower (on a side note, a full-scale review of security is urgently advised, with particular focus on the need for windows in key facilities) caused quite a media storm. The cleanup taxed our already fully stretched PR team to its fullest.

EXECUTIVE ASSESSMENT: No comment.

NAME: SPIDER-WOMAN

ART BY AGENT LEINIL YU

BACKGROUND: While Jessica Drew was held captive by the Skrulls, their Queen, Veranke, used her face to almost take over the world. Now the fake Spider-Woman is more famous than the real one ever was, and Drew is left to pick up the pieces of her life. She joined the New Avengers because she had nowhere else to go, and unsuccessfully sought to lure Director Osborn into a trap by claiming she wanted to defect. Our spies within S.W.O.R.D. (Sentient World Observation and Response Department) report that Drew has been recruited to their ranks to hunt the globe for remaining Skrulls.

ANALYSIS: AGENT HARROLD

Drew has experience with HYDRA, S.H.I.E.L.D. and now S.W.O.R.D. With years of experience in the intelligence field, and seemingly fickle allegiances, she could have been a considerable asset to H.A.M.M.E.R. However, as a result of her actions with the New Avengers, this should no longer be considered a viable possibility. In taking her down, our psychological profilers report that someone in Drew's position would be plagued with doubts over her identity and place in the world. Her face is one the world will forever associate with the Skrull devastation, and as a result her presence in the New Avengers is a valuable weapon against them in the ongoing media war. Our profilers also raise doubts as to whether even her own teammates could ever fully trust her. Any opportunity to play on those fears should be exploited to its fullest.

EXECUTIVE ASSESSMENT: Her knowledge of HYDRA, S.H.I.E.L.D. and S.W.O.R.D. make her a valuable asset in captivity.

USER: •••••••••

PASSWORD: •••••••••

ART BY AGENT BILLY TAN

NAME: **WOLVERINE**

BACKGROUND: Wolverine has of late split his time between the **New Avengers** and his many commitments to the **X-Men**. Since the incident in San Francisco, Wolverine and his fellow mutants have largely confined themselves to the island nation of Utopia. He was nowhere to be seen during recent confrontations with the New Avengers. Wolverine's son, **Daken**, has taken his father's name and old brown costume as well as a spot on Director Osborn's Avengers.

ANALYSIS: AGENT HARROLD

Wolverine's abilities are incredibly well documented – H.A.M.M.E.R.'s extensive files on what is known of his complex history occupy three Oscorp 10 terabyte hard drives. Without rehashing that here, there can be no doubt that the New Avengers are a more deadly prospect when Logan is on the team. While H.A.M.M.E.R. should clearly operate on the premise that Logan may find time to join the team should it involve itself in the Siege, it is highly probable his recent New Avengers absence means that he is one problem we will not have to deal with. While it won't be hard to find team members and other operatives who would welcome an opportunity to put Wolverine down for good, one among them stands out as an ideal man for the job: Daken. Wolverine has demonstrated a clear reluctance to use full force on his son, but Daken has no such qualms. Now Daken's claws are laced with metal from an ancient Muramasa blade – rumored to be the one weapon that can kill Wolverine – we have the ideal opportunity to cross Logan off the list permanently.

EXECUTIVE ASSESSMENT: If he turns up, let Daken go all Oedipal.

NAME: **MS. MARVEL**

BACKGROUND: Offered the opportunity to remain as team leader when Director Osborn took over the Avengers, Carol Danvers vehemently resigned, choosing instead to serve as deputy leader of the **New Avengers** team she had opposed during the Civil War. Danvers was apparently killed during a confrontation with her old nemesis **Ghazi Rashid**, an event carefully orchestrated by Director Osborn in which Danvers was actually split into four energy beings. With the aid of her Avengers allies, however, Danvers was able to use baby M.O.D.O.K.s to re-form herself and retake her place on the team. (Not making that last part up.)

ART BY AGENT
ED McGUINNESS

ANALYSIS: AGENT HARROLD

Since her return, Danvers seems more confident and assured. The attempt on her life may only have succeeded in making her a more powerful threat. With her array of powers, Danvers is the most dangerous of the New Avengers: Using an energy boost from Spider-Woman, she single-handedly took out the Hood's army. She also has considerable military expertise, and taking her off the board weakens her team in strategic terms just as much as it may in sheer power. She should be the initial target of any confrontation, with the Sentry identified as the most logical team member to engage her. Director Osborn will not be quick to forget that she had the audacity to turn him down. Nor the fact that she owes us a quinjet.

EXECUTIVE ASSESSMENT: Kill on sight. Again.

NAME: CAPTAIN AMERICA

BACKGROUND: Following **Steve Rogers'** apparent demise, his former partner Bucky Barnes was given the name and shield of Captain America, and he joined the **New Avengers** following the Secret Invasion. Following Rogers' recent return it is unclear whether Barnes will continue in his role as Captain America, or return to his previous guise as the **Winter Soldier**. Barnes has subsequently been spotted in action as Captain America, fighting alongside his partner the **Black Widow** against Mr. Hyde, suggesting that he will indeed be the one who wields the shield.

ANALYSIS: AGENT HARROLD

Barnes has impressed in the difficult job of living up to his mentor, not least with his adeptness at using the indestructible shield. It is thought that the bionic enhancements he received as the Winter Soldier have enabled this. He also carries a Luger, making him lethal at close and long range. While Barton appears

ART BY AGENT BILLY TAN

to be the New Avengers' notional leader, Barnes has been witnessed directing strategy in the field. It is possible that any confusion over the chain of command could be exploited in battle. S.H.I.E.L.D. files also report that, during his time as the Winter Soldier, Barnes was the subject of extensive mind control. It is possible that any lingering effects may make it possible to reeducate Barnes to our cause, meaning Director Osborn's goal of a Captain America to call his own may yet happen.

EXECUTIVE ASSESSMENT: Former Soviet assassin/spy, so many secrets. Would LOVE to get a shrink inside that head of his.

NAME: STEVE ROGERS

BACKGROUND: The plan to have a Captain America leading the Dark Avengers has failed. The **Red Skull** was defeated and is believed to have perished, and reports are that Steve Rogers is alive. According to intelligence gleaned from A.I.M. agents taken into custody, Rogers had been trapped in time by the Skull but managed to recover control of his mind and body before working with his Avengers allies to take his enemy down. His whereabouts and intentions are currently unknown.

ANALYSIS: AGENT HARROLD

We need to act fast before Rogers' return becomes public knowledge. The extent to which his reputation became tarnished during the Civil War was rendered irrelevant by his "assassination" and the outpouring of grief that followed. Public outcry would now make it almost impossible to try him for his rebellion. Captain America is a walking flag: In the ongoing battle for hearts and minds, Rogers could change everything. If he comes out against Director Osborn it could prove devastating to our regime. Our PR people have been

ART BY AGENT
BRYAN HITCH

working round the clock ever since Clint Barton went public with his grievances, so the last thing we want is Captain America fighting Iron Patriot on the nightly news. And all that is to say nothing of the galvanizing impact his return could have on the renegade superhuman population. When Rogers says "Assemble," they come running. Rogers could unite them, and at such a critical stage in our Siege planning, he needs to be neutralized.

EXECUTIVE ASSESSMENT: Handle with extreme care. This one's your call.

USER: ••••••••••

PASSWORD: ••••••••••

NAME: LUKE CAGE

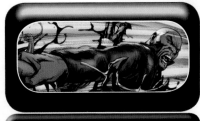

ART BY AGENT BILLY TAN

BACKGROUND: Luke Cage came to Director Osborn after his daughter with wife **Jessica Jones** was kidnapped by a rogue Skrull. He offered the Director "anything" in return, but reneged on the deal and fled to rejoin his New Avengers after the child was secured. After collapsing with heart pain as a result of Harrow's power drainer, he gave himself up to H.A.M.M.E.R. for treatment. His life was spared, and he was offered freedom for his wife and child in return for giving up his teammates. However, while the New Avengers distracted Director Osborn with an attack on Avengers Tower, a group of their associates carried out a rescue of Cage. The New Avengers somehow managed to find and remove a miniature explosive device attached to his heart – we suspect the involvement of Dr. Henry Pym – and used it to destroy one of Director Osborn's properties. When the Director decided to take matters into his own hands, to draft Cage into the Thunderbolts, he was rescued by another unwilling convert, Iron Fist. Side note: Cage's wife, many years ago the super hero **Jewel**, was recently identified in costume during the rescue of Clint Barton.

ANALYSIS: AGENT HARROLD

Cage has twice been the recipient of great kindness from Director Osborn and H.A.M.M.E.R., and twice thrown it back in our faces. He will not get a third opportunity to change his allegiance. But Cage is a formidable and durable opponent who will be very hard to kill. He is also very popular with the superhuman community, and can call a wide variety of powerful friends to his aid. However, his weakness is his heart, both literally and figuratively. While our doctors may have saved his life for now, it is difficult to predict the extent to which cardiac problems will affect him in the future. Perhaps more significantly, Luke Cage is a devoted husband and father who would give his life for wife and child. This should be exploited at the earliest opportunity.

EXECUTIVE ASSESSMENT: The way to Cage's heart is through his family.

NEW AVENGERS ALLIES

BACKGROUND: As well as the regular line-up of New Avengers, and their mystical reservists, their nebulous connections across the superhuman community have seen various other individuals join them in recent incidents. These include former member **Echo** and Luke Cage's long-time partner **Iron Fist**. In a recent battle with seemingly mystical beings in New Orleans, **Daimon Hellstrom**, the so-called Son of Satan, played a part. During the rescue of Luke Cage from H.A.M.M.E.R. custody, the **New Avengers** were joined by **Doctor Strange, Doctor Voodoo, Misty Knight, the Thing, Hellcat, Valkyrie** and **Daredevil.** (And since when did Hellcat go rogue from Alaska's Initiative outpost?)

ART BY AGENT STUART IMMONEN

ANALYSIS: AGENT HARROLD

If (or more likely, when) the New Avengers involve themselves in the Siege of Asgard, they can be expected to boost their ranks with every available superhuman they can get to join them. H.A.M.M.E.R. agents and our Avengers should be equipped with up-to-date intel on each of their known associates' abilities and weaknesses.

EXECUTIVE ASSESSMENT: They set 'em up, we'll knock 'em down.

USER: ••••••••••

PASSWORD: ••••••••••

NAME:

IRON MAN

BACKGROUND:

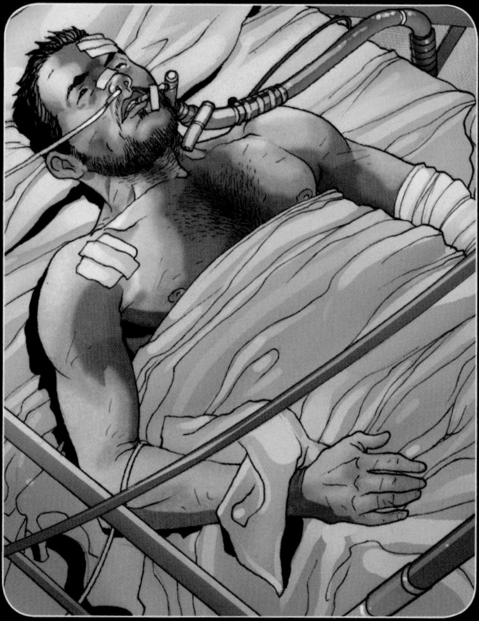

ART BY AGENT SALVADOR LARROCA

Since his powers were wrested by Director Osborn in the wake of the Secret Invasion, Tony Stark went underground in an effort to protect the registration database of superhuman secret identities; classified information that was legally the property of H.A.M.M.E.R., but was stored by Stark inside his brain. Aided only by his faithful assistant **Pepper Potts** and former S.H.I.E.L.D. Director **Maria Hill**, Stark set about systematically erasing his mind to delete the database forever. The gradual mind-wipe severely debilitated Stark's intellect, and he was forced to use more and more primitive iterations of his Iron Man armor as his brain regressed. By the time Director Osborn, as the Iron Patriot, caught up with him in Dubai, there was little fight in him, and no information left to salvage. The Director was forced to abandon the beating to avoid making a martyr of Stark on live television. But, with Stark left in a persistent vegetative state, his living will handed power of attorney to his personal physician, a doctor by the name of Donald Blake. Meanwhile, Potts, in her own set of armor and codenamed **Rescue**, was able to escape Avengers Tower along with Hill, **Black Widow** and an encrypted Stark Drive that H.A.M.M.E.R.'s tech team had failed to crack.

ANALYSIS: AGENT HARROLD

Stark is a spent force, practically brain dead. Director Osborn has decreed that he should be left to rot. However, it is recommended that his closest allies, Potts and Hill, should be monitored extremely carefully. (This Doctor Blake also warrants investigation. There must be a reason why Stark's physician is in Broxton, Oklahoma, the middle of nowhere.) If Stark was prepared enough to organize a series of safe houses across the globe he could use to effectively lobotomize himself, it is not beyond the bounds of possibility that he also envisaged a way back. That should be prevented at all costs. H.A.M.M.E.R. must also be prepared for the possibility of a Stark ally donning his armor, as has previously been the case with James Rhodes and, recently, Potts. However, this possibility may be inhibited by the fact that, as well as destroying all trace of the super-human database, Stark's condition also prevents the manufacture of the repulsor technology that is vital to power the Iron Man armor – and, as a result, the Iron Patriot. R&D has requested a tripled budget as they seek to reverse-engineer the spec.

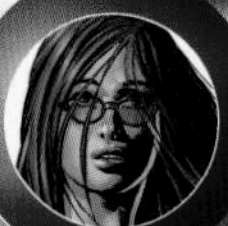

EXECUTIVE ASSESSMENT:
Not so invincible after all: Interference with Siege nil.

USER: ••••••••••

PASSWORD: ••••••••••

SIEGE
MIGHTY AVENGERS

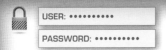

NAME:

WASP

BACKGROUND:

The former Ant-Man, Giant-Man, Goliath and Yellowjacket has now adopted the identity and powers of the Wasp, in tribute to his late ex-wife, Janet Van Dyne, who lost her life during the Secret Invasion. Pym himself was one of the superhumans captured and replaced by the Skrulls many months earlier, and his doppelganger played a key role in the invasion. Although reluctant to do so at first, he accepted the leadership of his own team, dubbed the **Mighty Avengers**. Reports are that Pym has made considerable strides with his size-changing Pym Particles, to the extent that he has now constructed a team headquarters in a separate dimension, dubbed the Infinite Avengers Mansion, which he can access from points across the globe.

ART BY AGENT BRYAN HITCH

ANALYSIS:
AGENT HARROLD

Dr. Henry Pym is often underestimated, dismissed as a second-rate super hero, or a poor man's Tony Stark or Reed Richards. However, indications are that we are now dealing with a very different Hank Pym – his latest identity is just the start. According to some of the more reliable Avengers newsgroups, Pym has been referring to himself publicly as Earth's "Scientist Supreme." Accurate or not, his extensive range of miniaturized weaponry – and the fact he has seemingly developed a headquarters we can't trace that enables his team to appear out of nowhere – is testament to his scientific expertise and achievement.

Accessing this technology, and taking this dimensional safe house for our own, could provide an answer to the recent series of infiltrations of our facilities. Pym now seems confident and mentally together, leading a disparate group of old and new Avengers to victory against a series of powerful adversaries, including Chthon and Zzaxx. It remains to be seen whether this is a permanent change in a man whose career has been blighted by times of emotional and psychological frailty, often highlighted – like his recent change to the codename Wasp – by a change in persona. It is possible that his ex-wife's death and the abuses the Skrulls carried out in his name remain ripe for exploitation, as does his reported emotional attachment to the robot Jocasta, who shares Van Dyne's brain patterns.

EXECUTIVE ASSESSMENT: Mess with his head, take his headquarters. Jocasta is his weak link.

USER: ••••••••••

PASSWORD: ••••••••••

NAME:

MIGHTY AVENGERS

BACKGROUND:

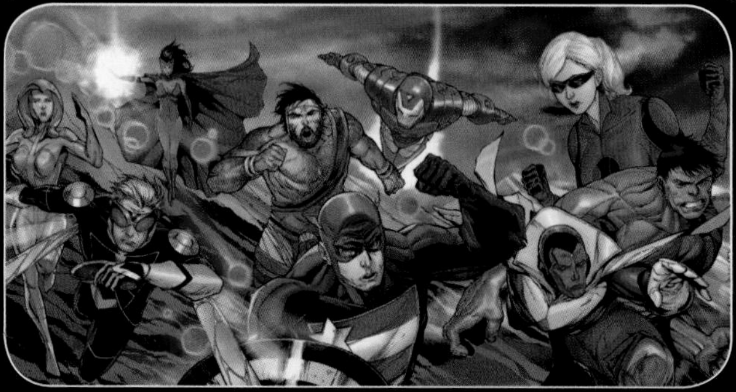

ART BY AGENT KHOI PHAM

Pym's Mighty Avengers line-up comprises former Avengers **Quicksilver**, **Hercules** and **USAgent**, and Young Avengers **Stature** and the rebooted synthezoid **Vision**. Working from a headquarters hidden in an alternate dimension, they have carried out successful missions across the globe to considerable acclaim. A variety of international media have reported that the wider world sees Pym's team as the "real" Avengers. Hercules' boy genius sidekick **Amadeus Cho** has also been seen with the Mighty Avengers, while references made on an internet blog attributed to Stature suggest that the robotic **Jocasta** and butler **Edwin Jarvis** also serve the team.

ANALYSIS: AGENT HARROLD

While this team is shorn of some of the Avengers' heavy-hitters, it nevertheless boasts considerable experience and power. You can't argue with their results, Pym's team having warded off threats including Terminus and an ancient Inhuman named the Unspoken who, according to intel the Chinese authorities tried to keep quiet, was more powerful than Black Bolt himself.

Hercules is the team powerhouse, and his long history of besting Ares is a concern. His brawn is now teamed with Cho's considerable brain, which S.H.I.E.L.D. files from the Hulk event demonstrate is a considerable threat. However, capture Cho and Hercules will be at our mercy.

There are other potential weaknesses to exploit. USAgent is a true patriot, and an authoritarian. It's one thing following Pym's directives on international soil, but here in America, the law is his boss. Quicksilver is a historically volatile team member, and in recent years appeared to be heavily involved in the M Day event and a major diplomatic incident with the Inhumans. He claims to have been an innocent victim of the Skrulls during the Secret Invasion, but, interestingly, we have yet to receive independent verification that he was on the Skrull vessel with the other replaced prisoners. Stature and Vision lack the experience of their comrades. It should be noted that, with Quicksilver, Vision and Stature – daughter of the late Scott Lang – on the team, relationships may be strained if the Scarlet Witch should ever resurface. Finding her and containing her remains high on H.A.M.M.E.R.'s to-do list. Until then, Loki has the greatest experience dealing with Avengers.

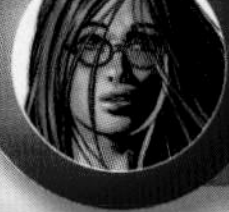

EXECUTIVE ASSESSMENT:
These clowns have only one thing going for them: Pym Particles. Do we have a tactical response?

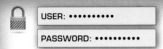
NAME:

SECRET WARRIORS/ NICK FURY

BACKGROUND:

In the wake of the Secret Invasion, former head of S.H.I.E.L.D. **Nick Fury** resurfaced after a long period of hiding, unsure of whom to trust. With the Avengers in disarray, he activated a number of young potential super-humans he had been keeping tabs on and led them into battle against the Skrulls. These **Secret Warriors** have remained together, trained by Fury, and are believed to include the offspring of numerous active super-humans. Among them, if reports are accurate, is Ares' son Alexander, using the codename **Phobos**. Other reported codenames include **Druid**, **Eden**, **Hellfire**, **Quake**, **Slingshot** and **Stonewall**.

ART BY AGENT ALESSANDRO VITTI

ANALYSIS: AGENT HICKMAN

Even though long-divorced from his one-time role as head of a global peacekeeping organization, Nick Fury has a tendency to find himself front and center in any kind of global conflict. Expect Fury to seek to involve himself extensively following the assault on Asgard. As someone who has unprecedented knowledge of many systems and protocols that remain in effect to this day, he poses a very serious threat to H.A.M.M.E.R.'s operational security in both the short and long term. As such, he was able to infiltrate Avengers Tower, lead H.A.M.M.E.R. to expose a security leak in the Treasury Department and waltz back out again, taking down several of our men and laying his hands on Director Osborn. An urgent review of all S.H.I.E.L.D.-era defenses and capturing Fury should be among our highest priorities. What limited reports we have of his Secret Warriors suggest that, while raw, they are a formidable group. If Phobos is indeed Ares' son then that fact poses an obvious complication, perhaps compromising the loyalty of one of the Avengers most vital to our strategic planning, to say nothing of the potential power level of a god's offspring in the wrong hands. It should be noted that there are rumors that Fury is also funding his former ally "Dum Dum" Dugan and his Howling Commandos, who have been operating as mercenaries since S.H.I.E.L.D.'s dissolution. After their assault on a H.A.M.M.E.R. facility led to the loss of several helicarriers, they are to be considered a viable and dangerous threat even though they have not yet acted in the US.

EXECUTIVE ASSESSMENT:
Contain Phobos. Kill the rest on sight.

USER: ••••••••••

PASSWORD: ••••••••••

NAME:

THE INITIATIVE

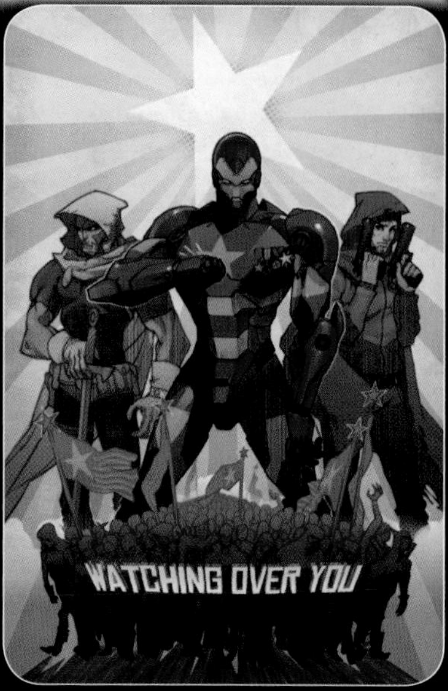
WATCHING OVER YOU

PROPAGANDA POSTER BY AGENT MATTEO DE LONGIS

BACKGROUND:

The Fifty State Initiative was established by former head of S.H.I.E.L.D. Tony Stark as a training ground for super-humans, staffing teams of protectors across the United States. Since taking control, Director Osborn has recruited hand-selected, reformed villains to the Initiative Training Program at Camp H.A.M.M.E.R. There they are being put through their paces by the Taskmaster, alongside those existing recruits who chose to remain.

ANALYSIS: AGENT GAGE

The Initiative Program has proven to be an invaluable resource. Career criminals view such benefits as health insurance, a steady, generous income, and the freedom to operate without fear of prosecution to be a brass ring they have no intention of letting go of. They follow orders without question, never raising qualms about tactics the mainstream media insists on calling controversial, such as enhanced interrogation techniques or the classification of detainees as enemy combatants. Of course, many of these individuals – while successfully branded as reformed in some cases (see file 2513A, **The Force of Nature**) and given new identities in others (see file 349F, **Boomerang/Outback**) – pose a significant risk of recidivism and antisocial public behavior. It is our determination that potential problems can be avoided if these impulses are directed toward the enemy (witness the highly successful apprehension of the rogue Initiative operative from Nevada's Heavy Hitters, Prodigy).

However, a comprehensive report commissioned by Taskmaster recommends that a future recruitment strategy be focused on young, pliable talent we can shape into more reliable soldiers. Concerns remain that a mole is feeding intel to the Avengers Resistance. A thorough evaluation of all members is recommended, including loyalty tests. Special focus on holdovers from the Stark administration (i.e., **Cloud 9, Diamondback, Bengal**). One of our legal teams has been assigned the task of assessing what current interpretations of the law will allow. We also need to keep constant watch on **Penance**, now that he has regained his memory of his life as Speedball. Though he chose to remain with us rather than leave with the Avengers Resistance following the battle with Nightmare, the prospect of rejoining his old New Warriors teammates must be a powerful lure.

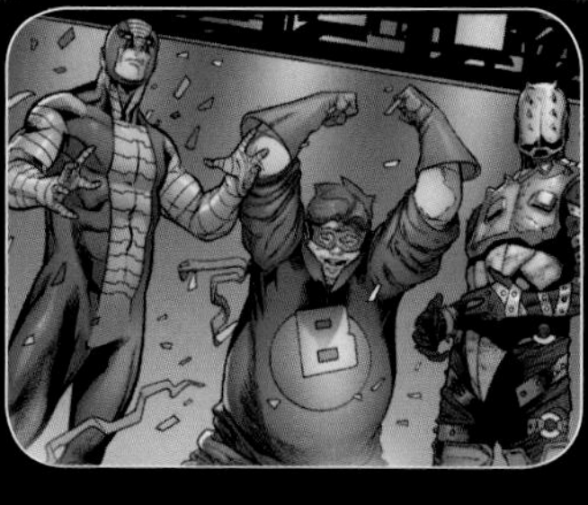

ART BY AGENT RAFA SANDOVAL

EXECUTIVE ASSESSMENT: Let Taskmaster sort out to what degree each of these "heroes" are expendable.

USER: ••••••••••

PASSWORD: ••••••••••

NAME:

AVENGERS RESISTANCE

BACKGROUND:

One of several homegrown groups of terrorist dissidents populated by former Avengers, this cell consists of a number of individuals who held key roles in the Initiative under Tony Stark, including **Justice**, **Tigra** and ex-Camp Hammond drill sergeant **Gauntlet**. Their ranks also include former Initiative recruit **Scarlet Spider**, Justice's colleagues from the New Warriors, **Rage**, **Slapstick** and **Ultra Girl**, as well as Donyell Taylor, who has adopted his late brother Dwayne's **Night Thrasher** identity. The Resistance has sought to undermine the Initiative and H.A.M.M.E.R. by carrying out attacks on our facilities, and releasing damning footage to the media.

ANALYSIS: AGENT GAGE

Given their inside knowledge of the workings of the Initiative, even the changes in security and operations protocols implemented under Director Osborn's leadership, may not prove enough to secure Camp H.A.M.M.E.R. from attack. Special care should be taken to guard against an assault during any operation that takes personnel away from the base. Security forces, both powered and non-powered, should always remain in sufficient numbers to repel an incursion. The knowledge evinced by the Resistance regarding classified data and Camp H.A.M.M.E.R.'s internal workings raises the disturbing possibility of a mole within the Initiative. However, in retaliation, we have managed to acquire our own double agent, compromising Night Thrasher by dangling the carrot of reviving his dead brother. We have also deprived the Resistance of significant resources from Night Thrasher's charitable Taylor Foundation. Hunted and on the run, dissension is inevitable, as reflected in reports that former member Debrii has left the group and fled to Europe. Either the Resistance will collapse from internal strife, or they will be goaded into attacking us prematurely. The stress they are under may also make certain members vulnerable to defecting; profiling is recommended to identify the most vulnerable members.

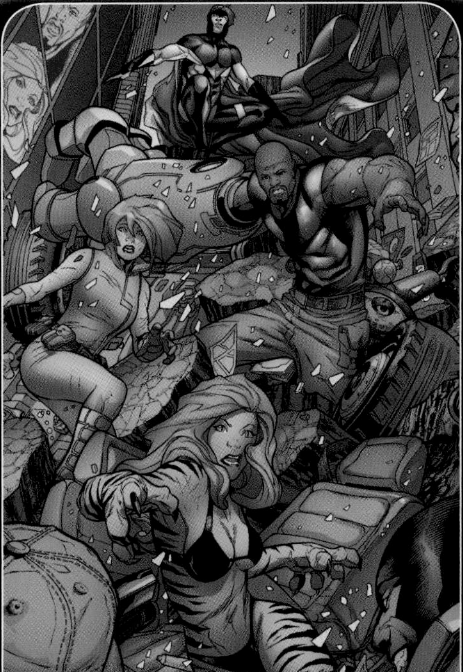

ART BY AGENT RAFA SANDOVAL

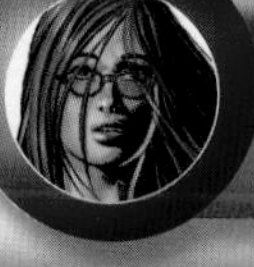

EXECUTIVE ASSESSMENT: This Resistance will find meddling with Siege irresistible. Plan accordingly.

USER: ••••••••••

PASSWORD: ••••••••••

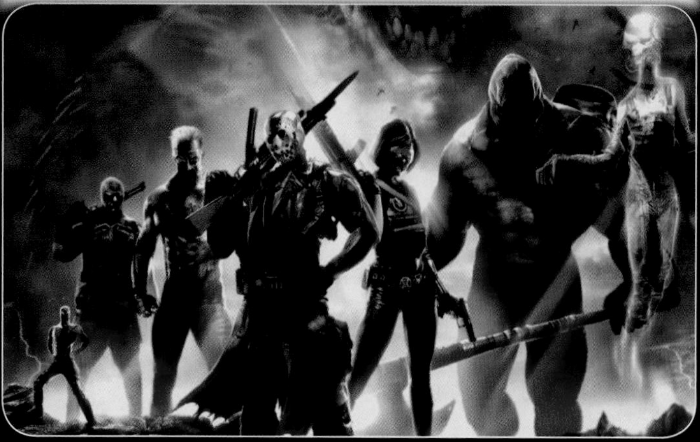

ART BY AGENT FRANCESCO MATTINA

NAME:

THUNDERBOLTS

BACKGROUND:

After promoting select Thunderbolts to his Dark Avengers team, and disposing of the rest, Director Osborn recruited a brand new team to be his personal squad of assassins. The present line-up is composed of Headsman, Ghost, Paladin, Mr. X, Scourge, Ant-Man and the recent addition, the Grizzly.

ANALYSIS: AGENT PARKER

The Thunderbolts are Director Osborn's personally assembled team, designated for the wettest of work. In their short history, they have proven themselves highly volatile and unstable, something that Director Osborn has attributed to inactivity. He has requested recommendations for future missions that he believes will encourage the team to maintain its focus. They are currently assigned to dealing with the Agents of ATLAS problem. Beyond that, they may be useful during the Siege on Asgard in a clandestine capacity, operating under the radar. Anything that uses their black-ops skills, and in particular Ghost's expertise at infiltration, would be ideal, though the addition of Grizzly to the line-up gives them some additional muscle, in case they need it.

Nevertheless, their effectiveness for vital missions may be compromised by numerous factors. Recent incidents suggest that the team might be sabotaged from within. Paladin has always been known for his mercenary nature, but there has come the possibility that even he has a line he's not willing to cross for money. Scourge, the former super-soldier known as Nuke, is perhaps the most unstable team leader the Thunderbolts has ever had – and that's saying something. Ant-Man (Eric O'Grady) gives the impression he's looking for a way out. And since Ghost is often invisible and almost always silent, it's easy to overlook whatever he's doing – he may well have an agenda that no one is picking up on.

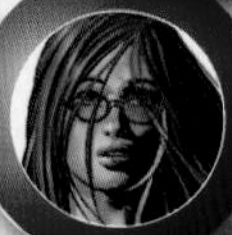

EXECUTIVE ASSESSMENT:
I think I have just the job for them...